THE NAZI OCCUPATION OF CRETE

1941-1945

G.C. KIRIAKOPOULOS

PRAEGER

Westport, Connecticut
London

Library of Congress Cataloging-in-Publication Data

Kiriakopoulos, G. C.
    The Nazi occupation of Crete, 1941–1945 / G. C. Kiriakopoulos.
      p. cm.
    Includes bibliographical references and index.
    ISBN 0–275–95277–0 (alk. paper)
    1. World War, 1939–1945—Greece—Crete. 2. Crete (Greece)—
History—Occupation, 1941–1945. I. Title.
D802.G8C75   1995
940.53′37—dc20   95–4290

British Library Cataloguing in Publication Data is available.

Library of Congress Catalog Card Number: 95–4290
ISBN: 0–275–95277–0

First published in 1995

Praeger Publishers, 88 Post Road West, Westport, CT 06881
An imprint of Greenwood Publishing Group, Inc.

Printed in the United States of America

The paper used in this book complies with the
Permanent Paper Standard issued by the National
Information Standards Organization (Z39.48–1984).

10 9 8 7 6 5 4 3 2 1

This book is dedicated to the late Mrs. Mary Demos
(née Varouxakis), a very dear Cretan lady and my mother-in-law,
whose inspiration made this book possible.
She is very much missed.

Contents

Contents

Preface

After completing my earlier book *Ten Days to Destiny—The Battle for Crete, 1941* (1985), in which I related the adventure, the audacity, and the horror of the first airborne invasion of an island-fortress in military history, and described the heroic involvement of the thousands of British Commonwealth soldiers and Cretan civilians who stood defiant in resisting the German invader, I thought that the story would end at that point. It was not to be.

My research into the whole subject of the battle and its aftermath revealed that the battle was only the beginning of the tale; that the story of the German occupation that followed the battle was an equally dramatic history of courageous human endeavor against the forces of oppression. It was a history that had to be related so that it could take its place in the scribed annals of the Second World War.

In writing *The Nazi Occupation of Crete*, I did not intend to present a total compilation of the many dramatic episodes that took place on the island during the years of that tragic occupation which began in 1941 and ended in 1945. Rather, I wanted to acquaint the reader with what happened on that island during that period of time, events that ultimately gave rise to the first organized resistance movement in Europe against Nazism by the oppressed people of that continent.

To complete my research, I sought to find the survivors or relatives of the survivors of that period in history, so that I might enter their stories into the record. Many narrated the events of their personal participation and documented them with diaries and letters, happy to note that at last their tale would be told. None had to prod their memories of those days of the occupation; I marveled at how they remembered facts and dates, even after all these years. I estimate that my travels exceeded 100,000 miles, taking me to many cities in the United States where Americans of Cretan ancestry had settled after the war; and to England, Germany, Austria, Switzerland, and Greece. And of course, I made repeated trips to the land where this story took place—Crete.

I am indebted to many people whose narratives fill the pages of this book:

To John Alexander, then living in New York and now in Florida, who narrated to me the Hollywood-like story of his experiences and of his personal quest to avenge the murder of his father.

To my dear friend, Tony Kokolas of Fresno, California, who put aside his busy schedule in order to escort me to the many homes of Cretan families where I sat and taped their stories of the German occupation.

To Penelope Simvoulakis, who hosted us in her home in Modesto, California, and spent many hours with us reviewing the letters her beloved late husband wrote to her while serving in the Office of Strategic Services (OSS) on Crete. His story appears in the latter pages of this text.

To George Tzitzikas of Sacramento, California, who met with me on several occasions and exhibited a remarkable memory in detailing the rise of the Cretan Resistance Movement, and of his insight into the character of the personages involved. Although he was personally involved as a bemedaled combatant during the battle and as a guerrilla fighter during the occupation, he modestly kept the aspect of his own participation to a minimum, stressing the overall picture of the resistance to the German occupation.

To George Psychoundakis, who sat with me on the terrace of his home in the village of Tavronitis, Crete, and told me about his exploits as a messenger for the Special Operations Executive (SOE) during the occupation. He graciously gave me permission to use excerpts from his book, *The Cretan Runner* (1955) in order to develop the story of life under the Nazi oppressor. I relied heavily on his diary to narrate the pathos, tragedy, and sometimes humorous episodes that took place on Crete during that period of time.

It was George Psychoundakis, who in 1975, as caretaker of the German Military Cemetery on Kazvakia Hill overlooking the old airfield at Maleme, introduced me to a fellow-caretaker, another hero of the Resistance Movement, Manoli Paterakis. And it was in the shade of the trees that lined the lanes of German dead in that cemetery, and later his home in Khania, that Manoli Paterakis told me of his "adventures" during the battle and later in the Resistance, and of his involvement in the kidnapping of the German general, Heinrich Kreipe.

In 1983, I had the pleasure of hosting Patrick Leigh Fermor in my home. During our discussions, he modestly, almost reluctantly, spoke of the Kreipe abduction. It was during a sight-seeing tour through New York that he revealed how his mother had heard on BBC radio that it was Fermor who had led the successful abduction of the German garrison commander.

To develop the story of the kidnapping of General Kreipe, I relied heavily on Leigh Fermor's narrative "How to Steal a General" and excerpts from William Stanley Moss's diary *Ill Met by Moonlight* (1950), besides the comments by Fermor, Psychoundakis, and Paterakis.

I am also indebted to the late Herakles Petrakogeorgis—Hercules Petergeorge—the son of the great guerrilla chieftain Kapetan Petergeorge. We first conversed at length by telephone in the United States, and later met at his home in Iraklion, Crete, when he spoke of his father's work during the occupation and later in peacetime. He gave me his father's diary with permission to use any part or all in telling my story in *The Nazi Occupation of Crete*. I found the material of this diary invaluable in understanding the life of the guerrillas in the mountains of Crete.

To the many others who sat patiently with me and generously related their tales of those distant days, I am greatly indebted. It is unfortunate that because of space limitations I could not include all those stories in this text.

I must include two other people who were of great assistance in the writing of this book: my wife Virginia, for her support and constant encouragement, and my daughter Stephanie, who assisted with the interviews and rendered her editorial expertise to my manuscript.

Introduction

This is a true story. It is the story of human endeavor and sacrifice, underscored by deeds of heroism, which marked a historic event that began in the early days of the Second World War and concluded when the pealing bells of victory announced to the free world that the great struggle in Europe against Nazism was over.

It is a story that takes place on the island of Crete, site of the great Minoan empire of ancient times. The tale begins on May 20, 1941, and concludes four years later, almost to the day, on May 23, 1945. It begins with a battle in which Crete took center stage in the conflict between the free world and Nazi Germany, by becoming the site of the first airborne conquest of an island in the history of modern warfare.

For ten frightful and terrible days in 1941, Crete became the battlefield for the struggle between the elite of the German invading army, the Fallschirmjäger—the German paratrooper—and the hardened Cretan civilian, struggling to remain free, while fighting beside his gallant British Commonwealth ally. With the battle concluded in defeat, the proud people of Crete stood defiant, together with their allies, against the Nazi conqueror.

In the four long years of the dreadful Nazi occupation that followed the battle, the people of this island suffered heavily under the yoke of their oppressor. From the first day of the occupation, which began on June 1, 1941, the Cretan population faced a terrible trial of terror and death. In time, not a single village, home, or family remained unscarred from the wanton executions and harsh imprisonment imposed on them in reprisal for their opposition to the Nazi invader. Soon the island was draped in black as the bereaved people mourned their dead.

These people of Crete, who had resisted oppressors including the Franks, Venetians, and Turks throughout the centuries, would not bow and kiss the boot of their latest conqueror. Instead, their hearts beat defiance, and their thoughts turned to resistance and revenge. They banded together, men and women, young and old, and formed an army of patriots that for four years was to fight a continuous battle against their enemy, the Nazi conqueror.

In this crusade against the Nazis, they were joined by select British military personnel of the Special Operations Executive from the British Mediterranean command in Cairo, who worked clandestinely with this gathering army of civilians. In time, this civilian army became the nucleus of the Cretan Resistance Movement that would set the example of resistance against the Nazis for the other conquered peoples of Europe. They took up their guns of defiance and fought for their freedom—a freedom that took four years to gain.

To better understand the enactment of human drama that prevailed in this tale of resistance, sabotage, and espionage, it is necessary to retrace the chronological events that led to the German invasion of the island of Crete, which in turn culminated in the occupation that followed.

The attack on the island of Crete took place on May 20, 1941. However, the events that led to the military campaign in Crete and the occupation that followed had begun eight months earlier.

It all began in the early hours of October 28, 1940, when Benito Mussolini, the fascist dictator if Italy, presented an ultimatum to Greece. It was a demand that Greece open its borders to an Italian occupation. The ultimatum had an expiration time of three hours from the moment of presentation, after which Greece would be attacked if it did not accede to Mussolini's wishes. The diminutive, bespectacled, professor-like premier of Greece, John Metaxas, electrified the world with his courageous reply. He simply said, "No!" In those early days of the war, no one dared defy the dictators of the Axis alliance.[1]

Thus, at 5:30 A.M. on October 28, not even waiting for the official three-hour expiration limit of the ultimatum, Italian troops crossed the Greco-Albanian frontier. The invasion of Greece had begun.

For many months following the beginning of the war in September 1939, Benito Mussolini, the senior partner of the Rome-Berlin Axis alliance, had stood in the shadows as the junior associate of the alliance, Adolf Hitler, became the master of all Europe. During those tumultuous early days of the war, Mussolini watched enviously as the German leader added Austria, Czechoslovakia, Poland, Norway, Denmark, the Netherlands, Belgium, and France to his ever-growing Nazi empire. These territorial acquisitions were accomplished with the power of the sword—the might of the Luftwaffe and the mobility of the Panzers. With the stroke of the pen Hitler had also added Hungary, Yugoslavia, Bulgaria, and Romania to the Third Reich. Up to October 28, 1940, Greece had been the only neutral state in the Balkans.

Mussolini, a political thespian who fantasized himself as a modern-day Caesar, hoped to add the whole Mediterranean to his modern "Roman empire." He considered the Mediterranean to be his own sea. But Mussolini was never allowed to participate fruitfully in Hitler's conquests. The Fuehrer repeatedly turned down his requests for the rewards of victory. It was insulting to Mussolini to see his "student" become the master of all Europe. Finally, with the German occupation of Romania accomplished without first informing Mussolini, the Italian dictator could no longer endure these affronts to his pride. In a frenzy, he ordered the invasion of Greece.

Thus, it came to pass that in the pre-dawn hours of October 28, 1940, Italy invaded Greece; Greece was no longer a neutral nation. Great Britain immediately dispatched military aid to Greece and established a defense garrison on Crete, with a naval flotilla at the natural harbor of Suda Bay.

Since November 1940, Adolf Hitler had instructed his General Staff to prepare for a military campaign against Russia, to be identified by the code name of Operation Barbarossa. Having abandoned his plans for the invasion of Great Britain, Hitler had turned his attention to his Eastern frontier. With the preparation for the Russian campaign uppermost in his mind, Hitler, above all, wanted peace in the Balkans. Mussolini had disturbed that peace with his invasion of Greece. Worst of all, the British, who has been cast out of Europe at Dunkirk in June 1940, were now back on the European continent. Hitler's once quiet southern flank in the Balkans was now in flames.

Mussolini's legions advanced slowly into Greece until they reached the Kalamas River. There, the hastily entrenched Greek troops waited for them. In a military campaign that surprised everyone in the Western world, the little Greek army struck back at the Italian goliath. Bloody battle after bloody battle, fought in the brutally cold, snowswept mountains of Northern Epirus, was crowned with victory for the aggressive Greek soldiers. Within a period of five weeks, not one of Mussolini's legions remained fighting on Greek soil; those remaining were either prisoners of war, or they were dead. The Greek army had chased the routed enemy back up into Albania. So total was the Italian defeat that Mussolini considered the possibility of asking Hitler to intercede in his behalf for an armistice with Greece.[2]

Hitler now realized that his Italian ally was incapable of completing what it had begun. It was obvious that Hitler would have to come to Mussolini's assistance in order to extricate him from a delicate and humiliating position, and to restore peace to the southern flank of Europe.

On December 13, 1940, the German leader issued Directive Number 20, code named Operation Marita—the invasion of Greece—to secure control of the Aegean coast.[3] As a result, Hitler's military campaign scheduled for Russia in that time frame had to be postponed.

On April 6, 1941, Hitler unleashed his military might against the Greeks. It was a short but hard-fought campaign. The tired, outnumbered Greeks were no match for the German war machine. Fighting valiantly together with their British, New Zealand, and Australian allies, they put up a gallant but futile struggle. By the end of April, Greece had become yet another nation that had fallen beneath the heel of the German conqueror. Now, the German soldier stood only 168 air miles from the island of Crete. The die was cast for the events that followed.

Chapter 1

The Hunters
from the Sky

The island of Crete, steeped in history and blessed with a natural virginal beauty, floats like a huge barrier reef halfway between Europe and Africa. Its location in the middle of the Mediterranean Sea gave it strategic significance throughout the centuries. This was particularly evident in 1941, when General Erwin Rommel and his Afrika Korps mustered an army of panzers for a strike across the torrid sands of North Africa in an effort to drive the British back and seize the Suez Canal.

Crete, the fifth largest island in the Mediterranean, possesses a very diverse topography. Beginning on its northern shore with a landscape that is verdant, being filled with multicolored flora, vineyards, and olive groves, the terrain rises gradually into a steep maze of gorges and crags until it reaches the near Alpine range of mountains on its southernmost coast. Ranging from the White Mountains in the west, to Mount Ida (the birthplace of the mythological Zeus) in the center, to the Lasithi Mountains in the east, they range from 7,000 to 8,000 feet in height. The whole range ends abruptly on the southern coast of the island in a sheer drop into the Libyan Sea.

In 1941, there was only one main road, located on the northern coast, that served to link, like a thin black ribbon, the three major cities of the island. It connected Khania (also written on maps as Chania or Hania) which was the capital of the island in the west, with its natural deep water harbor of Suda Bay, to Rethimnon in the center, and terminating in the largest of the three cities, Iraklion. Each of these three cities–they were actually the size of towns–had an airfield. These airfields, when viewed with the island's strategic location in the Mediterranean, had convinced the Operations Section of the German High Command—the Oberkommando der Wehrmacht—that Crete should be occupied.[1] The Operations Division of the German Naval War Staff issued a memorandum to that effect, but Hitler had no intention of extending his Greek campaign to include Crete. With Greece conquered, the German leader once again turned his attention to his plan for the invasion of Russia.

At this time, fate took a hand.

General Kurt Student, a Luftwaffe officer with a resplendent military career that dated back to the First World War, was the ingenious creator of the German paratroop units. He felt that the seizure of Crete would present a great opportunity for his paratroopers. When Student became aware that Hitler had no desire to take Crete, he rushed to his immediate superior, Reichsmarschall Hermann Goering, the commander in chief of the German Air Force. Goering, designated by Hitler as his heir and number-two man in the German hierarchy, listened intently to General Student's plan for the capture of the island of Crete.

Since the Luftwaffe's failure at Dunkirk in the Battle of Britain, Goering's reputation had diminished in Hitler's inner court. He was tormented with the idea that his beloved air force would play a secondary role to that of the Wehrmacht and Kriegsmarine. Goering hungered for an opportunity to prove that his airmen were capable of great things. When general Student approached him with the plan proposing the air invasion of Crete, Goering accepted without the slightest hesitation. The plan offered an opportunity for glory to his Luftwaffe and a greater glory to himself.

On April 21, Adolf Hitler listened to the proposal as presented by Goering and Student, but he did not share Goering's enthusiasm for the operation. He felt that the plan was unworkable. Actually, if Hitler was indifferent to Student's operational plan, it was because the invasion of Russia was continuously ringing like a bell in his mind.[2] Nothing else mattered. After one postponement necessitated by the invasion of Greece, he did not wish to delay it any further. But Goering was insistent, feeling that nothing was impossible for his paratroopers. After all, he argued, this would be entirely a Luftwaffe operation without the need for Wehrmacht troops. Hitler remained adamant. Only when General Alfred Jodl, chief of operations of the Armed Forces High Command, reminded Hitler of the memorandum from Grand Admiral Erich Raeder that the airbases on Crete, in British possession, were only four flying hours from the oil fields of Ploesti in Romania—only then did Hitler yield. He knew very well that the oil supply from Ploesti was the lifeblood of the German war machine.[3]

It was not until April 25, four days later, that Hitler finally gave his approval. On that date, Operation Mercury—the attack on Crete—was issued and ordered to be put into effect.[4]

While the Germans were planning the attack on Crete, the British were also making hasty plans for its defense. As early as October 1940, when Mussolini invaded Greece, the British prime minister, Winston Churchill, had ordered that Crete be converted into an island fortress.[5] The problem arose as to whether any effort should be made to hold the island. Churchill believed that it should be held, while the Imperial General Staff and the Middle East Command differed in that opinion. General Archibald Wavell, the commander in chief of the Mediterranean Command, short of military supply and personnel and facing Rommel in the western desert of North Africa, had little to offer in the defense of Crete.

In December 1940, Churchill again wrote to Wavell, inquiring, "What have you done for the defense of Crete?"[6] Wavell, heavily burdened and absorbed by the grave problems confronting him elsewhere in the Mediterranean, gave no positive reply. He had to clear up Africa and Syria first, so the immediate defense of Crete was shelved. When it finally became apparent that the Germans were in fact going to attack Crete, Churchill asked again, "What is happening in Crete?" Wavell, now realizing the consequences of his delay and neglect, lamely replied, "I have done my best under the circumstances."

In London, Churchill made a last effort to salvage Crete. He entrusted Crete's defenses to an old friend, Major General Bernard C. Freyberg, a New Zealander, who had achieved distinction as the bravest and most decorated soldier throughout the British Commonwealth.[7] Unfortunately for Crete, Freyberg had little enthusiasm for this assignment. He also felt, like Wavell and the Imperial General Staff, that Crete was a lost cause. He refused the call to duty. Only when General Wavell admonished him, reminding him that it was "his duty to serve in Crete and take on the job,"[8] particularly since the assignment came from his old friend, Churchill, did Freyberg accept. However, his defeatist attitude would eventually affect the fate of Crete. As the sands of time ran out, 40,000 defenders, comprised of British, New Zealand, Australian, and Greek troops, waited expectantly from day to day for the coming attack.

The plan for the German attack was completed after much arguing between General Student and the Luftwaffe General Staff. A compromise was finally arranged whereupon the invasion would be divided into two phases.[9] The initial attack would be scheduled for early morning on the western part of the island. The other phase would follow later in the afternoon when the second attack would strike the defenders on the eastern half of Crete. Student remained adamant that all objectives be attacked simultaneously until Goering interceded to establish the compromise that was acceptable to all members of his staff.

The specifications of the final approved plan dictated that a special Assault Regiment of approximately 2,500 men, comprised of three battalions of paratroopers and one battalion of glider troops, would strike the western part of Crete in the morning attack. The objectives of the men of this Assault Regiment would be the seizure of the airfield at Maleme village and its protective high ground—known locally as Kazvakia Hill—but destined to become famous during the battle as Hill 107.

The paratroopers that made up the only airborne division the Germans had, the Seventh Airborne, were considered to be the elite of the German fighting forces. However, the men of the Assault Regiment, all volunteers from all walks of life, were the elite of the elite.

These elite volunteers of the Seventh Airborne Division represented the other Luftwaffe force that was to be used in this invasion of Crete. The Third Regiment of this airborne division was ordered to land in a valley east of the airfield at Maleme and seize the capital of Crete, Khania, and its harbor at Suda Bay.

In that same afternoon, the second phase of the attack would be directed at the cities of Rethimnon and Iraklion in the eastern part of the island. The objectives of this latter attack would be the seizure of these cities and their respective airfields. The assault on Rethimnon was assigned to the Second Regiment of the Seventh Airborne Division, while the First Regiment had Iraklion and its airfield as the objective.

All these objectives were to be achieved by nightfall of the first day. Three days were judged to be ample time for the subsequent mop-up operations that would conclude this airborne campaign. It was to take them much longer than they expected.

In the bright, sunny morning of Tuesday, May 20, the Germans launched their attack.

The morning hours of May 20 witnessed a huge armada of 650 bombers and 500 transports, with 70 gliders in tow, leave the airfields on the Greek mainland and head for Crete. A little after 6:00 A.M., the bombers arrived over the island. For one whole hour, high-level bombers of Heinkel 111s, Dornier 17s, and Junker 88s, together with the dreaded Stuka divebombers, shattered the peaceful, beautiful island of Crete with their bombs. It was the greatest concentration of aerial bombardment since the Battle of Britain.

By 7:00 A.M., the bombardment ended. In the wake of the bombers came the low-flying troop transports, the roar of their tri-motors echoing over the hills of Crete. Once over their respective targets, the orders came for the paratroopers to jump.

From the ground, soldiers and civilians alike watched the blue sky above Crete fill with colorful, blossoming umbrellas, floating gently toward earth. There were thousands of them, from Maleme to Khania and from Suda Bay to the foothills of the White Mountains. It was a spellbinding sight. A cry was carried alarmingly from mouth to mouth: "They are coming!"

"ERHONTE"—"they are coming!" yelled the Cretans.

"Those bloomin' blighters are here!" exclaimed a New Zealander to his fellow defender at Maleme airfield.

"Those bloody Huns have come!" an English officer yelled, passing the alarm.

Everyone stared into the sunny sky in awe and silence. Then a shot sounding from somewhere in the distance broke the spell. The battle for Crete had begun.

Almost from the beginning, the Germans were in trouble. The airfield at Maleme, which had appeared deserted from the air, now filled with New Zealanders, shooting at the descending Germans. The hapless paratroopers were shot while still floating in air. Most of them were dead before their feet touched the ground.

At Kastelli, a village on the coast west of Maleme airfield, a detachment of seventy-two paratroopers descended amidst the men of the ill-trained and poorly armed First Greek Regiment. In a matter of one hour, all the invaders were dead except for seventeen survivors. Among the slain Germans was their commander. The New Zealand military adviser to the Greek regiment placed the survivors in the town jail to protect them from the wrath of the Greek soldiers.

Even the officers had their share in killing Germans. The colonel commanding the Twenty-third New Zealand Battalion, located in defense positions east of the airfield at Maleme, stepped out of his headquarters tent and fired his pistol five times—killing five descending paratroopers. His executive officer, sitting at his packing-box desk inside the open-sided tent, shot two Germans, without even rising from his desk.

But soldiers were not the only ones fighting and killing the invading Germans this hot morning in May 1941. At the village of Modhion, halfway between Maleme airfield and Khania, old men and women, children, and even dogs attacked the Germans. With axes, with shovels, and with their bare hands, they fought the invaders like ferocious beasts.

Manoli Paterakis, a gendarme by profession, left his family in his village located high in the White Mountains and descended to fight the invader. He joined a band of other irregulars and together spent the next days shooting German paratroopers.

Another Cretan, George Psychoundakis, a youth of small stature, lithe, agile, with soft dark eyes, also left his home in the village of Asi Gonia, located high in the mountains of central Crete, and set out to kill the invaders of his home island.

And there were thousands of others like Paterakis and Psychoundakis—who set forth that morning of May 20 to fight this foreign invader who attacked from the sky.

Throughout Crete that morning, the Germans faced the pent-up fury of soldier and civilian alike. It was a slaughter.

General Eugen Meindl, the field commander of the parachutists and glider troops in the Maleme area, realized that the situation was going against them. In a daze, he followed this early development in the battle. This veteran officer watched helplessly as his units were being decimated. It seemed to him like a nightmare. He had never conceived the possibility that German troops could be so quickly destroyed.

The glider troops, attempting to seize the vital Hill 107, had failed completely in their effort. Other glider troops, assigned to the capture of the airfield at Maleme and Freyberg's headquarters near Khania, also failed, suffering many killed, wounded, and captured. The Third Battalion of this Assault Regiment, comprised of paratroopers, was completely wiped out. Of the 750 men in this battalion, which had dropped onto the defense positions of the Twenty-third New Zealand Battalion located in the village of Pirgos, east of the airfield at Maleme, only a few remained alive after a few hours of battle.

A messenger brought further disquieting news for General Meindl. His best officers, all leading units with specific objectives, had been killed. The German general was stunned, for this was the worst blow of all. How could he succeed in seizing the objectives without the leadership of these officers, now dead? Meindl momentarily considered abandoning the attack, but he knew that he had to go on. He decided that the only chance of success lay in the capture of Maleme airfield and its commanding height, Hill 107. These objectives had to be taken at all costs, and these paratroopers, the elite of the German army, knew how to fight as no other soldiers. They had been well trained and well disciplined. Meindl's order went out to them: "Attack!"

The Germans rushed forward toward the airfield and up Hill 107. The first ranks were cut down by the blistering fire from the New Zealand defenders, but the second and third waves leaped over the bodies of their fallen comrades and succeeded in capturing the western perimeter of the airfield. Simultaneously, they gained a foothold at the base of Hill 107. It was a frenzied attack! Bullets fell like heavy raindrops with mortars exploding in a cacophony of sound, as the Germans pressed the attack. The whole hill was ablaze with the smoke of battle.

The men of the Twenty-second New Zealand Battalion, defending Hill 107, were hard-pressed and were taking heavy losses. Colonel Andrew, the commanding officer of this battalion, requested assistance from the Twenty-third Battalion, located three miles to his right rear, but no help was forthcoming. The defenders of Hill 107 were on their own. Beneath the blazing hot Cretan sun, the struggle for this valuable piece of real estate continued throughout the whole day.

By late afternoon, Colonel Andrew decided to launch a counter-attack in order to dislodge the Germans from the base of the hill. With a handful of men—mostly artillery men who had lost their guns or were out of ammunition—he ordered the attack. It was a brave attempt and the men fought magnificently, however futile. The paratroopers clung feverishly to their positions like a shipwrecked sailor clings to a raft. The Germans knew that withdrawal in the face of this attack would mean the loss of the battle.

When the two tanks that led the counterattack—derelicts sent to Crete from the desert battles of North Africa—broke down, the surviving attackers withdrew. Having failed in his counterattack, Colonel Andrew informed his brigade commander, General Hargest, who was headquartered two miles to the east of Hill 107, that if he did not receive reinforcements immediately, he would be obliged to withdraw from Hill 107. His requests for reinforcements were again denied. Instead, he received the startling reply: "If you must withdraw, then withdraw."[10] It was a shocking comment from a brigade commander who never left his headquarters to go to the battlefield for a personal inspection. It is axiomatic in infantry tactics that the high ground must be held at all costs. Yet, without a second thought, Brigadier Hargest sanctioned the withdrawal. As night approached, Colonel Andrew planned for the withdrawal of the Twenty-second Battalion from Hill 107.

With nightfall, the sound of battle diminished. The Maleme area appeared to be asleep. The moonlight cast its bright light on the bodies of the dead who had fallen during the day's hard fighting. The Germans were hungry, thirsty, and tired, but no one was able to close his eyes. The atmosphere was tense and uneasy. Most of the Germans were scattered, alone or in small groups. They made no movement. They just lay there glued to the ground, under the olive trees and vines, waiting for whatever the night might bring.

General Meindl was apprehensive, for he expected a New Zealand counterattack at any moment. Only fifty-two of his paratroopers held the lower part of Hill 107. He knew that if the New Zealanders made a spirited attack that night, the Germans would be swept away like leaves before an autumn wind. But there was no movement evident from the New Zealand positions.

When the British commander, General Freyberg, was asked by the New Zealand division commander, General Edward Puttick, if he would permit a counterattack that night, Freyberg responded with the order, "The positions of the forces will remain unchanged." That thoughtless command sealed the fate of the battle for Maleme, and subsequently for the island of Crete.

In that twenty-four hour period of battle, Crete had been won and later lost. The battle was lost because the British commander did not realize that he had won it. With the fall of Maleme airfield and Hill 107, the defense of Crete was destined to defeat. It was a fateful decision by Freyberg, whose earlier attitude that Crete could not and should not be held now undoubtedly affected his decision. It was an unfortunate decision, for the opportunity for victory was irretrievably lost.

What General Freyberg did not know was that the German High Command had informed General Kurt Student that if his paratroopers did not succeed in securing a single airfield by the next morning, *the whole operation would be withdrawn.*[11] That is how close the British Commonwealth troops, who had fought so bravely with such heroic determination on this day of May 20—together with the ill-equipped Greek troops and hardened Cretan civilians—had come in inflicting upon the Germans their *first* land defeat of World War II. But the British command ordered no counterattack that first night. Instead, Freyberg ordered a meeting of his area commanders to take place the next morning. It was a meeting in which his commanders dictated self-serving and often contradictory requests to Freyberg, instead of receiving clear-cut orders from their commander in chief.

With no counterattack planned for the night of May 20 and no reinforcements forthcoming, Colonel Andrew, amidst objections from his gallant, hard-pressed officers and men, ordered the Twenty-second New Zealand Battalion to withdraw from Hill 107. Before sunrise the next day, a patrol of paratroopers crept up the hill in a surprise attack. To their own surprise, not a single shot was fired against them. The men of the patrol found the trenches empty, except for the dead. What they could not capture by force of arms during the day, they received as a gift that night. With the seizure of Hill 107, Maleme airfield fell under the control of the Germans.

Crete was lost in the Maleme area of the island, but in the eastern sector, it was a different story. At the towns of Rethimnon and Iraklion, the Greeks, British, and Australians were successful in their defense against the invader from the first attack in the afternoon of May 20, until the last day of the battle.

German paratroopers were dropped into this area, in this the second phase of the invasion, in the late afternnon of May 20. From the first moment of the attack, the situation was under the control of the Allied defenders.

At the town of Rethimnon and its adjacent airfield, the Australian defenders, together with two Greek regiments and the cadets from the Royal Gendarmerie Academy under the command of Colonel Ksifakis, kept the city and the airfield out of German hands. At one point, the paratroopers of the Second Regiment of the Seventh Airborne Division were surrounded, while the regimental commander was captured with his whole staff by the Australians.

As at Maleme, the Cretan civilian population of Rethimnon rose en masse to fight the invader. Everyone fought the Germans except one. That noncombatant was a naturalized American citizen by the name of Nicholas Alexandrakis. He had been born in Rethimnon but had emigrated to the United States where he had married and raised his family. He even had Americanized his name to Alexander. He had returned to Crete with his American family to visit his parents, when the war clouds came. Now he was stranded on Crete. He felt safe inasmuch as he was an American citizen, and the United States was still a neutral nation in that period of time.

To show the Germans that he was an American national and a neutral, he exhibited the American flag from a pole in front of his house and from the roof. Fate would rule otherwise, however, and Nicholas, together with his whole family, comprised of his wife, two daughters, and son John, were destined to face tragic tribulations of the occupation that followed the battle.

At Iraklion, the British, Australian, and Greek units fought ferociously against the paratroopers of the First Parachute Regiment. They fought with such determination that the German attackers became the defenders. The whole German regiment was split in two and isolated. Not only were they under constant pressure from the Australian and British units, but they were also constantly harassed by the sniping of Cretan irregulars. Manoli Paterakis, who had left his village and family high in the White Mountains to fight the invader, was one of those snipers.

Day after day, the ring of Allied steel drew tighter around the weary Germans. All the German paratroopers could do was to desperately hold on and pray for a miracle. The city and airfield of both Rethimnon and Iraklion remained securely in the possession of the Australian and British battalions until the end of the ten-day battle.

Once again, as in the Maleme and Rethimnon areas, the civilian population rose to fight the invaders. Even monks and priests joined the struggle. So fiercely did the Cretan people oppose the enemy that the Germans in furious frustration swore revenge.

On May 24, they gathered at random forty-two civilians from the villages around Iraklion and summarily executed them in reprisal for the valiant defense taken by the Cretan population. These hostages were comprised of men, women, and children. They were the first Cretans to face a German firing squad. They would not be the last. It was a portent of what was to come.

With the capture of Hill 107, General Student decided to concentrate the spearpoint of the German attack in the Maleme area. With the airfield now in their possession, troop transports began to arrive in a steady stream, bringing in new reinforcements. By the end of the second day of battle, more than 5,000 Germans of the Fifth Mountain Division had landed on Crete via Maleme airfield. The British Command, from the commander in chief, General Freyberg, in his headquarters near Suda Bay, to Brigadier Hargest, in his brigade command post east of Maleme, belatedly realized the major tactical error in allowing the airfield to fall into German hands. Freyberg now ordered a counterattack for the purpose of recapturing Hill 107 and the airfield, but it was too late! The commander in chief's hesitation in ordering the attack on the first night of the invasion gave the enemy the opportunity it sought to ferry in fresh troops. The Germans were now too strong to be dislodged from their positions.

With their strength increasing by the hour, the Germans returned to the offensive. They launched a series of attacks that caused the New Zealand troops and the remnants of the Greek regiments to withdraw. Village after village quickly fell to the newly arrived Mountain troops. But every square yard of the retreat was stained with the blood of the attacker and defender alike. There, under the gnarled olive trees, a drama of life and death took place. Glittering bayonets plunged and stabbed like a tireless machine as men fell like wheat before a scythe. It was a bloodbath.

The greatest bloodshed was spilled in the struggle that took place at the village of Galatas. This small, picturesque, hilltop village stood like a sentinel over the southern approach to the capital of Crete, Khania. If Galatas were to fall, the door would be wide open for the fall of Khania.

In a three-pronged attack, the fresh troops of the German mountain division, together with the surviving remnants of the paratroopers, struck the Galatas defenders. Maddened with the fury of battle and enraged by the stout resistance of the defenders, the Germans fought mercilessly. The ensuing battle was furious and fiery. Charge and countercharge left dead German bodies at the entrance to the village. The attackers gave no quarter, and none was given in return. Any captured soldier was slain on the spot. A group of New Zealanders, surrounded in a stone house, raised a white flag, but the Germans burned them alive with flamethrowers. One survivor tried to escape, but was caught and thrown barbarously back into the flames. The battle was fought foot by foot, yard by yard, street by street, room by room, house by house. It was a carnage.

While the central prong of the attack was sweeping through Galatas, a similar attack was taking place south of the village. It was directed at a strategic hill held by a company of New Zealanders from the Eighteenth New Zealand Battalion. The New Zealanders craftily held their fire until the Germans were right on top of them. The effect was devastating. Caught in a crossfire, the Germans were decimated. The assault was repulsed, but it was not over. They turned their attention to the flank of the hill position which was held by the Sixth Company of the Sixth Greek Regiment. This was a bedraggled, ill-armed unit that the New Zealand commander had earlier referred to as "malaria ridden chaps."[12]

"You must hold the line," the New Zealand company commander beseeched the captain of the Greek company.

"We shall!" he replied tersely.[13]

The Germans rushed the Greek defenses. They were greeted with a sporadic but brief defensive fire. Then the Greek weapons, already short of ammunition, were empty. The Germans pressed their advance. As one man, the Greeks rose from their trenches. The New Zealanders watched in shock. They thought that the Greeks were retreating.

In a sweep that reminded the New Zealand company commander of an old-fashioned cavalry charge, the Greeks raced down the hill with their bayonets sparkling in the afternoon sun. From their throats came the inspired shouts of "Aera"—the battle cry of the historic kilted Evzones. Their yells, similar in pitch to the Confederate shouts of the American Civil War, startled the Germans. They stood momentarily in mesmeric surprise, then fell back in full retreat. The Greeks followed them into the olive groves, slashing and killing. The German attack had been shattered. Among the German dead was their battalion commander.

Meanwhile, the village of Galatas had fallen, and now the Germans surged past the village and up the remaining hill, which stood as a final barrier in the New Zealand defense line. The New Zealanders, in the face of this heavy, overwhelming attack, broke and fell back in retreat.

Colonel Howard Kippenberger, the commander of the Tenth Brigade defending this perimeter, watched in alarm as his men trickled back from the defense line. They were wild-eyed, without their helmets or rifles. Kippenberger recognized the symptoms. It was not a retreat—it was developing into a rout. As more of his men came over the hill, he rushed into their midst, waving his arms and shouting, "Stand for New Zealand!"[14]

With an electrified response, the men awakened from their momentary lapse. The retreat had been stopped, and the New Zealanders turned to counterattack. Now, it began all over again—the same slaughter in reverse. Bayonets drawn and drunk with the taste of their own blood, the New Zealanders tore into the Germans. In the twilight hours that remained before nightfall, the New Zealanders recaptured the village of Galatas. These gallant men, from the distant land below the Southern Cross, had written the finest pages of their history that day at Galatas.

In his headquarters at the Grande Bretagne Hotel in Athens, General Kurt Student, the commanding general of the German forces attacking Crete, stared thoughtfully out the tall windows of his office. He looked upon Constitution Square and the Tomb of the Greek Unknown Soldier, but was too deep in thought to focus. Student was worried. He had promised Adolf Hitler that he would capture Crete in three days; Hitler gave him five days. The attack had been delayed from the original date of May 15 to May 17, and finally to May 20. Now, eight days later, Crete was still in British hands. His forces were advancing, but the progress was painstakingly slow with heavy losses to his beloved paratroopers. Student knew that time was very important in Hitler's plan for his scheduled attack on Russia. Even General Franz Halder, chief of the General Staff of the German army, had written him a memorandum that the delay in Crete might cause another postponement in Operation Barbarossa—the attack on Russia.

On May 27, General Student received a painful message. It read:

FRANCE FELL IN EIGHT DAYS, WHY IS CRETE STILL RESISTING?[15]

It was signed by Adolf Hitler.

On that same day, General Freyberg requested permission from General Wavell to evacuate Crete. He wanted to disengage his forces and retreat to the southern coast, where they might be transported to Egypt. He stated that "his troops had reached the limit of their endurance."

Freyberg's earlier attitude of defeatism had now surfaced. He had no communication with his forces in Rethimnon and Iraklion to learn of the defeat that his Australians and British troops, fighting side by side with the Greek irregulars, had inflicted on the Germans. Nor did he seem to acknowledge the determined resistance and gallantry exhibited by his New Zealanders at Galatas. He thought only of withdrawal from Crete.

In spite of Churchill's continuous exhortations that Crete be held, Wavell convinced him that further battle was futile and that the troops should be withdrawn. Churchill reluctantly acceded to Freyberg's request.

The question remained: "Would the Royal Navy assist us in the evacuation?" This was the question put to the chief of the Mediterranean Fleet, Sir Andrew Cunningham. Once again, as at Dunkirk and later in Greece, the Royal Navy rose to the occasion. In distinct Nelsonian tones, Admiral Cunningham declared that "it take sthe Navy three years to build a new ship, but it takes three hundred years to build a new tradition."[16]

The brave men sailing the ships of the Mediterranean Fleet played their greatest role in Crete since the days of Dunkirk, but they paid a heavy price for their heroism. In the sea battle around Crete, the British were destined to lose nine ships sunk and fifteen ships damaged. In no other sea battle fought in the Second World War had the Royal Navy lost as many ships in any single battle.

The order to evacuate was passed to the British Commonwealth troops. Suddenly, everyone—British, Australian, and New Zealander—felt the desire to leave this once beautiful, peaceful island. The flames of war had converted it into a cauldron of death and desolation.

Khania was abandoned amidst the shattered houses of that beautiful city. The last defenders stood, fought, and died in their tracks, in rear guard resistance, while the rest of the troops left Suda Bay for the southern coast.

The dusty, dirty route south to Sfakia became choked with columns of ragged, defeated soldiers. They struggled forward, stumbling over each other in battle-weary exhaustion. General Freyberg, leading the retreat, looked sadly at the brave but battered remnants of his proud command. They had fought a good fight; he could ask no more of them. When Sfakia was finally reached, the Royal Navy was there waiting for them. In the next few nights, using the cover of darkness to avoid attacks from the ever-present Luftwaffe, the Mediterranean Fleet was able to remove a total of 16,511 men from Crete.

By June 1, the evacuation had ended. Five thousand soldiers were left behind to surrender to the Germans. For them, the battle for Crete was over.

But what of the Cretan civilians, who had fought the German invaders like soldiers? Their agony was just beginning. In the next four years of the occupation, it was to become the Calvary of Crete.

Chapter 2

With Victory
Comes Revenge

With the battle concluded, an eerie silence fell over the land. No longer was the roar of exploding shells heard, spewing death and destruction in their wake. There was no bark of rifles nor was there the rapid burp sound of machine guns, no more the cacophonic din of battle, just silence.

At first, many of the island's inhabitants believed that with the cessation of hostilities they would be able to resume their lives, even though they barely survived amidst the rubble of what was once their homes, their villages, or their cities. They would bury their dead, grieve over their losses, and then go on with their simple pastoral lives, even though they were now under the heel of the German invader.

However, General Kurt Student, who had fathered this airborne invasion, could not forget the scene that had assaulted him when he first visited Crete in the middle of the ten-day battle. He could not erase from his memory the sight of his beloved paratroopers sprawled in every grotesque position of death, with their blackened, bloated bodies rotting in the hot sun and covered with fat, green flies.

In almost two years of war, the triumphant legions of the German army had occupied most of Europe, and everywhere the conquered civilians cowered with fear before the presence of the German soldier. Just the sound of his hobnailed boots striking the pavement was enough to instill terror into the heart. Yet, here on Crete, the civilian population had risen in bitter opposition and had fought with a snarling ferocity this invader who sought to deprive the Cretan of his free spirit and of his liberty.

Kurt Student could well understand the valiant and stubborn

resistance of the New Zealand, Australian, British and Greek *uniformed* troops during the battle, for they were *soldiers* who had been ordered to resist the enemy. It was their sworn duty to stand and fight their enemy to the bitter end, but the resistance of the civilian population was a complete surprise. It was an inexplicable surprise because during the planning stage for the Cretan invasion, Admiral Wilhelm Canaris's Bureau of Military Intelligence, the Abwehr, had reported to Student that the Cretans were Germano-philes who would greet them with open arms.

The Abwehr intelligence staff had failed to evaluate the past history of Crete in its bitter struggle against another oppressor—the Turks. All that an Abwehr agent had to do was step into a Cretan home, simple and austere as it was, and observe the family portraits that adorned the walls. Portraits of grandfathers, fathers, husbands, and sons—the Kapetans, an honored title which in Crete denoted a leader, of Cretan tradition—dressed in their native costume, rifle in hand, pistol and knife at the belt, and bandoleers across the chest— would have given him an indication of what to expect.

Student had read reports from General Julius Ringel, the commanding general of the Fifth Mountain Division, who had arrived in Crete with his troops in order to reinforce the dwindling numbers of the harassed paratroopers. These reports stated that Cretan civilians were picking off German troopers from rooftops, from behind windows, walls, and trees. It angered Student to learn that no German was safe from the danger that lurked everywhere; that death was a common denominator in the hands of Cretan civilian sharpshooters. He had heard of the episode involving the Cretan civilians at the village of Modhion, near Maleme airfield, who had attacked a platoon of paratroopers with axes, scythes, knives, and bare hands, slaughtering many of them before forcing the survivors to flee.

He had yet to discover to what extent such civilian resistance had affected the battle in areas like the strategic village of Galatas, where civilians joined the Sixth Greek Regiment and the Eighteenth New Zealand Battalion in totally decimating the Second Parachute Battalion; or at the village of Alikianou where civilians joined the Eighth Greek Regiment in impeding the advance of the German Engineer Battalion, inflicting heavy losses on them and, in doing so, keeping the Germans from outflanking and encircling the New Zealand defense perimeter. Had the Germans been able to break through the defense line at that village of Alikianou, there would have been no opportunity for withdrawal and subsequent evacuation of the Commonwealth forces from the southern shores of Crete. Nor had Student heard of the resistance in the city of Rethimnon, where the civilian police held the Germans of the Second Parachute Regiment at bay; or in Iraklion, where the citizens of the town attacked the Germans of the First Parachute Regiment with such fury that they almost brought the invader to a point of surrender.

In addition, there were reports from the village of Kastelli, in the western part of the island, where civilians had joined the men of the First Greek Regiment in decimating a detachment of paratroopers. The reports added that the bodies of the German dead showed evidence of having been brutally executed *after* their surrender. The dead paratroopers had apparently met their demise not by bullets but by distinct slashes and punctures of knives or swords, or by having their skulls bashed. The report erroneously concluded that these were acts of *atrocity*.

It never occurred to the Germans that the civilian defenders had no rifles or pistols with which to repel the invader and had resorted to the age-old weaponry of knife, sword, and club. It was an act of defense, not an act of atrocity.

Although there were international regulations governing the treatment of enemy soldiers in uniform, the Geneva Convention made little reference to civilians—whether men, women or children—fighting as soldiers without uniforms. During the Franco-Prussian War of 1870, French civilians fighting the Prussians were called *franc-tireurs* by the Germans, who did not hesitate to shoot on sight these "French-shooters." That same word was revived to describe the resistance of the Belgian civilians during the German invasion of their land in the First World War. The wholesale atrocities committed by the invading Boche against the Belgians is recorded in the history of that war. In this Second World War, those civilians who rose to resist the Nazi invader were labeled guerrillas. As in the instances of the earlier wars, the Germans reacted with the same response. It was to be no different here on Crete in 1941.

As early as May 23, while the battle for Crete was still in its third critical day, General Ringel issued a memorandum from his headquarters at the Fifth Mountain Division with this information:

THE GREEK POPULATION, IN CIVILIAN OR GERMAN UNIFORMS, IS TAKING PART IN THE FIGHTING. THEY ARE MUTILATING AND ROBBING THE CORPSES OF OUR GERMAN SOLDIERS.

Then the memorandum, which was distributed to all the echelons of his divisional command and to the paratroopers, ordered that

ANY GREEK CIVILIAN TAKEN WITH A FIREARM IN HIS HANDS IS TO BE SHOT IMMEDIATELY.

And, finally, the words that would begin the program of senseless punitive executions, first in Crete and later in other occupied countries:

HOSTAGES (MEN BETWEEN 18 AND 55) ARE TO BE TAKEN FROM THEIR VILLAGES AND IF ACTS OF HOSTILITY TAKE PLACE AGAINST THE GERMAN ARMY WILL BE SHOT. TEN GREEKS WILL DIE FOR EVERY GERMAN![1]

This memorandum became an edict for murder that the German troops of occupation lost no time in promulgating.

General Student endorsed this edict.

He was to govern Crete only twenty days after the cessation of hostilities before he was recalled to Germany by Hitler. However, in those twenty days Student was determined to punish the civilian population of Crete. He wanted no magnanimity shown to the vanquished—no mercy, only revenge.

Student's surviving paratroopers were among the first to wreak their vengeance against these Cretans who dared to resist them. They could not and would not erase from their mind the sight of their dead comrades killed at the hands of these civilians. They fell on the coastal towns and villages of their latest conquest with an insatiable thirst for vengeful blood. They sacked and they looted the improverished homes of the villages and towns, which in their austerity had little to offer in the form of wealth to these soldiers from Hitler's Germany. Finally, in their frustration, these paratroopers killed many innocent hapless civilians for the sake of killing. It became a bloodbath. However, this was not to be the end; it was only the beginning.

From the first day of the occupation, June 1, 1941, the peace that momentarily prevailed with the cessation of hostilities was again torn asunder by the sound of rifle fire echoing through the verdant hills and valleys of Crete, as German death squads, obedient to Student's orders, marched from village to village collecting hostages at random for execution.

One such unfortunate village was Kontomari, located in the

western part of the island, just off the main northern highway, one mile east of Maleme airfield.

On Monday afternoon, June 2, a platoon of German paratroopers approached the outskirts of this village. All of them still wore the camouflaged combat uniform that they had worn in combat, and it still clung to their bodies like wet tissue paper soaked with perspiration. Many of them had cut their trousers off above the knees so as to gain some cooling relief from the searing heat of the Cretan summer. Many still wore the round steel helmet that so characterized the German paratrooper, while others had changed to a cooler white pith helmet.

Kostas Mavridakis was sitting under the shade of an old, gnarled olive tree, together with three other villagers. He had celebrated his twenty-seventh birthday the day before with these same three friends. They all heard the sound of a motor, and they assumed it was a passing aircraft. When Kostas looked again, he saw army trucks approaching the village.

"Germans are coming this way, wonder what's up?" he remarked in a low tone as if his voice would be heard by the Germans over the roar of the approaching motors. There was, however, a note of alarm in his question.

"They are probably coming to take us for labor gangs to bury their dead," one of Kostas's companions opined.

Kostas's friends rose and approached the side of the road to watch, filled with a curiosity that was unbridled by any apprehension of what was to follow. The trucks stopped suddenly in front of the three, and amidst the gutteral shouts of commands, German paratroopers jumped off. They immediately seized Kostas's friends and herded them off toward the village.

Kostas lingered behind, saw the Germans approach his friends, and quickly rolled behind a thick bush. Still unseen by the Germans, he remained hidden behind the bush, later making his escape among the olive groves. He had no wish to serve the Germans in any labor gang. It was a decision that saved his life, for these paratroopers represented the first of many death squads sent out to exact punishment on the Cretan population.[2]

The commanding officer of this execution squad was Oberleutnant Horst Trebes. It was First Lieutenant Trebes, who, during the first night of battle on May 20-21, had led a platoon of paratroopers from the elite Second Assault Battalion in an attack to seize

Hill 107, only to find the defense positions left empty by the retreating Twenty-second New Zealand battalion. He had survived the battle and had returned now to fulfill General Student's edict of revenge.

While his troopers encircled the village of Kontomari, Trebes waited in the village square, examining a bloodied German tunic. He tried to determine whether the soldier who wore it had met death by bullet or blade. The slash in the center of the bloody stain indicated the entry of a knife or sword. It was enough evidence for Trebes to assume that an "atrocity" had been committed against a German soldier.

The paratroopers went from house to house collecting all the men and women—young and old—and all the children, and herded them like cattle in the village square. Many of the men were working in the fields when they were seized and forced to join the rest of the villagers in the square. In a short period of time, all these villagers, dressed as they were in their drab garments of everyday wear, stood with a look of uncertainty and bewilderment in their eyes.

One villager, with a piece of paper in his hand, stood apart from the group. Trebes spoke to him several times but did not order him to join the rest of the villagers. It appeared that he was an informer.

Now the paratroopers began to separate the old men, the old women, and all the children from the rest, and crowded them to one end of the village square. The remaining group, comprised of the village males aged 18 to 55, was huddled into a nearby grassy field under some olive trees. Kostas Mavridakis's three friends were among this latter group.

One old woman at last realized what the paratroopers were planning and turned to rejoin her son in the huddled group on the grassy field. Unmindful of her tearful, pleading eyes, a paratrooper stopped her and forced her to return to the group of older villagers, while her white-bearded husband stood aside, stoically, yet defiant, in the face of the treacherous deed that was soon to take place.

As the Germans positioned themselves in a semicircle around the twenty-five ill-fated young men of Kontomari, one of the condemned approached Trebes. The platoon leader eyed him aloofly, noting that he was the only one wearing a tie and jacket. The youth pleaded with the German, explaining that he was not from this village but had come here on a visit.

Trebes listened but ignored the youth's plea, his cold eyes sighted beyond him, staring at the crowd of elders in the village square. Finally, he turned to the youth as if to reply, but instead shouted in a loud voice for all the villagers to hear that "because you have killed some of *my* men in your village, now I will kill *your* men!"

The young visitor from another village continued his pleas with Trebes, but to no avail, and was brusquely returned to the condemned group of men that were gathered in the grassy field. He must have been frustrated at his ill luck, for he welled up in tears and sobbed openly.

A young boy ran up to a sergeant standing next to Trebes, and pointing at a grey-haired man leaning against an olive tree at the outer edge of the grassy field, cried out: "That is my father . . . please let him go!" One of the paratroopers grabbed the boy by the shoulders and forcibly led him back to the group of elders in the village square.

Trebes looked at his sergeant and nodded.

The old men in the square grimaced with torturous pain, while the women—the mothers, wives, daughters—screamed in anguish as the paratroopers fired volley after volley into the young men in the grassy field.

Some fell where they stood, still defiant even in death. Others sought refuge amongst themselves, embracing each other, as the bullets tore into their bodies. The shortest of the group hid behind the trunk of an olive tree, while another kneeled behind him, both hoping that the trunk would protect them from the searing bullets. One paratrooper stepped up and fired point blank at both, until they too fell dead. Some tried to run, but were quickly brought down. Then, there was silence.

The bereaved, shocked villagers in the square rushed forward only to be held at bay by a circle of Germans menacing them with their weapons. Then the anguish rose again, as the syncopated bark of a pistol told that an officer was delivering the coup de grace to each young man's head.[3]

Their task completed, the Germans mounted their trucks and left the village of Kontomari leaving behind them orphans, widows, and bereaved parents.

Like the village of Kontomari, other villages were soon to suffer a similar fate in order to satiate the German thirst for revenge. In some cases, the ordeal was greater.

So it was with the village of Kandanos.

Back on May 25, during the height of the battle, armed civilians from the surrounding villages concentrated high in the escarpments of the White Mountains near the village of Kandanos. They ambushed an approaching battalion of mountain troops, holding it at bay for three days, while inflicting heavy casualties on the Germans. It was a unique battle in which untrained civilian mountaineers, armed with old vintage hunting weapons, surrounded the professional, elite mountain troops and slew them one by one. When they ran out of ammunition, they used the weapons taken from the German dead. The Cretans also had suffered casualties, though much fewer than the invader. After the third day of intense battle, the Cretans withdrew to the higher protective escarpments of the White Mountains. The Germans licked their wounds but dared not follow. They were satisfied with the capture of the village.

On June 3, the Germans came back to Kandanos.

The villagers were warned, via the mountain grapevine, of the German approach and of their intentions. Most of them left the village for the safety of the rugged mountains. The Germans found only seven villagers who had remained behind, unmindful of the danger they faced. Their fate was to be the same as that of the twenty-five young victims executed the previous day at Kontomari. A young girl of 12 years faced the terror of execution together with the six other hostages. Once they were executed, the Germans systematically razed the village to the ground. In its place, they erected a sign, in German and in Greek, which proclaimed that it was done

IN ORDER TO PUNISH THE ARMED MEN AND
WOMEN RESIDENTS WHO KILLED GERMAN
SOLDIERS AT THIS SITE. . . .FOR THIS KAN-
DANOS WAS DESTROYED![4]

Village after village underwent in 1941 what the Czechoslo-vakian village of Lidice suffered in 1942. The whole free world had heard of the tragedy of Lidice, but little became known of what had occurred in the villages of Crete. Little was heard of the wanton killings of innocents and the willful burning of their homes.

Even individual Cretans who had fought as spirited patriots in the defense of their homes were no exception to the German pogrom of punishment and revenge.

Men like Nicholas Manolakakis, from the village of Spilia, located southwest of the airfield at Maleme, had waged a one-man war against the German invader in order to avenge the death of his wife and his beloved son, who had been shot by the paratroopers on the first day of the invasion. In that period of ten days, Manolakakis had personally killed some forty paratroopers. Now, the Germans were searching for him and had placed a bounty on his head. They had announced that if he did not surrender himself immediately, they would execute ten hostages from his village for each day's delay. Manolakakis heard of this proclamation, he returned from the safety of the White Mountains and surrendered himself. The Germans made him dig his own grave, and when he had finished, they executed him.[5]

The same fate befell another Cretan named Antoni Skoumbakis. During the battle, he had shot three paratroopers near the village of Perivolia (translated as the village of the gardens) just outside Khania. In one day, a platoon of paratroopers surrounded the village, collected thirty hostages, men and boys aged 18 to 55 years, and executed them. When they realized that Skoumbakis was not among the slain, they placed a bounty on his head. If he did not surrender, another thirty hostages would be shot from the village. Skoumbakis, safely hidden in the distant village of Keramia, heard of the bounty and decided to return. The next morning, he presented himself to the local police precinct in Khania and asked that he be taken to the German Kommandatura. Two days later, in a field behind the German military police headquarters, Antoni Skoumbakis was executed.

The afternoon prior to his execution, two young men from a neighboring village were walking past and saw him digging. They did not realize that he was digging his own grave. An armed German guard stood nearby. They greeted Skoumbakis, and he stopped digging long enough to offer the youths some cigars which the Germans had not taken from him.

"Will the guard let us accept them?" they asked.

"He will. He is a good boy from Austria," Skoumbakis replied. The two youths lit their cigars and then asked him what he was digging.

"My grave," he replied.

The two youths were struck speechless. They sought to quickly get away from this poor man who spoke of his own death so indifferently. "He smells of death," one youth whispered to the other.

"Do you want us to tell anyone in the village?" they asked him.

"No," was his response, as he dug out another shovel full of dirt. "I have written to them. Just tell them to forgive me."

The young men departed, saddened to tears, and Skoumbakis continued to dig out his grave.[6]

Nor did the German executioners have any respect for the clergy.

On June 4, another group of paratroopers surrounded the village of Skalani, south of Iraklion. At that moment, the Right Reverend Fotios Theodosakis was conducting a funeral service for his elderly aunt.

When all the inhabitants had been collected in the village square—as was the Germans' routine before choosing those who would become the victims of the execution—their officer stepped forth. Father Fotios recognized him. The German lieutenant still wore the bandage on his face which Father Fotios had placed there when he had treated his wound during the battle. Now, the German had returned with the grim look of revenge etched on his face.

The German officer selected the priest and three other villagers to be shot. He remembered that they were the most active during the battle.

"So this is how you repay kindness," Father Fotios said to the lieutenant. "God forgive you!"

The lieutenant ignored him and ordered that the four be marched to the neighboring village.

It was long, hot, exhausting march for Father Fotios, still dressed in his heavy, black clerical robes. When they reached the next village, the four hostages were brought before the commanding officer for judgment. They stood accused; there was no salvation for them. All the interrogating officer wanted to know was who else in the village of Skalani had participated actively against the Germans.

That night, the four were thrown into a makeshift prison where they rested their weary bodies on a pile of manure. They were hungry and thirsty, for all forms of sustenance had been denied to them. Finally, a young sympathetic German guard heeded the priest's pleas and furtively threw him a canteen of water.

Just before dawn, Father Fotios awakened his fellow prisoners and made them pledge not to reveal to their interrogators who else in the village was involved in the actual skirmish against the paratroopers.

"We are lost," he said to them, "but let us not be the cause for any one else in our village to die." The men, who loved and respected the priest, agreed.

Early the next day, the Germans marched the four back to Skalani village. They had already sent orders ahead that three graves were to be dug by the villagers. By the time the four condemned hostages reached the village cemetary, all the villagers had been forcibly gathered there to witness the execution.

At the last moment, the officer in charge pulled one of the four prisoners out of line and kicked him aside. There were only three graves dug, and that error had saved the villager, Kosta Tsanakis, from execution.[7] The remaining three hostages, Father Fotios, George Tsikaloudakis, and Angelo Louloukakis, were disrobed and summarily shot by rifle bursts from the three paratroopers who comprised the firing squad.

The villagers gazed in horror at the bloodied corpses, as they lay in their graves, and made the sign of the Cross. The officer in charge forbade them to bless themselves. They were not to make the sign of the Cross to honor the memory of these dead hostages, he ordered, nor would they be allowed to place flowers on their graves. The German revenge would be total.[8]

Father Gregory Progoulis, the 24-year-old parish priest of the Church of St. Demetrios in Platanias village in the Khania sector, was selflessly busy in the days that immediately followed the battle. During the battle, his village of Platanias was the site of the New Zealand Brigade headquarters and of very heavy fighting.

The young priest still marveled at the miracle that had saved his church from destruction during the devastating bombardment that had taken place during the battle. It was during one such bombardment that a 1,000-pound bomb had fallen in the dirt patio outside the church entrance and had failed to detonate. Considering that brigade headquarters was just down the road, Father Gregory was thankful that the Germans had not concentrated an additional air attack in this vicinity.

During the days that followed the battle, Father Gregory attended his parish, offering prayers and communion to whoever requested them, and saying many prayers for the dead, for death was all around him.

One afternoon, word reached the young priest that three wounded New Zealanders were hiding in the wine cellar of a home that belonged to George Zoforianakis. When he learned that the house had been abandoned and that the wounded soldiers had no food or water, the tireless young cleric decided to go to them. Taking a loaf of bread and a small jug of wine, he set off across the fields, dressed in his flowing black rob with his ever-present round black hat on his head.

Unfortunately, a German patrol happened to observe him as he hurriedly crossed the fields and became suspicious. The sergeant leading the patrol watched him for several minutes through his field glasses and decided to follow him to his destination.

It was a long hike under the hot Cretan sun, and when Father Gregory finally reached the Zoforianakis house, he was saturated with perspiration. The tired priest was unaware that the German patrol was close behind. He found George Zoforianakis standing there, staring sadly at the roofless, blasted masonry that once had been his home.

"Where are our friends?" inquired the priest.

Zoforianakis led him into a wine cellar that had been built into the side of a small hill.

The three New Zealanders greeted him respectfully. They hungrily ate the bread and washed it down with the wine, warm as it was. Though the young priest did not understand their words of gratitude, he comprehended their appreciation from the look in their eyes. He turned to Zoforianakis: "Bring me some water. I want to wash their wounds."

Zoforianakis went out to fetch water from the well. Without warning, a burst of machine-gun bullets ripped across his back. No sooner had the echo subsided than three Germans rushed into the cellar with their tommy guns trained on the priest and the three New Zealanders. A huge German grabbed the priest and gruffly threw him out of the cellar. Hatless and bruised, he staggered to his feet. Not far from him lay the lifeless body of the slain Zoforianakis.

Father Gregory uttered a cry of grief as a burst of machine-gun fire echoed from the depths of the cellar. The distraught priest stood there with his eyes closed and a prayer on his lips, waiting his turn to be shot. But the Germans had other plans. Tying his hands before him, they dragged him back to the village of Platanias.

Father Gregory Progoulis was executed that same night. The reason given was that he had given aid to enemy soldiers. When his family requested the body, the German local commander refused to give it up for burial. Instead, they let it lay at the site of the execution for three days, under armed guard, in order to teach the villagers a lesson of what happens to those who render assistance to the enemy.[9]

Thus, it continued throughout the island, day in and day out. Execution followed execution, either individually or en masse. In that first month of the occupation—June 1941—more than 2,000 Cretans faced the terror of death before German execution squads.

The Germans said that "they were avenging the thousands of slain brothers-in-arms who now filled the whole island with their graves." This was their justification for these executions. This is what General Kurt Student had ordered them to do—to punish the Cretan population for their resistance.

The Cretans, however, could not and would not accept this as justification. With agony, anguish and sorrow—not to mention fear and terror—they had seen their fathers and brothers shot to death. They had seen their children killed in their mothers' arms. They saw men and women—young and old—fall before German bullets. They witnessed the burning of their villages and of their churches; the destruction of all that was sacred to them in their lifetime.

These barbarous deeds, exacted on the Cretan people by the German occupation forces on a daily basis, created a state of constant persecution that brought death and desolation to almost every family throughout the island. However, the German plan to punish the Cretans with these persecutions failed in its purpose. The Germans were soon to learn that these brutal acts of inhumanity, instead of terrifying the Cretans into submission, created in them a raging hatred, bolstering the Cretan spirit with defiance and arming them with the weapon of revenge. In time, their wrath would prevail until the yoke of the oppressor was destroyed.

Chapter 3

Fight to the Last
Drop of Blood

When General Kurt Student departed from Crete, he left behind a land whose soil was saturated with the blood of approximately 2,000 innocent civilians who had been executed in order to satiate the conqueror's thirst for vengeance as punishment for having opposed the soldiers of the Third Reich.

In his place came General Alexander Andre who would be the new senior military commander of the Fortress of Crete—as the Germans now called their latest conquest.

The Cretan political leadership in the capital city of Khania had been informed that General Andre was not a National Socialist or a member of the Nazi party. Before the war, he had been a member of the Social Democratic party and had been one of its representatives in the Reichstag, before Adolf Hitler, as the Fuehrer, abolished all political parties. With that fact in mind, the political leaders in Khania formed a committee and requested an interview with the new commandant. In their hearts sparked a glimmer of hope that they might be able to pursuade the new commandant to put an end to this inhuman slaughter of innocent civilians.

This committee met with General Andre at his military headquarters in the village of Pelikapina, which was located a few miles beyond the western exit of the capital city of Khania. This tall, stately mansion had formerly been the residence of King George II of Greece in the days before the invasion. Inasmuch as this was the best and largest house in the village, the Germans had comandeered it for Student's succesor. Constantine Manos, the original owner of the mansion, had graciously presented it as a residence to his monarch when King George had fled the mainland of Greece for the safety of Crete. Now, the Germans brusquely evicted Manos and converted the residence into Andre's headquarters.

The committee, which was comprised of a bishop, the mayor of Khania, and two of the city's leading citizens, arrived at the German headquarters riding on donkeys. The smirking German guards were expecting them, but kept them waiting in the outer foyer for almost an hour. Finally, they were ushered before the new German military commander of Crete.

Resplendent in his dress uniform, the general did not rise when they entered but remained seated behind his desk. On his desk lay a huge map of Crete.

Although the members of the committee were there on a mission of mercy, they entered the main room of the commandant's office with a certain degree of determination evident on their faces. They stood before General Andre, not humbly but rather hopeful that they would succeed in their mission. All they wanted was to reason with him and have him understand the plight of the Cretan citizenry.

The general took note of this and studied them for several minutes before he spoke. He did not invite them to sit, not even the bishop.

"I have read the history of Crete," he began as an opener, "and I must say I admired your heroic opposition to the Turks."[1]

Andre's opening remark startled the committee. The four exchanged rapid glances with each other. It was a good beginning, they thought. Perhaps this new commandant was appreciative of Cretan lore and history, and because of this appreciation might understand why the Cretan people had resisted the parachute invasion of their island so stubbornly.

Bishop Xirouhakis, the leader of the committee, was the first to respond. In soft, mellifluous tones—as if he were speaking before his congregation—he stated that "the Cretan people wanted nothing more but to be left alone, to rebuild their shattered homes, and then go on with their daily life; they wanted only that these mass executions cease, and that *hereafter let each person be responsible for his own actions.*"[2]

The other members of the committee nodded their concurrence but kept silent.

Andre, still seated, looked sternly at the bishop. In momentary silence, as if evaluating the bishop's words, he opened a gold cigarette case and placed one of its contents between his lips. His aide, who was also his interpretor, jumped forward to light it. He took a few puffs and blew the smoke upward. The elderly bishop, tiring, shifted his stance.

"I must repeat that I admired the way the Cretan people opposed the foreigners who came to conquer you in the past, but *why* did you oppose *us*? Why did you not oppose the Englanders who came here before us? You knew that they are our enemy!"

The youngest member of the committee lost patience with the general's remark. He spat the words out.

"What did you expect us to do—cross our hands and surrender?" He continued, "the British are our friends, while you came to drive us out of our homes, dishonor us, and kill us with your planes and cannon. Our spirit forbade us to surrender—*you* read our history!"

General Andre's eyes flickered in anger as he rose from his chair for the first time. The bishop threw a furtive, angry look at the young committeeman and raised his hand to silence him.

The German commander placed his cigarette in a tray, blew out a wisp of smoke, and stared fixedly at the bishop. He totally ignored the young man who had uttered such unfriendly words with such arrogance.

"We did not come to your island because we wanted to—the war brought us here—this war against the English. We shall try to administer justly and we shall assist you in your daily work, but we ask for your patience."

The bishop nodded understandingly. In his heart, the same spark of hope rose again in that the German might finally accept their plea and order all executions to cease, in spite of the previous speaker's antagonizing remarks. After all, this was the purpose of their mission, and not to be contentious. Unfortunately, this hope lingered for only a second, before being quashed by the commandant's final comments.

"I cannot declare an amnesty as you request. You must assist us in our work here peacefully, and when I see cooperation on your part—only then will I consider such a proposal."

Andre's facial features hardened, and his tone became more emphatic as he continued, "Germany has the power to enforce her will in your land, and God help those who resist! The list of penalties has not ended yet. It depends on you . . . and I ask you to cooperate for the good of your people!"

He stood before the committee, one hand on his hip while the forefinger of his other hand drove home the full meaning of his words. There was no need for the translation, for the bishop and the other members of the committee had understood the meaning from the vehemence of his tone. The bishop took one step forward, pleadingly with tears glistening in his eyes. The general turned his back.

When the interpretor had completed the translation, Andre nodded to him just once, the signal that the audience was over. The committee was dismissed.[3]

So the executions continued. On the first of August 1941, the greatest mass execution took place. Squads of Germans motored out from Khania on the roads that led southward toward the villages of Koufos, Vatolakos, Skines, Fournes, Ourthouni, and Nea Roumato. In each village, they collected all the male inhabitants and then marched them to the village of Alikianou.

It was at Alikianou village that the tattered and ill-equipped Eighth Greek Regiment had held the German Paratroop Engineer Battalion at bay so long and so well during the battle. It was a defense that kept the Germans from breaking through and rolling up the flank of the New Zealand defense perimeter. Now the people of Alikianou and the surrounding villages were to pay the price.

At the bridge over the Kerites River, the Germans selected their victims. They huddled 142 of these hostages onto the small stone bridge and executed them with machine-gun fire. This was the largest number of any previous single mass execution. It also differed from all the countless other executions because this group included an octogenarian, a youth of 14, and a 15-year-old girl.

It appeared that General Alexander Andre wanted to underscore his remarks to the committee when he stated that "Germany has the power to enforce her will in your land!"

With the new military commander in Crete came the Geheime Staatspolizei—the security state police—better known as the Gestapo. The major cities of Khania, Rethimnon, and Iraklion were now infiltrated with members of the Gestapo—members who were nurtured on suspicion and raised on deceit. But although these were inquisitorial functionaries, the most dangerous Gestapo members were the anonymous spies, the paid informers, who noted "overheard" conversations, opened letters, tapped telephone lines (the few that existed), and passed on scraps of information that accumulated into dossiers.

In Crete, these Gestapo informers were instructed to uncover the names of the dissenters who were involved in clandestine activity against the German occupation. They were also ordered to learn the names of any Jews who inhabited the cities or the villages of the island.

The campaign to obliterate the very existence of the Jews of Europe had been set in full motion by the summer of 1941. Reichsfuehrer-SS Heinrich Himmler, the director of the dreaded Gestapo, had promulgated a program through which all the Jews of Europe would eventually be exterminated. It was designated by the code name, The Final Solution.

Throughout the Nazi-occupied lands of Europe, Jews were gathered for shipment to concentration camps to die from disease, starvation, hard labor, and firing squads, and in the dreaded crematoria. It was a modern-day pogrom for the mass murder of a hapless and innocent people. When the Germans occupied Greece, that same program was extended to include the Jews of that ancient land.

There were not too many Jews living in Crete in 1941. Only a few resided in the capital city of Khania, and none in Rethimnon. Most lived in Iraklion which was more cosmopolitan.

There was no distinction between the Jews and Christians of Crete as a people. Most of the islanders were Greek Orthodox in religion, who respected their Jewish brethren in the pursuit of their faith. Most of the Jews were wealthy merchants with Cretan names. There was no distinction between Christian and Jew, and it was unthinkable to bear hatred for their fellow citizens, the Jews of Crete. It was not until the German invasion of the island that the Christian Cretans realized the hate that the Germans bore for the Jews.

The first Jews known to die in Crete at the hands of the Germans was the family of Rabbi Ben Israel Sholub, his young wife, and two children. It occurred on May 22, 1941—at the height of the battle—when the invading paratroopers of the First Parachute Regiment were forced to withdraw from Iraklion by the persistent attacks of the British Black Watch Battalions and the harassing tactics of the Cretan civilian irregulars. Frustrated by this defeat, the Germans vented their fury on the civilian population by seizing forty-two hostages. Rabbi Sholub and his family were among them.

Born and raised in Germany, the rabbi fled during the early days of the Nazi rise to power. He traveled to Greece and settled in the large Jewish community of Salonika, Greece's second largest city. It was in Salonika that he married and raised his children.

When the Germans invaded Greece, he and his family boarded a steamer for Egypt but were transported instead to Crete for his appointment with destiny. His flight from Nazism finally ended at the execution wall in Iraklion.[4]

When the Gestapo arrived on Crete, they sought to victimize the Jews. It proved difficult, for the Jews of Crete had names indistinguishable from other Cretans, and the Greek Orthodox Cretans would not reveal who were the Jews in their community. It was a human brotherhood united against the Nazi oppressor. However, the Gestapo had many methods of finding out, one of which was through the utilization of paid informers.

Many of the older Jews of Iraklion were executed together with other victimized Cretan civilians without the Germans ever realizing that they were, in fact, shooting Jews. When the Germans did succeed in identifying Jewish hostages, they were quickly shipped to the Greek mainland for transportation to Germany and subsequent internment in concentration camps. Other Jews were sent to Aghia prison in Prison Valley, in the western sector of the island, to die from starvation, disease, or execution.

Many Orthodox Cretans sympathized with the Jews in their plight, even though they knew that they faced the same danger of death. Many of them jeopardized their own lives in order to offer succor to their fellow humans.

Anthony Kastrinakis knew that his next door neighbor was a Jew, and he knew what the Germans ultimately planned for him, his wife, and three boys. In spite of the danger that threatened himself, his wife, and his own two boys—if discovered—he took his neighbor into his own home. He passed the family off as his cousins and nephews who had been visiting him from Athens when the invasion of Crete occurred. For many months, Kastrinakis succeeded in this ruse until the day when an informer betrayed him.

It was dinnertime when the Gestapo troopers burst into the apartment. Amidst heated protests by Kastrinakis, the Germans gathered the males into the living room of the house and ordered them to drop their pants. One cursory glance at the circumcized males identified the Jews.

The screams of the women echoed into the street, when the Gestapo soldiers opened fire with their machine guns. The bullets cut down the Jewish father and his three boys, just for being Jews. The same fate was meted out to Kastrinakis and his two boys for giving shelter to a Jewish family. The women were shipped off to serve in the labor gangs of the death camp prison in Prison Valley.[5]

The spacious home of Doctor Anastasios Karvoulakis in Iraklion proved to be the haven for two Jewish families. He had hidden one family of four in the attic of his home, while the second family of three lived a secluded life in the basement. Each day he sought to find whatever food was available in order to feed his own family and the two Jewish families in his charge. Each day, he would cut a huge loaf of bread—which he usually purchased on the black market—into three pieces. One piece was for his family, and the other two were relegated to those hidden in his attic and basement.

Doctor Karvoulakis was successful in keeping his sheltered guests out of the hands of the Gestapo up to the German withdrawal from Crete in 1944.[6]

Many others, however, were not as fortunate. Their names were added to the list of all the civilians who were executed during those four dreadful years of the occupation.

One of the most feared and hated representatives of the Gestapo on Crete was Sergeant Fritz Schubert, who in the Gestapo held the rank of unterscharfuehrer. Schubert had been assigned as an interpretor to the military commander in charge of the garrison in the city of Rethimnon.

At first glance, this short, dark-complexioned Nazi noncommissioned officer appeared to be a nondescript soldier of the Third Reich. However, he differed from the rest of the Germans, whose attitude toward the Cretan civilian population was one of indifference, one of soldiers following orders. In contrast, Schubert bore an innate sense of hatred for the Greeks. In the next four years of the occupation—first in Rethimnon, then in Iraklion, and later in Khania—this hatred drove him to atrocious excesses. In time, he was cited as being responsible for at least 1,000 civilian executions on his orders, not to mention the innumerable victims of his sadistic torture devices.

In the beginning, Schubert was an enigma to the people of Rethimnon, for they did not know how to judge him. He was a German, who spoke fluent Greek but with a thick Turkish accent, while on his tunic he wore several Turkish crescent-shaped medals. He also spoke Turkish, besides German and Greek, but he indicated a preference for Turkish over the other languages. For this, the Cretans nicknamed him "The Turk."

In fact, Fritz Schubert was a Greek born in Smyrna, now Izmir, Asia Minor, in 1900. His real name was Peter Constantine, or Petros Constantinidis. In his early twenties, he went to Germany, became a German citizen, and adopted his new name of Schubert. Later, he returned to the city of his birth and worked with the Turks on behalf of the German government. There is evidence to indicate that he served with the Turkish army in the sacking and burning of Smyrna in 1923.

In 1937, he found his niche in the order of life and became an active member of the German National Socialist paty. He became a dedicated Nazi. Why Schubert, born a Greek, went to Germany, and as a German citizen joined the ranks of the Turkish army to fight the Greeks, will never be known. Nor will it ever be known why he bore such a hatred for anything Greek. But in Crete in 1941, he was in a position to exercise this feeling of hate to the utmost.

Day or night, he walked, or rode on his white horse, through the town looking for the slightest infraction by the townspeople of military regulations or curfew. He would stop a passerby at random and ask for identification. If the papers were not in order, Schubert would arrest him gleefully and without hesitation, and drag him to Gestapo headquarters. There, he would take pleasure in torturing the poor victim during interrogation. If Schubert was convinced of the person's innocence, he would release him; if not, he would imprison him or have him shot. Often, the inhabitants of Rethimnon were seized and detained for torture without cause—just to satisfy Schubert's sadistic tendencies. In time, the name of Fritz Schubert became anathema to the people of Rethimnon, as he would be to all of Crete. His nickname "The Turk" was now equated with barbarity.[7]

John Alexander and his family were among many Americans of Greek ancestry who were caught in the middle of the European war. They witnessed the bloody battle of Crete and later suffered the German occupation of the island. As Americans, they were neutral, for the United States was at peace, and Pearl Harbor was still six months away.

John was born in Wheeling, West Virginia, and had come to Crete in 1940 with his parents and sisters on a visit. His father, Nicholas, had come to the United States from Greece in 1919 and in due time became a naturalized citizen. So proud was Nicholas of his new homeland that he Americanized his family name from Alexandrakis to Alexander.

He worked in a local grocery store in Wheeling, which he later purchased when his employer died. The years were good to Nicholas Alexander; he married a local girl, whose parents lived in Iraklion, and raised two girls and a boy. John was the youngest of the three.

In June 1940, Nicholas Alexander decided to visit his parents and in-laws who were still living in Crete. A week after John's graduation from high school, Nicholas and the whole family departed for a three-month trip to the land of his roots. He had been warned against the trip because of the danger of war that threatened the continent of Europe, especially since Benito Mussolini was making menacing overtures against Greece. But Nicholas Alexander was adamant. He was advised at least to register with the American embassy once he arrived in Greece.

After a lengthy sea voyage that took them from the Port of New York to Naples, to Piraeus, Greece, and thence to Suda Bay, Crete, the Alexander family finally arrived at Nicholas's paternal home on Grigoriou Street in Rethimnon. In his anxiety to arrive at his destination and see his birthplace once again, he forgot to register with the American embassy in Athens.

Nicholas Alexander found the island to be as primitive, beautiful, and peaceful as it has been when he had left it in 1919. Unfortunately, that peaceful existence was marred when war came to Greece four months later as Italian troops crossed the Greco-Albanian frontier in Mussolini's attempt to expand his proclaimed new Roman Empire.

John Alexander saw many of his new young friends depart for military service, having been conscripted to serve in the Fifth Cretan Division, which was sent to the Albanian frontier. As an American, John was neutral.

During the German airborne assault on Crete in May 1941, the Alexander family left for the safety of the southern mountains, hiding in caves during the heavy air bombardments that ensued. With the battle over and the occupation begun, this American family returned to its home on Grigoriou Street.

To show the German occupying forces that he was an American, as noted earlier, he hung the Stars and Stripes from a pole in front of his house, and a second one from the roof. He was proud to be an American, and he wanted to show his patriotism for his adopted land. It was also a security measure, to remind the Germans that his home was neutral territory.

During one of his rounds through the village seated as usual on his white horse, Sergeant Fritz Schubert noted the American flag flying in front of the Alexander home and sneered at what he called *typical American arrogance.*

"As far as I am concerned," he confided to a civilian Gestapo agent assigned to his headquarters, "that damned Alexander clan is Greek and as such bears watching. See to it!"

In time, the Alexander family's path would cross that of "The Turk"—Fritz Schubert.

With the battle concluded, there were many New Zealanders, Australians, and British soldiers of all ranks whose fighting spirit would not allow them to surrender to the German victor. Approximately 1,000 men were able to escape from the stricken island in some manner or other, while 11,835 others remained behind to become prisoners of war. However, there were still 500 Commonwealth soldiers who roamed the hills and mountains of Crete seeking sustenance and shelter from the Cretan population—an assistance that they received heartily and without qualm or question.

The Germans called these stragglers "deserters" and sought to apprehend them. With the arrival of the Gestapo on Crete, a program was initiated that became ruthless in its enforcement not only for the hunted escapees but also for the civilians who harbored them.

One night, two Australians were brought clandestinely to the home of Nicholas Alexander for refuge. The guide who brought them reasoned that no one would suspect that the neutral American would harbor stragglers. The plan was to keep the two Australians secluded until the appropriate opportunity arose to transport them to the southern coast of Crete for evacuation by boat to Egypt.

Private John Carr and Corporal James Matthews of the Eleventh Australian Battalion were apprehensive, for they did not wish to endanger the lives of the Alexander family. But Nicholas Alexander welcomed them, alleviated their fears with his good-natured warmth, and secluded them in a hidden room, entry to which was by a trapdoor in the wall of the main bedroom.

Nicholas shared his family's meager meal with his two guests, and at night, his son John—who had developed a close relationship with them—would take them out into the backyard for fresh air. Unfortunately, one night they were observed by a neighbor.

The neighbor innocently and thoughtlessly spoke of his discovery at the local coffee house. It was overheard by one of Fritz Schubert's civilian agents, an informer masquerading as a visitor from another village. It was his function to sit and listen, and unobservedly eavesdrop on all conversations. When he heard the whisper about the two Australians and the Alexander family, he rushed to file his report with Schubert.

The next day, two Volkswagen jeeps skidded to a halt amidst a cloud of dust in front of the Alexander house on Grigoriou Street. Schubert and three Gestapo troopers rushed the house, smashing the door in with one blow from a rifle butt.

Schubert entered behind his three Gestapo men, pistol in hand, glowering at Nicholas Alexander, who was seated with his wife, son, and two daughters at the table in the main room. The surprise created by this noisy and abrupt intrusion into their home was evident on their faces and immediately replaced by apprehension. They thought of the two Australians in the hidden room. Mrs. Alexander cast a quick glance toward the bedroom with its trapdoor.

Nicholas Alexander rose from his seat slowly. "What do you want here?" he inquired of Schubert in a voice one would use to challenge a trespasser.

Schubert looked at him with hate-filled eyes, his dark complexion turning red with rage. "How dare you question me, you Greek, who dares hide under the American flag!"

With a motion of his hand, Schubert ordered two of his men directly to the bedroom where they quickly found the trapdoor. John caught his father's look and followed the Germans, just in time to see them enter the hidden room. The two Australians were seized and roughly dragged out of the house. John ran after them, only to be stopped at the door by the third German.

It was obvious that they had been betrayed. Later, John learned that the guide who had brought the Australians to the Alexander house had been captured and tortured. It was obvious that he had revealed the secret before he died.

Nicholas Alexander overcame his initial shock and protested vehemently. "You cannot enter this house without permission! I am an American citizen. So is my family!"

Schubert stared at Nicholas, surprised that this Cretan had the audacity to speak to him so authoritatively, and enraged that he had dared to sequester Australian stragglers, contrary to German occupation restrictions.

Nicholas rushed to the drawer of his desk and took out two American passports—one of himself and his wife, and the other which pictured his three children.

"Here, we are American citizens—neutrals!" he shouted angrily at Schubert, and with that he leaned forward to show the documents to the Germans. "The Turk's" eyes blazed at the arrogance of this man who did not cower before him.

Schubert turned abruptly and with a snap of his wrist fired his pistol at Nicholas Alexander.

Whether he meant to frighten Nicholas or kill him will never be known. The bullet struck the elder Alexander in the forehead over one eye, propelling him backward. A splash of blood splattered the nearby wall and flowed from the large wound in the back of his head, where the bullet had exited.

Katina, his wife, fainted and the two daughters screamed in terror. John, recovering quickly from the initial shock of seeing his beloved father murdered, threw himself at Schubert, grabbing him by the throat and epaulets. The third Gestapo trooper quickly stepped in and knocked John into unconsciousness with a blow from the butt of his rifle.[8]

Angered and livid that a civilian dared lay hands on his person, Schubert ordered the guard to take John Alexander to Gestapo headquarters, together with the two Australians. As he walked out of the room, he cast an indifferent glance at the dead man lying on the floor in a spreading pool of blood, with his wife collapsed beside him, and the two girls sobbing hysterically at the tragedy meted to them by this evil Gestapo man.

Sergeant Schubert returned to Gestapo headquarters distressed. His commanding officer, Major Fuchs, must not learn that he had shot an American citizen. If the American legation were to find out, there would be repercussions. To cover up, he realized that he must not keep John Alexander in the Rethimnon prison. In order to be rid of him, he ordered two Gestapo troopers to drive the American to the prison compound at Aghia, in Prison Valley, well west of the city of Rethimnon, located in the Khania area. There, without a passport to prove his American origin, he would die from disease or firing squad. In either case, John Alexander's death would cover Schubert's indiscretion.

The prison complex to which John was sent consisted of a group of one-story buildings in a valley south of the village of Galatas, just east of Aghia village. The British always referred to it as Prison Valley, whereas the local inhabitants spoke of it as the prison at Aghia. Before the war, it was an agricultural rehabilitation prison. In either case, it was a camp where all prisoners faced death or disease, and most often both. One section of buildings housed the Commonwealth prisoners of war, while in the other buildings were the civilian detainees, crowded together like cattle.

It would be difficult to envisage the conditions that prevailed in the Prison Valley complex where civilians were tortured and executed without trial. There were the screams of the tortured and the sobs of the sick and feeble, soon to die. Daily, in groups of ten, they were taken out and shot in the field beyond the prison complex. The prison had become a death camp.

John Alexander, sitting in a corner of the building into which he had been cast, still had not fully recovered from the shock of seeing his father slain. Tragedy had entered his young life quite suddenly. His sorrow was compounded by his concern for the welfare of his mother and two sisters. Their friends in the United States were right, he thought, when they had advised his father against traveling to Europe at a time when the threat of war was so imminent.

He still nursed the cut at the side of his head caused by the rifle butt that had knocked him senseless. It was a cut that would leave a permanent scar. Yet, at this time, that cut and the event that had preceded it back at Grigoriou Street awakened in him a feeling he had never known before. It was a feeling of fuming anger that slowly turned to hate.

For John Alexander, that moment marked the end of the innocence of youth and the beginning of the maturity of manhood. He vowed to avenge his father's death, and he swore revenge on Schubert and on the rest of the Nazis who had brought death and sorrow into his family.

It became a vow that he would nurture each day of the war. To fulfill that vow, however, John realized that he would have to escape from this hellish prison before he, too, became a victim. Then, he would return to Rethimnon, kill that Turkish Gestapo beast, Schubert, and rescue his mother and sisters. But first he must escape.

Within a few days, John Alexander noted that there was a daily detail of prisoners selected by the guards from the more able-bodied. It was a burial detail chosen to bury the many who had died the previous day from disease or firing squad. He toyed with the idea that this might be a way for him to escape from this hell. On the fourth day of his imprisonment, John volunteered for the morning burial detail.

There were two other young Cretan men in the work detail that day, Dino and Dimitri. John never learned their last names. Together, they pulled a two-wheeled cart on which, with saddened respect, they placed the corpses, many of which were already swelling and rotting with a terrible stench from the searing heat of the day.

As he and his companions bent to pick up the decomposing body of a young woman, Alexander whispered furtively to Dino that at first opportunity he was going to escape. Dino looked at him, without stopping what he was doing. Momentarily taken aback by the thought of escape, he grunted and agreed to join him. They passed the word to the other young man in the burial detail, Dimitri, but he was not as agreeable.

"Why are you talking?" the guard shouted, pointing his rifle at them. Dino picked up the corpse's brassiere and with a sheepish smile showed it to the guard. The German's lip turned down in distaste. Dino's quick thinking had fooled the inquisitive guard.

Later that afternoon, as the three youths dug the huge crater that was to serve as a common grave for the corpses, John reminded them that it was now or never and beckoned the guard to come closer. Curious at John Alexander's motion, the guard approached, and as he looked down into the grave site, Dino swung his shovel. Struck a full blow at the back of his head, the guard fell into a heap into the crater. He lay there motionless.

John and Dino dropped their shovels and fled, heading southward toward the mountains. Dimitri stood there shocked at what Dino had done. He realized that he could not stay behind, for he would be accused and shot. Though fearful and hesitant, he had no choice but to follow the other two, although he followed at a distance.

They traveled all night until they reached the deep gorges and crags of the White Mountain range, where they felt some degree of safety. They were certain that as soon as the Germans discovered what had happened they would pursue.

The next morning, they stopped at a home on the outer fringe of a village. They feared to enter the village lest there be Germans about. The three refugees thanked the hosts for their hospitality and left that night, circumventing the village.

They hiked all night, moving very slowly among the mountain trails, carefully picking their way over the rugged rocks, aided by the bleak light of a quarter moon. They continued climbing until fatigue had sapped their strength to the point of exhaustion. On a narrow plateau between two huge escarpments they found a sheepfold. All three crawled in and immediately fell into a deep sleep.

The sun was high in the bright blue sky when the three still-exhausted young men were awakened by a gruff voice. Its owner jabbed a rifle into John Alexander's ribs. John squinted at him through bleary eyes and assumed that they had been caught by the Germans. When the three stepped into the sunlight, they were relieved to see that he was not wearing a German uniform.

When they explained to him who they were and what they had done, he smiled and remarked with some pride that he was a runner for a guerrilla group that tenanted these mountains and that he would guide them to safety.[9]

He was not much older than John, Dino, or Dimitri and introduced himself as George Psychoundakis from Asi Gonia near Rethimnon. This short, lithe, bushy-haired guerrilla runner raced far ahead of the struggling trio, skipping from rock to rock, jumping over crevices like a mountain goat, climbing ever upward over the rugged terrain of the Cretan mountains, leading the three refugees to safety. They hiked with little rest for two suns and three moons, until they finally reached the southern coast of Crete.

Out of the darkness there loomed a huge edifice, built on a gentle slope and cradled between two protective escarpments. John Alexander felt a cool breeze flow past his hot cheek, a clean refreshing wind that blew in from the Libyan Sea.

"You will be safe here," Psychoundakis assured them. "These monks will take good care of you. Tomorrow, you will meet the abbot, Father Agathangelos Lagouvardos."[10]

"But where are we?" John asked the young guerrilla.

"You are at the Monastery of Preveli, south of Rethimnon."

For the first time in a week, John Alexander lay comfortably in a bed with a full stomach and free from the fear of death. And for the first time he realized that he did not know the full name of his two fellow escapees. In fact, he was destined never to see them again.

When Fritz Schubert learned that Alexander had escaped from prison and that a guard had been killed in the process, he was furious. In his rage, he sought to seize John's mother and two sisters, even his grandparents, as hostages. But much to his chagrin, he discovered that they had left for the safety of a village deep in the southern mountains, well out of his reach. In angry frustration, he ordered that any villagers held in the Rethimnon town jail be shot. Fifteen such innocent victims met their fate by this order. For Schubert to order an execution in the Galatas-Aghia area, where the escape had taken place, was out of his jurisdiction. He would not be assigned to the Khania area until 1944.

The executions continued at random throughout the island.

Soon an outcry of despair rose from the Cretan population. Nonetheless, their freedom-loving spirit would not yield in the face of such brutal oppression. Instead, they left their cities and villages for the safety of the rugged heights of the southern mountains, where they banded together to form an irregular army of resistance fighters. From the heights of these mountains they pursued a ferocious struggle against the Germans. The mountains and valleys soon echoed with the din of battle as skirmishes turned into bitter but short engagements. Many Cretans died in these struggles against a well-armed enemy, but the toll of the German garrison was greater. Many areas of the island became unsafe for a German soldier to tread. Germans who went in fearlessly seldom came out alive. But the Germans still had their scapegoat—the Cretan civilian population—those that still remained in the villages. Eventually, the Cretan agony and despair became a cry for revenge. It became an outcry that reached the ears of the guerrillas, who vowed to fight and destroy the oppressor of their land. Thus, the stage was set for the creation of what was to become the best organized and most effective movement in the Cretan struggle for freedom.

At first, the Germans did not have the manpower or the

organized administrative coordination to police the whole island thoroughly. The tired combat troops had already been relieved and replaced by fresh garrison soldiers which, unfortunately for the Cretans, included SS units and the Gestapo. However, these reinforcements were not sufficient in the face of the rising resistance movement.

General Alexander Andre, the German occupation commander, needed more troops to help police the island and defend against these newly formed Cretan bands whose sting was beginning to be felt. His requests for additional men fell on deaf ears in the German High Army Command—the Ober Kommando des Heeres. The German General Staff was more concerned about the need for more men and supplies to strengthen General Erwin Rommel and his Afrika Korps in Libya, who at this time was striking toward the gates of Egypt. Additional troops were also needed to feed the massive effort of Operation Barbarossa which had begun on June 21-22 in order to bring Russia to its knees. There would be no more troops available to help police Crete.

The German commandant of Crete now realized that if he offered amnesty to the Cretans, as had been requested earlier by the select civilian committee that had met with him, perhaps the civilian population would accept peaceful coexistence, and perhaps the newly formed guerrilla bands would desist from the nuisance attacks against German outposts and patrols. The question that arose in General Andre's mind, however, was how he could consider this proposition of amnesty without losing face, in view of his earlier refusal. In granting such an amnesty, the Cretans might feel that it was being offered from a position of weakness. After careful review, he decided not to yield to this proposition. The executions would continue.

Assistance in this matter now came from an unexpected source. Back on the Greek mainland, the vice-president of the Greek puppet government of General Tsolakoglu had heard the appeals regarding the daily slaughter of the inhabitants of Crete, appeals that stemmed from some of his own ministers in the puppet government. Vice-President Logothetopoulos agreed to make a personal appeal to General Andre on behalf of the Greek puppet government.

While in Crete, he also met with the select civilian committee from Khania which had initiated this request for amnesty. Bishop Xirouhakis, who had led the committee in an earlier meeting with

General Andre, together with Nicholas Scoulas, the mayor of Khania, met with the vice-president in a schoolhouse in Khania.

The Greek vice-president pressed on the committee the urgent need for a peaceful coexistance between the Cretan people and the German occupying forces.

"Do not oppose them," he advised. "Remember, the war for us in Greece and in Crete is over. Let us live in peace."

The bishop lowered his head and frowned at the futility of the vice-president's words. The remark did not impress the mayor of Khania.

"Let us live in peace with them?" he shouted angrily at the vice-president. Then he added sarcastically, "Tell that to the Germans!"[11]

General Andre was somehow impressed with this latest effort for peaceful coexistance which resulted from the meeting between the Greek puppet vice-president and the select Cretan committee. He therefore agreed to issue a decree of amnesty only if the Cretan population would surrender all their weapons. But the Cretans had no intention of surrendering their weapons; they did not trust the German commander.

"Suppose," they argued, "we *did* give up all our weapons—and if the German goes back on his word, we would then be defenseless and at the mercy of our enemy."

Indeed, the Cretans had in their possession many rifles and machine guns which they had seized from the dead paratroopers during the thick of the fighting. Even during the last days of the battle, back on May 30-31, a delegation of old men had approached the headquarters of Brigadier B. H. Chappel of the Welsh Regiment, commanding the defense forces at Iraklion, and had asked Chappel for arms to continue the fight after the British evacuation. Chappel was so moved by their pleas that he ordered that all available weapons in the armory be given to them.

To conform with Andre's proposal and thus gain a reprieve from this slaughter of innocent civilians, Bishop Xirouhakis and his committee were able to collect approximately 1,800 weapons, 70 percent of which were old vintage rifles of an earlier era, while the remainder were defective. The modern weapons remained hidden for use by the guerrilla forces.

The promise of peaceful coexistence, added to this collection of weapons, satisfied the German commandant. He had saved face and in so doing issued a decree of limited amnesty. Thus, a momentary cessation of executions went into effect in the early fall of 1941. It was not destined to last long.

This amnesty came too late to soothe the grief, pain, and bereavement felt by the thousands of Cretans who had lost so many relatives in the bloodbath that had begun on June 1, 1941. It was too late to quell the hatred that had welled up in the Cretan heart. This hatred, coupled with the earlier cry for revenge that came from the victims of this Nazi slaughter, had reached the ears of those who had earlier fled to the mountains, and they intended to respond.

The early attacks on German outposts and patrols were disorganized, even though they had a telling effect. After several such engagements, it became obvious that the movements of the guerrilla forces were desultory. They needed organization, and to gain such organization they turned to several outstanding men who had already established themselves as patriots in the cause of freedom.

Men like George Petergeorge—or Petrakogiorgis—a businessman from the village of Megarikari, who had fought in the battle for Crete in the Maleme-Khania area and had lost a son in the battle; Emmanuel Bandouvas from the village of Asites, who also had fought in the ten-day battle with outstanding heroism in the Iraklion area; and Anthony Grigorakis, better known as the fearless Kapetan Satan, became leaders of three of the most effective guerrilla* forces on Crete. All three men were given the honored title of "Kapetan" which in Crete denoted a leader, in this case a guerrilla leader.

In early August 1941, these three Kapetans met with other guerrilla leaders, such as Stefanogiannis and the heroice Mixali Xilouris, who had exhibited great leadership against the Germans of the Second Parachute Regiment at Rethimnon in the heat of the battle for the island. They met in the village of Asites located southwest of Iraklion, deep in the crags of Mount Ida. These leaders met to plan an organized strategy of attack and resistance against the Nazi garrison that occupied Crete.

The meeting was lengthy, and the plans were well formulated. Before parting, they all took an oath which they vowed to keep to

---

*The Greek word for *guerrilla* is *andartes*; however, the synonymous term *guerrilla* is used throughout this text.

the end. They clinked their wine glasses and swore "to fight the enemy of their land to the last drop of blood and until their island had gained its freedom, and the Cretan people their liberty."[12]

The Cretan Resistance Movement was now officially organized.

Chapter 4

The Baker Street Irregulars

While the Cretan guerrilla leaders organized their forces, and while John Alexander remained secluded within the secure walls of the monastery, other events were taking place that would eventually affect both the guerrilla movement on Crete and John Alexander in his quest to avenge his father's murder.

Across the vast land expanse of Europe and the moat that separated Europe from Great Britain, other men gathered in London for the similar purpose of forming a resistance army that, like the Cretan guerrillas, would carry the war into the Nazi backyard. These men planned to form an army that would fight its war in the shadows.

In the spring of 1941, a small bronze plaque was bolted into place at the entrance of a building at number 64 Baker Street in London. The letters on the plaque glittered the announcement that this building housed the Inter-Service Research Institute. The preponderance and multiplicity of service uniforms that entered and exited from this building was in keeping with the military atmosphere of wartime London.

Further down the western side of the same street, at number 84—closer yet to the famous residence of the legendary fictional detective Sherlock Holmes—was the administrative offices of the Marks & Spencer department store, housed in a building that bore the name of Michaelhouse.

These Baker Street addresses with such nondescript pseudonymous titles concealed the operation of an extraordinary organization with extraordinary members, who collectively were referred to as the "Old Firm." Because many of the buildings that housed their activities were on Baker Street, the members also bore the name of "The Baker Street Irregulars." The official title of this organization was the Special Operations Executive, or the SOE.[1]

The SOE was not officially founded like any other organization; rather, it evolved in the summer of England's darkest hour, 1940. In that year, Great Britain stood alone against the might of Hitler's conquering armies. Flushed with victory—after the successful campaigns in Norway, Denmark, Holland, Belgium, and France—the Wehrmacht now stood on the French shores of the English Channel and eyed the White Cliffs of Dover. They were waiting for the order that would carry them across this body of water in what would be the first invasion of the British Isles since William the Conqueror in 1066. They waited and waited, and with them waited anxiously the people of Great Britain and those of the free Western world.

In spite of this ominous danger that was certain to burst on their shores, certain military and civilian members of the British government met to discuss the formation of an organization whose sole purpose would be to harass the German in all the lands that lay under the Nazi boot.

Winston Churchill, then newly appointed as prime minister, favored the formation of such a group. He felt that such an organization would train specially selected personnel as secret agents and then parachute them into German-occupied territory. Subsequently, other specially trained indigenes—like the guerrillas on Crete—would be formed into an army of the underground that would rise and strike the Nazi conqueror.

In this meeting which took place on July 1, 1940, the British High Command, represented by Lord Gort, who was at that time the chief of the Imperial General Staff, met at the Foreign Office with Lord Halifax, the foreign minister. Gort and Halifax, together with several other cabinet ministers, agreed on forming just such an organization that Churchill had recommended. Dr. Hugh Dalton, at that time the minister of economic warfare, serving under Churchill, best describe the conclusions of the meeting:

> It is quite clear that an organization on this scale and
> of this character is not something that can be handled
> by the ordinary departmental machinery of either the
> British Civil Service or the British military machine.
> What is needed is a new organization to coordinate,

inspire, control, and assist the nationals of the oppressed countries who must themselves be the direct participants.[2]

In that single paragraph Dalton had expressed the very essence of this new organization. All who were present at that July 1 meeting concurred that such an organization needed a director with "almost dictatorial powers."

Lord Halifax took these conclusions to the prime minister.

With his glasses resting at the tip of his nose, Churchill read the minutes of the meeting and gleefully accepted them. They expressed collectively his own views on the need to create such an intelligence service.

Churchill assigned the final details that would establish the charter of this organization to his predecessor, Neville Chamberlain. Chamberlain, who now served as lord president of the Council, turned over the office of the prime minister to Churchill on May 10, 1940, leaving that position under a shadow cast first by his appeasement of Adolf Hitler at Munich in 1938, and subsequently by the turbulent and tragic events that brought Hitler's army to the shores of the English Channel.

In the final draft of this newly created organization, the former prime minister exhibited nothing of his earlier reticence or appeasement. In fact, he established the new organization's founding charter, which was signed on July 19, and stipulated that "a new organization shall be created forthwith to coordinate all action by way of subversion and sabotage, against the enemy overseas."

Chamberlain even gave this new independent intelligence service its name. He referred to it as the Special Operations Executive.[3]

With the formation of the SOE, a rivalry developed between the various British intelligence agencies. To resolve this problem, Winston Churchill appointed his minister of economic warfare, Hugh Dalton, as director, with absolute powers. Dalton would be responsible primarily to the prime minister, to his war cabinet, and to the chiefs of staff for the purpose of strategy.

Churchill gave Dalton only one standard order, *"set Europe ablaze!"*[4]

Hugh Dalton, a balding six-footer, with a loud voice and forceful personality, quickly overcame the problems of bitterness and infighting that he encountered from the other governmental intelligence agencies.

He was not very popular—in fact, he was disliked by many of his colleagues. Even Churchill found it difficult to be civil to him. But Dalton did his job well, handling the problems of this new service either by the forceful persuasion of his dominant personality or by the multiple talents of his associates working under him.

One such associate was Brigadier Colin Gubbins, a small, slightly built but wiry Highlander, who wore the toothbrush-styled moustache that identified him as a former officer of the Royal Artillery. He was an unusual soldier: neat, well organized, well read, well traveled, fluent in French and German with a comprehension of Russian. He had served in the First World War and had been decorated for gallantry. He was experienced and well versed in the concepts of guerrilla warfare and had authored two pamphlets on the subject, aptly entitled "The Art of Guerrilla Warfare" and "The Partisan Leader's Handbook."

In November 1940, Dalton brought Gubbins into the SOE as director of operations and training. Sir Alan Brooke, who in 1941 had become chief of the Imperial General Staff and later chairman of the Chiefs of Staff Committee—himself an artillery officer—liked Gubbins. This friendship with Gubbins ensured that the SOE would always have a positive hearing from the all-important Chiefs of Staff Committee. Financing this new organization posed no problem. Ample monies were available for all its needs, coming from a special fund that did not require parliamentary appropriation.[5] In other words, the SOE was independent of government bureaucracy.

Gubbins accepted the appointment as field director of these extraordinary members of the SOE, who came from all walks of life and who worked out of Baker Street. That is why they came to be known as "The Baker Street Irregulars," after the young urchins described by Conan Doyle in his Sherlock Holmes adventures.

Initially setting up headquarters on Caxton Street, not far from Baker Street, Gubbins formulated the first plans by which he would send agents behind German lines in the occupied countries of France, Belgium, Netherlands, Yugoslavia, Greece, and now Crete.

The Mediterranean office of the SOE was set up in Cairo. A special section of the SOE in Cairo was the *Crete Desk*. All operations that were to take place on Crete would originate from this section.

With Crete now under German control, the British were not going to let them use the island as a depot to supply Rommel's

Afrika Korps. Gubbins planned to send his agents into Crete and harass the Nazis' occupation force. At last the cry of the Cretan people would be answered.

The SOE agents who were selected to participate in the secret missions that would infiltrate and work behind German lines, particularly on Crete, came from all walks of life. They served in all branches of the British army and were chosen for this type of work because of their willingness and of their suitability. Suitability was based on the agent's knowledge of the native language and of the environment, knowledge that would readily allow him to fade into the background. However, not all agents easily satisfied this essential criterion. In Crete, the agents had to have at least a smattering of modern Greek, or even a readable knowledge of ancient Greek, which allowed them somehow to communicate with the local population.

In civilian life, most of these select men were distinguished scholars, writers, teachers, historians, and adventurers. Of all the SOE agents sent into Crete during the German occupation, only two of them were regular army soldiers. Most of them were in their early or mid-twenties, young enough to be brave, too young to know fear.

The first SOE agent to arrive on Crete was Commander Francis Pool, who disembarked from the submarine HMS *Torbay* on July 17, 1941. When he later departed from the island, he took with him a small contingent of New Zealanders, Australian, and British stragglers that had been left behind when the evacuation was terminated on the night of May 31. Among these evacuees was a young officer named Lieutenant Jack Smith-Hughes, who was to play a major role in the SOE missions on Crete.[6]

The first surface sea trips across the choppy waters that separated North Africa from Crete were run by navy lieutenants Michael Cumberlege and John Campbell, who commanded a small piratical flotilla of caiques named the *Hedgehog*, the *Porcupine*, and the *Escampador*. They operated out of Bardia in North Africa, and when that town was captured by Rommel's panzers, they moved their base to Mersa Matrüh, and later to Alexandria in Egypt.

Mike Cumberlege had left a deep impression on the Cretan guerrillas with whom he had come into contact during these trips. They admired his buccaneerish air, his humor, and his Hollywood-like good looks. Most of all, they smiled at the single gold earring he wore which was so symbolic of his piratical nature.

Sadly, Cumberlege was captured by the Germans in 1942 while on a sabotage mission and spent the next three years as a prisoner of war in Flossenburg prison in Germany. Only five days before liberation by Allied troops, he was taken out and executed by firing squad. It is said that he was smiling with a fearless defiance even as the bullets snuffed out his gallant life.[7]

Cumberlege was a sparkling example of the type of heroic men who served in the SOE in this clandestine war against the Germans on Crete. Like Cumberlege, these agents were high spirited and dauntless. For the Cretan people, they were symbols of the free world. They became important figures in the Cretan's daily life, for these men, at great danger to themselves, had come to help the Cretans fight for their freedom. The guerrillas showed their gratitude by baptizing them with Cretan names; these local appellations brought these gallant men into the circle of the Cretan family, showing that they were to be given love, respect, succor, and hospitality.

Captain Xan Fielding, nicknamed Aleko by the Cretans, was one of the earliest arrivals. He was assigned to command the SOE agents that had been infiltrated into the western part of the island.

Another agent was Captain Thomas Dunbabin—O Tom to the Cretans—described as the most raggedy of the guerrillas, who was a distinguished classical Greek scholar and a fellow at All Souls College during peacetime.

And there were many others: Corporal Alec Tarves, the only one of two regular army men to serve as an agent on Crete; Corporal Matthew White (O Matthaios) to the Cretans—who with Tarves arrived on the island as radiomen. Then came the writer Captain C. M. Woodhouse (O Monti), who later left Crete to assume command of the entire SOE mission on the Greek mainland. Others included Lieutenant John Stanley (O Yannis) and the writer and lawyer, Captain Arthur Reade, known as O Leftheris. To this list should be added the schoolmaster Captain Dick Barnes (O Pavlos) with Sergeant Harry Brooke (O Harris), his radioman, who, like Tarves, was the only other regular army man in the SOE to serve on Crete.

Still other agents were Major Bruce Mitford (O Mitsos) who had left his professional chair at Cambridge to serve in the SOE on Crete; Lieutenant Steven Varney (O Stefanos) who because of the horror of the executions on Crete later entered the clergy; and the writer and correspondent Captain Sandy Rendel (O Alexis) who served in the eastern part of the island.

The list of men who served with the SOE on Crete could not be complete without the name of Sergeant-Major Dudley Perkins of the New Zealand Division. He was nicknamed Vasili by the Cretans and loved and honored for his heroic exploits. He was known to his fellow SOE colleagues as Kiwi while he served as Captain Xan Fielding's second in command. He left legendary tales of heroic guerilla escapades on Crete until he met his death in a German ambush.

There were others, among whom the name of Patrick Leigh Fermor gleams because of his exploits. At the conclusion of the battle on May 30, 1941, he was evacuated by ship with other British troops from the Iraklion area. As a member of the SOE, he returned to Crete on Lieutenant Campbell's boat for the first time in June 1942 and served in the western part of the island. The second time he came to Crete was to accept the voluntary surrender of an Italian general after Italy's surrender and to escort him off the island, avoiding capture by the Germans. The third time, he returned to lead a special commando team that kidnapped the German garrison commander, General Heinrich Kreipe and took him off the island as a prisoner of war. The whole world would marvel at the audactiy of this exploit.[8]

On October 20, 1941—more than three months after he had first left Crete as an escapee—former lieutenant, now promoted to captain, Jack Smith-Hughes returned to Crete.

After the battle for Crete had ended, 22-year-old Smith-Hughes was taken prisoner by the Germans and sent to Aghia prison in Prison Valley. It did not take long for him to escape and head for the mountains.

Once within the rugged heights of the mountains, he reached the village of Vourvoure where the local villagers directed him to the home of the Papadakis family for refuge. Papadakis subsequently turned Smith-Hughes over to a relative, a tall, balding, blue-eyed guerrilla leader who bore the lengthy name of Petrakas Papado-petrakis. Kapetan Petrakas had already established himself as a courageous guerrilla leader. Because of his heavy blond moustache, the British had given him the code name of Beowulf.

The tall guerrilla leader, together with fifteen of his band, escorted Smith-Hughes southward toward Preveli village. They were guided by George Psychoundakis, the same guide who earlier had found John Alexander in the sheepfold with Dino and Dimitri, and had brought them to the Monastery of St. John at Preveli for safety. Now, he guided Lieutenant Smith-Hughes and his escort to the same monastery.

Smith-Hughes was subsequently taken off the island by submarine, together with other evacuees, by the first SOE agent to alight on Crete in the person of Commander Francis Pool.

While in Cairo, Smith-Hughes informed the SOE command of the Cretan population's terrible suffering from the German reprisals but emphasized that they remained defiant against this Nazi oppressor. He added that the seeds of resistance had taken root but needed direction. He was ordered back to Crete to help organize this resistance under British leadership.

He returned to Crete by boat and brought with him another Englishman, his communication sergeant, Ralph Stockbridge. Much to the marvel of the local Cretan guerrillas, who greeted their arrival, Sergeant Stockbridge carried his wireless transmitter secreted in a suitcase.

Despite his disguise as a Cretan native—in baggy black trousers with high boots, black shirt, and a black fringed turban on his head—Smith-Hughes still stood out as an Englishman. His attempt to fade into the local environment was an utter failure. Thus the local guerrillas took extra precautions to ensure that his presence would not be betrayed to the Germans by any local inhabitant who might be in the pay of the Gestapo.

The Cretans readily accepted Smith-Hughes and Stockbridge into their midst and quickly dubbed Smith-Hughes Yanni and called Stockbridge, first Michalaki and later sifi, so as not to confuse him with Leigh Fermor who was known as Michali. As noted earlier, the Cretans showed their love and respect for these brave Englishmen by attaching their own sobriquets to each man.

In the relatively brief time that Jack Smith-Hughes served on Crete, he formulated the basic concepts of the underground resistance under British direction: infiltration, supply, communications, assault, and evacuation. He was later withdrawn from the island, and once back in Cairo he was given command of the Cretan Desk of the Special Operations Executive.[9]

Thus, the British secret missions to Crete had begun. Nighttime landings by caique, trawler, or submarine, followed by silent infiltrations and forced marches across German-occupied plains, around German outposted villages and up the rugged heights of the near alpine peaks of the mountains brought each man to the safety of a sheepfold or a cave somewhere above and beyond the enemy's reach.

Here, each officer, together with his communication sergeant, would eventually settle down, and with the help of Cretan guides and runners—like George Psychoundakis—would begin his clandestine war against the enemy.

The Special Operations Executive command, with the concurrence of the commanding general in the Mediterranean, decided that all military and civilian personnel involved in these operations would be grouped into a specially designated unit that would bear the title of Force 133.

These brave men of Force 133 on Crete were ready to set the island ablaze.

Chapter 5

Force 133
to Crete

No sooner had Jack Smith-Hughes been placed in charge of the Cretan Section of the SOE, when the gears of the underground operation began to turn. Reviewing the list of SOE agents who were available and who would best fit into his plans, his eyes settled on the name of Patrick Leigh Fermor.

Born of English and Irish ancestry in the second year of the First World War, Patrick was left behind as a young boy when his mother sailed to India to join her husband who was on duty there. During the long years of the war, the young boy was left behind and alone, to be raised by relatives who possessed a kind and simple nature. Neither a stern word nor any admonitory reprimand was ever directed toward him so as to help mold him during his formative boyhood years. He was allowed to do whatever he liked, and thus uninhibited, he ran wild. Since he lacked any degree of discipline, his early school years were best described as "stormy."

While in his late teens, he left school and decided to travel through Europe on foot. For the next year and a half, he journeyed from England to Constantinople in Turkey, through the Balkans and the Greek Archipelago, and in that time learned more about life than he could ever have gleaned from textbooks. In that period of travel, Leigh Fermor acquired a deep interest in languages and in the cultures of the people whom he met during that peripatetic journey.

When the Second World War began in 1939, Fermor enlisted in the Irish Guards. Now he found that the freedom of travel that he had enjoyed was very different from the discipline of army life. He had that "closed in" feeling again which he had experienced in school during his boyhood years. But fortune came to his rescue: having developed a good knowledge of languages during his travels, he was assigned to the Intelligence Service. Thus it was that he was able to exempt himself from the "spit-and-polish" garrison life of the infantry.

His tour of duty took him to Greece during the German invasion of that country and later to Crete, where he fought with the Iraklion garrison, until his unit was evacuated to Egypt. Now, at age 26, Lieutenant Patrick Leigh Fermor was back on Crete as an agent of the SOE.[1]

In June 1942, he was smuggled into a cove on the southern coast of the island via a small trawler commanded by Lieutenant John Campbell. Fermor had been sent to Crete to take over command of the western part of the island from his friend Aleko—Captain Xan Fielding.

Fielding reviewed with Fermor the dangers and problems he had encountered during his tour of duty on the island. The worst problem of all, which Leigh Fermor soon discovered after a few hours of hiking over the rocky crags of the rugged mountains of Crete, was that the rocks tore their shoes to bits.

"Between that and the Germans, you'll survive," Fielding joke with his successor.

"I leave you one legacy, at least, Paddy," said Fielding as he threw his pack over one shoulder and started to leave, "and that is my runner and guide who has been of great service to me. You'll meet him tomorrow!"

"What is his name?" Leigh Fermor shouted after him.

Fielding had already started down the trail that would eventually take him to the southern coast for embarkation to Egypt. He heard Fermor and turned to reply. "His name is George . . . George Psychoundakis."[2]

The ever-present George, who weeks before had guided the young American, John Alexander, to safety amidst the confines of the Monastery of St. John at Preveli, and later guided Jack Smith-Hughes and his escort to the southern shores for evacuation, now became Leigh Fermor's official guide and runner.

Lieutenant Fermor first met his new guide while hiding in a cave high in the White Mountains, well out of reach of the Germans. One evening, he heard the sound of someone moving about in the brush. He reached for his pistol and took a position behind a huge boulder at the entrance to the cave and waited anxiously, wondering if someone had betrayed his presence to the Germans.

Crawling on all fours through the bushes and thorn trees that led to the cave, his clothes tattered and his face dripping with perspiration, George Psychoundakis popped through the small opening. He removed the fringed handkerchief that served as his hat and bowed before the amused Leigh Fermor. The young lieutenant sat there quietly, studying this short and agile individual whom he had recently inherited from Xan Fielding.

What first caught Fermor's eye about this youth were his boots. They were torn, just as Fermor's boots had been after the first few days of hiking over the rocks of those mountain trails. The young runner had patched them by securing the semidetached soles of his boots to the upper part with a strand of wire. It was a clever improvisation that Fermor noted and planned to do for his own boots, until new ones arrived.

The young Cretan runner looked at Fermor with huge dark eyes set below a bushy mop of black hair. His face bore a melancholy expression until he smiled, and then under that thin trim moustache glowed a set of pearly white teeth. When he laughed, it was so infectious that Leigh Fermor could not help but laugh with him.

The 21-year-old Psychoundakis—he looked more like 16—had just completed a 40-mile hike to reach this cave, bringing messages from SOE agents in other parts of the island. Though tired, he masked his fatigue with his nervous energy. With the comic flourish of a conjurer, he handed Leigh Fermor a half-dozen bits of twisted paper that he had hidden in different parts of his clothing. Each time he did so, he threw furtive glances over his shoulder in a comic caricature of clandestine security. The Englishman laughed at Psychoundakis's sense of humor.

Fermor replied to those messages, and George safely stowed them in little hidden tears in his clothing. With nightfall, the youthful Cretan runner was ready to depart for another long trip over the mountains. Before he left, he took a last swig of Cretan raki, a locally brewed clear liquid of fiery taste which burns all the way down from the throat into the stomach.

"Another drop of petrol for the engine," he commented in Greek with a sheepish grin. Fermor, who understood and spoke the language well, joshingly advised him to take a second swig, for he had a long trip before him.

At the small opening to the cave, Psychoundakis turned, rolled his eyes, and placing a forefinger to his lips, whispered in the few words of English he knew, "the Intelligence Service!" Then he disappeared into the brush.

From just the first few hours of acquaintance with his new guide and runner, Leigh Fermor realized that Psychoundakis was obviously enraptured by the secret life of an SOE agent. Fermor watched him as he hopped through the brush like a rabbit. Within a few minutes, Fermor was able to discern in the moonlight the small figure of his runner sprinting across the foothills of the mountains.

One of the messages that Psychoundakis carried on his person was an order to the abbot of the Monastery of St. John at Preveli to gather as many straggling Commonwealth soldiers as possible for evacuation to Egypt.[3]

When the battle for Crete had ended, many Commonwealth soldiers did not accept the order to surrender to the Germans. In the weeks that followed, more and more such soldiers reached the shores of North Africa singly, in pairs, and in groups. They did not wish to become inmates in a prisoner-of-war camp. Some of them were successful in leaving the island, some failed, and still others faded into the environment of daily Cretan life.

One soldier who succeeded in leaving was Major R. Sandover, an Australian who had commanded the Eleventh Battalion at Rethimnon. He informed his superior officer that he was not going to surrender and led a group of Australians across the tall mountains southward to the village of Sfakia on the southern coast. There, under the cover of darkness, they commandeered a caique and made their escape to North Africa.[4]

Another who succeeded was Private D. McQuarrie of the Eighteenth New Zealand Battalion who had been wounded at the battle for Galatas and was now confined to a hospital encampment in Khania. He decided to escape and finally did so on June 18. Racked with pain from his wound, he trekked southward to the village of Meskla where he stayed with a Cretan family for two weeks, until his wound healed.

Fearing for the safety of his Cretan hosts who were now in danger of German reprisal, he left for the surrounding hills where he met another New Zealander, Private B. Carter. The two wandered over the escarpments of the mountains for a week, after which they headed north to Suda Bay. There they were joined by two other Australians, and when they reached the coast they found an abandoned dinghy. Setting off on July 16, with a strong wind blowing them southward, they miraculously reached Sidi Barrani in North Africa in four days.[5]

These soldiers, like hundreds of other stragglers, were successful in reaching safety within British lines, after harrowing journeys. There were others, however, who were not as successful.

Private E. Phelan of the Royal Marines spent fifteen months roaming the hills and mountains of Crete. In that period of time, he had made sixteen attempts to find a boat. He had set sail twice, but the first time the boat sank, and the second, the engine broke down. Each time he returned to his friends, the Cretan family with whom he stayed those many months.

In a final attempt to escape, he and four other Australians overpowered the crew of a trawler and set sail for North Africa. But fate willed otherwise, and when they landed on Gavdos Island, a few miles off the southern Cretan coast, to repair the caique's motor, they were captured by the Germans.[6]

Private William Siely, a New Zealander, was so shocked by the Germans' reprisals against the Cretan population who offered assistance to escapees that it bothered his conscience. He had escaped three times from Prison Valley, and each time the very thought of those brutal, inhuman reprisals made him return to prison voluntarily. He did not want his escape to bring suffering to these brave hospitable people.[7]

There were also those who could not find the means to escape but instead faded into the Cretan environment.

Private John Babcock had been in the midst of battle from the first day of the invasion. He had seen his best friend die from bullets that had been meant for him. When the order came for the men to withdraw to the southern beaches for evacuation, Babcock joined the mad rush. Somewhere along the way he got separated from his unit.

It was an arduous struggle to reach the southern coast. When at last on June 1, he half-crawled, half-climbed up the last escarpment overlooking the village of Sfakia and felt the cooling breeze of the Mediterranean soothingly strike his flushed perspiring face, Babcock was shocked to find the inlet empty of ships. There below him masses of men stood about the beach, while here and there a white flag fluttered. He was too late!

Exhausted beyond endurance from lack of food, water, and sleep, the discouraging sight before him was too bitter to bear. At that moment, he heard the crunch of a boot behind him. He turned abruptly in alarm, but his fatigue finally overwhelmed him and he fainted. He fell into the arms of two tall Cretans. They hid Babcock for the day in a nearby cave, leaving food and water for him. That night, they returned and carried him to their village.

Babcock stayed hidden in that village for the whole four years of the German occupation. In all that time, he remained in seclusion in the home of the two Cretan brothers who had rescued him. He learned to speak Greek and Cretan with its heavy dialect, readily adapting to all his hosts' customs. He became so astute that he even fooled the Germans into thinking he was just another villager. In time, he became engaged to the daughter of the family with whom he lived.[8]

Like John Babcock, Corporal Edward Nathan, known to his comrades as Ned Nathan, also was given refuge by a Cretan family.

In the counterattack on Maleme airfield by the Twenty-eighth Maori Battalion in the first days of the German invasion, Ned Nathan had been wounded in the hip and eye. While being evacuated to Egypt, the barge in which he sailed was attacked and sunk by Stuka divebombers. with many others, he made it to shore, only to find Commonwealth soldiers on the beach surrendering to the Germans. Exhausted with fatigue and from his wounds, Nathan collapsed. When he awakened, he found himself in the home of the Cretan family Torakis.

They nursed his wounds, and he stayed with them a long time. Like Babcock, he learned the Cretan dialect and moved about freely, even among the German soldiers. Twice he had been detained for questioning by the Gestapo, and twice he had fooled them—convincing them that he was truly a Cretan. The third time the Gestapo detained him—upon the word of an informer—they exposed him to be a New Zealander. They beat and tortured him in order to discover the name of the family that had given him shelter and sustenance all these weeks. He never told them. He would not betray his beloved Katina, to whom he had become engaged, nor the other members of the Torakis family.[9]

For all those who succeeded in fleeing Crete, rest and relaxation awaited them in Egypt, at least until the next call of battle. While they relaxed, they could not help but remember that back among the fields, valleys, and mountains of Crete, they had left behind their friends and comrades.

The commanding general of the British forces in the Mediterranean, General Archibald Wavell, did not need the SOE or his army intelligence service to inform him about the innumerable British Commonwealth soldiers who were roaming at will the mountains of Crete with the intent of finding some vehicle via which they could flee the island. Each time a group of men landed safely behind British lines on the northern shores of North Africa, they reported that many others had been left behind, who also sought to escape.

At a staff meeting held at Wavell's headquarters in Cairo, it was decided to dispatch a representative to Crete with orders to contact the Cretan underground and initiate a plan to collect these soldiers for evacuation from the island. The person chosen to lead this mission was Commander Francis Pool, another agent of the SOE.

On the night of July 26, 1941, a tall, well-booted Cretan, dressed in semi-military garb, stealthily approached the Monastery of St. John at Preveli. His knock on the door was answered by a monk, whose eyes showed relief when he observed that the nocturnal visitor was not a German. The stranger requested an audience with the abbot of the monastery, Father Agathangelos Lagouvardos.

A short while later, the dignified, white-bearded abbot appeared. The stranger, still standing at the door, identified himself as a villager from the village of Loutro near the hamlet of Sfakia.

"My name is Stratis Liparis," he remarked, introducing himself, "and I am in the service of the British."

Father Lagouvardos raised his lantern high enough to cast a bright light on the stranger's face, eyeing him suspiciously.

Liparis, sensing the abbot's suspicion, explained the reason for this midnight visit. "I have just come from a submarine in the harbor of Limni with a British naval officer. He is in hiding, waiting for my signal to approach."

The abbot remained silent and motionless, while Liparis continued. "The officer's name is Commander Pool, and he says that you know him and that he knows you."

Still suspicious and careful that this might be a German ploy, the abbot replied, "We have no English here, only Germans! However, if he wants, let him come for coffee." There was no harm, he thought, in offering coffee even to a German, if he *was* a spy.

Liparis returned moments later in the company of a tall Englishman who greeted the abbot warmly as he was being introduced. The abbot remained carefully aloof, but invited them both into the austere reception room of the monastery.

"Reverend Father," the Englishman began, speaking in fluent Greek, "I bring you greetings. I landed by submarine a few hours ago in response to your signals. I have hidden my dinghy amongst some rocks nearby, and I have brought you some canned preserves as a personal gift."

The abbot studied the Englishman carefully, his penetrating eyes delving deeply into his, almost to the very soul, to determine if this tall night visitor was telling the truth or whether it was a ruse to trap him.

"Why have you come here?" he asked.

"I have been sent here on a special mission to help organize and evacuate any British soldiers in the area."

The elderly abbot rose, crossed the room, and stopped before an icon of the Virgin Mary, making the sign of the Cross. Then turning to the Englishman and waving his arms in feigned anger, he remarked loudly, "I know nothing of all these things you say! I have given no signals, and I do not want to know where you came from, where you are going, or what you are doing here! As I said before, we have no English here, only Germans."

Commander Pool was surprised by the priest's vehemence, and he looked away dejectedly, saddened by his failure to convince him as to his identity and the purpose of his mission. He understood the abbot's distrust. Of course, Father Lagouvardos *had* to take precautionary measures, for too many lives were at stake. Yet, Pool must convince him. After a moment's silence, Pool tried a different tactic.

"I served ten years as director of the airport at Elounda, before the war. That is where I learned my Greek. Believe me, Reverend Father, I *am* Pool, and I am here under orders to collect our soldiers and get them off the island. We would not have come if we had not seen your signals."

Still suspicious of entrapment, the abbot put Pool to the test. "If you have served ten years at Elounda, as you say you have, then you must be able to identify some of my friends there . . . who they are . . . their duties . . . what they look like . . . even their relatives!"

Commander Pool's face lit up. At last he found a basis by which he could prove his identity. For the next hour, he cited ecclesiastical, political, and local personages with whom he had contact while at Elounda. To questions put to him by the abbot, he was able to describe their duties, their habits, even their facial characteristics. The old priest's stern features softened, for he seemed almost convinced. When Pool stated, in addition, that he carried a special message from his superiors for Captain John Pendlebury, the old priest smiled and nodded approval.

The name of John Pendlebury erased all suspicions that the abbot might have had, for Pendlebury was one of his dearest friends whom he had known for many years. Pendlebury was a giant of a man, a distinguished Greek scholar, an archaeologist, who before the war had worked with Sir Robert Evans at the ancient Minoan excavations at Knossos. Tall, athletic, and always smiling, even when he wore the black patch instead of his glass eye, he had lived on Crete for many years and was much loved by all who knew him. The Abbot Lagouvardos loved Pendlebury like a brother.

Satisfied at last that Pool was indeed who he said he was, and not a German spy, Father Lagouvardos embraced him and kissed him on both cheeks in the formal sign of welcome.[10]

From June 1 until July 20, 1941, many of the British, Australian, and New Zealanders who roamed the mountains of the southern coast of Crete signaled each night, hoping that perhaps a passing British ship would observe them and send a landing party for evacuation. Their flashes were indeed observed, for on the afternoon of June 6, a British aircraft flew over the area and dropped canisters filled with food. This response heartened them.

When the Germans became aware of these signals through their paid informers and of the wandering Commonwealth soldiers—whom they termed "deserters"—they set up patrols on the shores of the southern coast in order to prevent any landings or evacuation. These patrols began on June 9 and remained in place until July 20, when they were withdrawn because they were needed elsewhere to defend German outposts against increasing attacks by Cretan guerrilla bands.

The abbot of the Monastery of St. John at Preveli, through the local grapevine, knew exactly what prevailed in his area. In fact, Father Lagouvardos was the unheralded and unofficial leader of all anti-German activity in the area. Yet, he played a clandestine role, for as far as the Germans were aware, he was just the local abbot, a cleric following his religious order and indifferent to secular life.

On July 20, the day the Germans withdrew their patrols from the southern coast, Father Lagouvardos received the message from Patrick Leigh Fermor—brought to the monastery by George Psychoundakis, Fermor's runner—that he should establish a system of nightly signals seaward for the ultimate purpose of evacuating British soldiers.

The abbot turned to his interpreter, Steven Kaffatos, who spoke English well, and who, unknown to the abbot, was already helping the British stragglers send their signals. The abbot asked Kaffatos to send nightly signals from a building near the monastery. Kaffatos had already secured a naval lantern, but the batteries were running low. They would need new batteries, and the only place to obtain them would be in the city of Rethimnon. Father Lagouvardos turned to George Psychoundakis for assistance. George had remained at the monastery for two days to rest before returning to Leigh Fermor's cave. Now he was off again, this time to Rethimnon for batteries.

Once in Rethimnon, the young Cretan runner had no difficulties getting the batteries from his contacts. Getting through the German outposts on his return trip to the monastery would be another story.

They gave him an old donkey for the trip back. George examined the beast and wondered if it was strong enough to make the trip south over the mountain trails. He threw a saddlebag onto the donkey's back and hid a radio transmitter for Leigh Fermor's signaler on one side, while placing the heavy batteries in the other. He then covered both sides with some 40 pounds of wheat. The donkey groaned under the heavy weight and, straining forward, began its slow trek toward its destination.

Psychoundakis avoided the villages lest he encounter Germans who would take the wheat from him and in so doing would discover the radio and the batteries. He knew that if this were to happen, it would be sudden death for him. There was one village, however, that he had to enter in order to continue on the trail to the monastery. To circumvent this village meant that the overburdened donkey would have to ascend a precipitous trail that could prove impossible for this old beast of burden to bear.

No sooner had he reached the village square, when two German guards followed him, teasing him about his old donkey.

"Poly xylo avto"—"Too much whipping"—one of the guards chided George in fractured Greek. George nodded, trying to ignore them and hoping that they would go away, but they continued behind him. The young Cretan's heart was beating rapidly, and he prayed as he had never prayed before.

"Poly xylo, no faghi"—"Too much whipping, not enough food"—the second guard added as they now walked beside the donkey, examining it.

"Ochi, gaidaros kaputti!"—"No, donkey done for!"—George replied.

"Ochi, no kaputt!"—"No, not done for!"—the first guard remarked and laid his hand on the left saddlebag that contained the batteries.

Just then he spied two local village girls standing in front of their house. They were watching him and his pitiful donkey and were giggling.

Psychoundakis nodded to them as if in greeting and pleaded, "Get these devils off my back, will you!"

The girls immediately understood his dilemma and began to flirt with the two Germans, beckoning to them. The guards finally left George's side for the better company.

Psychoundakis arrived at the Monastery of St. John with the batteries late the following night. Miraculously, the old donkey had survived the trip.[11]

With the new batteries providing ample energy for the lantern, Morse code signals for SOS were flashed every hour each night as soon as darkness fell until one hour before dawn. The commander of the British submarine HMS *Torbay* observed the signal on the night of July 26, whereupon Commander Pool disembarked and began his special mission.

Pool's first request of Abbot Lagouvardos was for word to go out to all available British, Australian, and New Zealanders in the area that they should arrive at the harbor of Limni below the monastery at Preveli by the next night, July 27, for evacuation. The word flew like the wind from mouth to mouth, better than a wireless.

That night, Commander Pool and the abbot sent their signal from a small chapel near the harbor. At about 1:00 A.M., the waters of the harbor were broken by the appearance of a conning tower as the submarine *Torbay* surfaced 70 meters from the shore.

On that first night, seventy-three British soldiers were evacuated.

On July 28, Father Lagouvardos and Pool left the safety of the monastery and traveled by donkey over the rocky trails of the mountains, stealthily bypassing German outposts, finally arriving at the village of St. Apostle, which was the elderly abbot's birthplace.

At this village, they met with leaders of several guerrilla bands that occupied that sector of the mountain range. Together, they formulated plans for mustering all remaining British Commonwealth stragglers for one final evacuation.

After the meeting, Commander Pool spoke with one of the guerrilla leaders, Antoni Grigorakis, who bore the nickname of Kapetan Satan. It was from Kapetan Satan that Pool learned of the tragic death of his close friend, Captain John Pendlebury. The tall Greek scholar had been shot by the Germans as he lay wounded while leading a raid by Cretan guerrillas against the German garrison of Iraklion. The news saddened Commander Pool and brought tears to Father Lagouvardos's eyes.

During the night of August 19, the *Torbay* returned for another evacuation sortie. The men gathered by the shore of the harbor as early as 11:00 P.M., anxiously and excitedly waiting for their turn to embark. In response to the usual light signal from shore, the submarine's signaler fired a flare in acknowledgment. That drew suspicion, for it was the first time that a flare had been used as a signal. The men on shore went into hiding, fearing that the signal might have come from a passing German patrol boat.

When the misunderstanding was finally corrected by the use of the regular Morse code light signal, the date for the final evacuation was reset for the next night. On August 20, thirty British soldiers and twelve civilians went on board the submarine. Also aboard was Commander Francis Pool, his mission as an SOE officer having been successfully completed.

On board the *Torbay* was another passenger, the young American, John Alexander.

From the first night of his arrival at the Monastery of St. John at Preveli, Father Lagouvardos had taken him under his personal care. The elderly abbot had kept a close watch on him, offering him the austere comfort and security of the sanctified monastery.

John Alexander insisted that he had to return to Rethimnon and look after his mother and two sisters. The wise, elderly abbot recognized another reason for Alexander's determination to return to Rethimnon—to avenge his father's murder by killing Fritz Schubert.

The grapevine had informed the abbot that Schubert had placed a bounty on Alexander's head. To keep this young American from losing his life in a misadventure, he asked Commander Pool, as a personal favor to him, to take John Alexander with him to Egypt.[12]

The abbot was destined to meet Alexander again in Cairo. On August 20, 1941, Father Lagouvardos did not know the role that this young American would play in the Cretan struggle for liberation, while seeking to avenge his father's murder by the Gestapo.

Chapter 6

Return to
the Land of Minos

When the HMS *Torbay* made port in Alexandria, its passengers were met by a billeting officer who quartered them in a second-rate hotel that served as a dormitory.

John Alexander, as an American in a British environment, felt lost. Here he was, an 18 year old, separated from his family for the first time in his young life. His father was dead, while his mother and sisters, back on Crete, were in danger of imprisonment, or worse, at the hands of the Gestapo. All alone in a strange land, John wished that he and his family had never left the United States. He sat on his cot and cried the tears of a lonely boy, tears of despair and tears also of loneliness, fear, and abandonment.

The next day, he felt better, although he still harbored a deep concern for the welfare of his mother and sisters. A poster on the wall of the hotel's dining room caught his eye. It advertised the British army's need for enlistees in its fight against the Nazis. John had taken a vow to fight the Germans if only to avenge his father's death. The brutal scene that had taken place in his home in Rethimnon, the day his father was murdered, was emblazoned in his mind. He clenched his teeth in grim determination that somehow, sometime, he would return to Crete and fulfill that vow.

He heard rumors—though unfounded, as most rumors usually are in any army—that British forces planned to invade and retake Crete. For Alexander, this rumor kindled a hope, and so the next day, he volunteered for service in the British army.

For the next six months, Private John Alexander sweated and toiled in the heat of the desert as he trained in the searing sands of Palestine. He excelled in every aspect of the rigorous training that he underwent. He was first in marksmanship, both pistol and rifle;

first in hand-to-hand combat; and first in the use of the bayonet. Each time he thrust the blade of his bayonet into a straw-filled dummy, he would repeat the name of Fritz Schubert. It was enough to boil his blood beyond the heat of the desert sun. It was enough to push him beyond human endurance in his determination to excel. In time, his efforts were noted by the training cadre who cited him as the best soldier in the brigade.

With his training completed, Alexander was assigned to a British liaison unit attached to the headquarters of the Greek army-in-exile in Cairo. His knowledge of Greek came in good use in this assignment, and in a short time he was promoted to the rank of corporal.

Alexander, though an American in the British military service (the United States was still at peace, for Pearl Harbor was two months away) was no longer lonely. Now he had both comradeship and a purpose. He was on active duty, serving with the British in their stand against the Germans. However, he did not like his rear echelon assignment and sought reassignment to a combat unit. There was one frustrating desire that remained uppermost in his mind. He was still determined to return to Crete and face Fritz Schubert.[1]

His wish was soon to be fulfilled.

In the port city of Alexandria, there was another person who was determined to return to Crete. He was Lieutenant Colonel Robert E. Laycock, who commanded the Special Service Brigade of Commandos. Colonel Laycock had fought in the ill-fated battle on Crete with a special brigade of his commandos and never quite accepted defeat.

Back in March 1941, a special force of the Seventh, Eighth, and Eleventh units of commandos arrived in Egypt at the time when General Erwin Rommel and his Afrika Korps was beginning his massive attacks in the steaming desert of North Africa. These three commando units were initially used as a reserve brigade of the British Eighth Army that opposed Rommel.

The Seventh Commando unit was designated as "A" Battalion of a brigade in the Sixth British Division. Its sister battalion, the Eighth Commando, was designated as "B" Battalion. The ranks of the "B" Battalion were comprised of men from such outstanding historic units as the Household Cavalry, the Somerset Light Infantry, the Royal Marines, and the Foot Guards. Collectively, these units were designated as "Layforce" after their commanding officer, Colonel Laycock.

In early May of 1941, the Eleventh Commando of Layforce—known as the "Scottish Commando"—was detached and assigned to garrison the island of Cyprus, which at that time was a British possession. Later the same month, the remaining two units of Layforce, augmented by a brigade of four battalions, were shipped to Crete to fight the German paratroopers in the airborne invasion of that island.[2]

The Layforce commandos landed at Suda Bay successfully on May 26-27, even though they were continuously divebombed and strafed by German Stukas and Messerschmitts. In that battle, Laycock's battalions fought resolutely and heroically in a rear guard action that allowed the rest of the Commonwealth troops to retreat to the southern coast of Crete for evacuation.

The Layforce commandos positioned themselves astride the single road that led southward to the village of Sfakia. By dividing themselves into small combat patrols, they attacked the advancing Germans fiercely with bayonets. In skirmish after skirmish, the commandos sent the Germans reeling back, thus permitting the British, Australian, and New Zealand troops to continue safely on their trek to the southern beaches.

It was, however, a hotly contested rear guard action.

In one skirmish, Captain F. Nicholls of G Troop of "A" Battalion led a sharp bayonet attack that drove the Germans off an enfilading hill position. In another, the advancing Germans overran commando headquarters, whereupon Colonel Laycock and his brigade major jumped into nearby idle tank and, with the tank still swathed in camouflage netting, drove it into the enemy formation, dispersing them. Laycock succeeded in routing the enemy but was almost captured in the process. He escaped through sheer good fortune.[3]

On the night of the May 30-31, the commanding general of the defense garrison on Crete, General Bernard Freyberg, was ordered to leave the island and fly to Cairo. He was instructed to turn the command over to the next ranking officer, General Edward Weston of the Royal Marines. When Admiral Andrew Cunningham, the commander in chief of the Mediterranean Fleet, decided to suspend evacuation operations that same night, General Weston was also ordered to leave Crete aboard a Sunderland flying boat. The next ranking officer was Colonel Robert Laycock.

"I am ordered out tonight," Weston informed Laycock, "and I have been instructed to pass the command to the next senior officer."

Laycock had a premonition of what was to follow. "I am offering you the command of the remaining troops," continued Weston, "and am authorizing you to negotiate their surrender."

Laycock thought for a few moments before responding. When he finally spoke, he refused the offer. "I did not come to Crete," explained Laycock, "to surrender to the Hun. I believe I can be of greater service with my commando brigade than as a prisoner of war."

It was a remark typical of the feisty Laycock. Weston nodded his head understandingly. He had not *ordered* Laycock to take the command; rather he had *offered* him the command.

"Very well, then, Laycock, *you* pick the officer who is to negotiate with the Germans."

Colonel Laycock selected an officer in his command, the leader of "D" Battalion of Layforce, Lieutenant Colonel G.A.D. Young. The sad task and final burden of surrendering the island to the Germans fell to this young officer. When Laycock flew out of Crete with Weston that same night, he was filled with remorse.[4]

Laycock was never to forget that episode. He intended to return to Crete someday and avenge that insult.

Robert Laycock was a remarkable officer, tough and resolute, as befitted an officer of the Royal Horse Guards. He demanded the highest standards of courage, initiative, and discipline, and in this respect he himself set an unswerving example. These qualities of leadership made him the formidable commander of a formidable brigade of commandos. His Layforce with its daring exploits had made history in the Mediterranean even before the heroic stand on Crete. He had proven the worth of his specialized brigade through several missions against the Axis forces.

In January 1941, Laycock had led a commando raid against Italian installations in Bardia in North Africa. In June of the same year, he directed a commando attack against Axis troops in Vichy-held Syria to clear a path for the advance of Australian units. And on November 17, Laycock was to lead another daring raid, this time on German headquarters in Beda Littoria in North Africa, in an attempt to kill or capture the "Desert Fox"—General Erwin Rommel.

It was in early 1942 that Colonel Laycock finally decided to send a commando raiding party against the Luftwaffe installations on the airfield at Iraklion. Laycock was going back to Crete.

The raiding party was to be commanded by Major Charles Duncan-Moore, formerly an officer in the Coldstream Guards and a close friend of Colonel Laycock, with whom he shared Laycock's military attributes of courage and initiative. Laycock had assigned the command of this raid to his friend, even though he felt that it could develop into a suicide mission. However, Duncan-Moore was an intrepid officer who could be trusted, and if anyone could succeed, Laycock felt, it would be Charles Duncan-Moore.

Robert Laycock wanted to lead this mission in person with Duncan-Moore as second in command. Laycock felt that this raid was no more perilous than the one in which he had participated the previous November at Beta Littoria. Even though he did not consider the raid at Beta Littoria—to kill or capture Rommel—as perilous, it was pointed out to him that of the whole commando raiding party, only he and another soldier survived to return within the safety of the British lines. It was Wavell's chief of staff, probably expressing the opinion of his superior, who forbade Laycock from leading this raiding party to Crete.

By this time. most of Layforce had been disbanded because no new recruits had volunteered for this specialized service to replace the men lost on Crete. The survivors were returned to their original units, but a few were retained to become the nucleus of a new force designated as the Special Air Service. A smaller force, which was designed to wage amphibious warfare in the Mediterranean, remained under Laycock's command. It was from this small amphibious force that Laycock and Duncan-Moore selected the personnel that were to participate in the raid on Iraklion airfield.

By the time the plans for this raid were prepared, the men selected, and all other administrative and logistical details concluded, it was May 1942, almost a year to the day that Layforce had faced defeat on Crete.

In the course of his duties as British liaison to the headquarters of the Greek army-in-exile in Cairo, John Alexander had made many friends, both Greek and British. The young American, who spoke English with an American accent in an English environment, and who felt quite at home with the Greek language, became known and liked by the officers and enlisted personnel with whom he had come into contact. Most of them had heard of the tragic tale of his father, and they knew of his vow to return to Crete.

One of the British noncommissioned officers who had befriended the young American was a communications sergeant assigned to the operations section of the Cretan desk of the SOE. Corporal Alexander knew him only as Sergeant Joseph Dickason, but was not aware of his relationship with the SOE. Dickason knew of the preparations for the commando attack on Crete through the many requests from Laycock's headquarters for maps and topographical details of the area surrounding Iraklion airfield.

Dickason's immediate superior was a British officer of Greek ancestry, Captain Denis Ciclitiras. Ciclitiras was a member of the SOE and had just returned from Crete with all the information that Laycock's raiding party would need. There was one specific request that Colonel Laycock had made of Captain Ciclitiras. Laycock needed a British soldier who was fluent in Greek so that there could be some degree of communication with the Cretan guerrillas who were to meet them on the beach. Sergeant Dickason recommended John Alexander to Captain Ciclitiras for this assignment.

Ciclitiras reviewed Corporal Alexander's army file, noting that this young American had volunteered for service in the British army in order to fight the Nazis at a time when the United States was still at peace with Germany. Although Alexander was not trained as a commando, his file carried a letter from the commanding officer of his training brigade commending his excellence above all the rest, a commendation that made him a good recruit for Laycock's Special Services. The file also contained a notation about his parents and about what had happened back in Rethimnon to his father. The young American had motive and determination, and, above all, he spoke Greek fluently. In view of all that information, Ciclitiras did not hesitate to authorize Alexander's transfer to Laycock's commando force.

Alexander was ordered to report to Captain Ciclitiras at the Rustom Buildings, located in the Sharia Kast-el-Aini section of Cairo, where the Cretan Section of the SOE was housed. Alexander had no inkling why he had been summoned, and when he was told, his heart started skipping beats from the excitement. At last, after innumerable requests, he was being transferred to a combat unit. Not only that, but his prayers had been answered. He was going back to Crete, this time as a commando.

"Remember, Alexander," Ciclitiras commented in a sharp, warning tone as the interview concluded, "you will be under the command of Colonel Laycock's group, and as such, you are follow *their* orders at all times. Your personal feelings relative to whatever happened in Rethimnon have no bearing with your new assignment."

"Sir!" replied Alexander rather subdued, his initial excitement about going back to Crete now somewhat dampened by Ciclitiras's admonition.

Ciclitiras's eyes softened momentarily, for as a British officer of Greek ancestry, he felt the pain that this young American must be bearing in his heart.

"If you survive this mission, Alexander," he concluded, "and it will be rather risky, I might add, then, perhaps I can arrange to have you remain on Crete and work with one of our SOE agents there."

When Ciclitiras returned Alexander's salute, the young American noted a mischievous twinkle in the captain's eye as if he shared Alexander's thought that fate might still present him with the opportunity to confront his father's murderer.[5]

The next day, Corporal John Alexander reported to the headquarters building in which the operations office of Colonel Robert Laycock's unit was located. He was to meet, for the first time, the senior officer of the commando force that was to raid Iraklion airfield, and it was to be his first briefing on the raid.

A huge, broad-backed sergeant escorted Alexander into a brightly lit conference room and introduced him to Major Charles Duncan-Moore. Alexander, in dress uniform as instructed by Captain Ciclitiras, snapped to attention and saluted smartly. Duncan-Moore eye the young corporal, irritated by the interruption.

"You're late!" he snapped at him. "Take a seat there," he pointed with his crop, "and listen sharply!"

Alexander reddened, for he felt a sense of annoyance in the major's voice. He was correct in his assumption, for Duncan-Moore did not appreciate having a combat-inexperienced addition to his raiding party. Besides, although John Alexander was a British soldier, he was an American, and Duncan-Moore disliked Americans, whom he referred to as "colonials." However, he had no choice, for he needed an interpreter and time was running out.

Alexander studied the major to whom he had just had an inauspicious introduction. Duncan-Moore stood before the group straight as a ramrod; he was a well-built man of average height, with the stern countenance of a disciplinarian. What surprised Alexander was that the major was out of formal uniform. Alexander was used to the strict military dress code of his previous headquarters assignment and was puzzled by the major's informal dress. Even though everyone in the room was dressed formally, he wore no tunic, just a pullover sweater over cuffless army trousers, the crease of which fell over the laces of civilian shoes. However, the stern look in the major's eye, though belied by his informal appearance, was the look of a hardened, experienced officer.

Alexander looked around him viewing for the first time the men who were to be the members of the raiding team. There were thirteen men—one lieutenant, one sergeant, two lance-corporals, and nine privates. An unlucky number, thought Alexander, but with the addition of the major and himself, it brought the number to fifteen.

He studied their faces, all rugged and tanned, with eyes that spoke of combat service. Alexander realized that he was outclassed by these combat-experienced soldiers. Even though he had qualified as the best soldier during his training period—a distinction that did not escape Duncan-Moore's eye when he reviewed Alexander's service record—he had never faced the trial of combat. But a youthful spirit kindled in his heart, and he swore that he would show Duncan-Moore and the rest of these men that he could be as tough as they, for the determination within him had hardened him to face whatever lay ahead.

Duncan-Moore resumed the briefing. "We will be met on shore by Cretan guerrillas who will escort us to a safe house from which we will make all further plans for the actual attack."

For the first time, the major introduced Alexander to the rest of the team. "This is Corporal John Alexander, Gentlemen!"

The men greeted him with smiles, nods, and murmurs.

Then turning to Alexander, he revealed the role that he would play in the raid, "That is where you come in, Corporal! You are to make chit-chat with these locals!"

"Sir!" Alexander responded, acknowledging the major's reference to what was expected of him.

The commando leader continued, "After we receive the signal from the beach, you, Alexander and Lieutenant Forrester, here, will go ashore in a dinghy to speak to these people and make certain that it is not a trap!"

Alexander was pleased to learn that he would be the first to land on Cretan soil during this raid, never for a moment considering the danger that might be present. His heart radiated satisfaction knowing that the first phase of his vow—the return to Crete—was soon to be fulfilled. Once on Crete, finding and confronting Fritz Schubert would be the second phase.

"Study your notes and maps, Gentlemen! The show goes on the road tomorrow at 1800 hours!"

The next afternoon, at 6:00 P.M. of June 3, the Duncan-Moore commando team of fifteen men mustered on the quay in Alexandria harbor for embarkation. There was a tall bemedaled officer standing next to Duncan-Moore, conversing with him at length. His epaulets bore the insignia of a full colonel. It was the first time that

John Alexander saw the famous leader of the Layforce Commandos, Colonel Robert Laycock.

Alexander smiled when he recognized the submarine that was moored at the pier. It was the HMS *Torbay*, the same boat that had taken him off Crete many months earlier. It was a stroke of irony, he thought, for the same one would now take him back.[6]

Chapter 7

They Came
from the Sea

The submarine HMS *Torbay* lay off the dark northern coast of Crete. It had traveled on the surface all night to reach its destination, using the darkness of a moonless night for protection. Fortunately, the seas were calm, allowing the *Torbay* to make good time. When it approached its destination, it submerged and waited for the appointed hour when the signal would be received to go ashore.

Gathered in the cramped quarters of the forward torpedo room were the men of the commando raiding party. By now, John Alexander had become acquainted with each of the enlisted men.

The senior NCO of the group was Sergeant Harry Feldmann, a British subject of German ancestry, who spoke German as fluently as a native. He had fought in Crete under Laycock and had been retained by the colonel for this special force. Under Feldmann were eleven men of lesser rank, mostly privates. They all had several points in common, especially combat service as members of commando battalions that had fought in earlier battles in the Mediterranean, and as demolition experts. The latter experience could come in good use on this mission.

The other men of this raiding team consisted of Lance Corporals James Barlow and Edwin Greene, and privates Jock Nathan, George Terry, Emery O'Connell, Jerry Keely, Jack Stirling, Paddy Leech, Mike Lewis, Ronald Kirk, and Johnny Keyes.[1]

The officer commanding this team was, of course, Major Duncan-Moore. His executive and second in command was Lieutenant Harvey Forrester, formerly of the Royal Engineers. Both officers spent the whole trip in the ward room with the sub's captain, thus maintaining the dichotomy between   officers   and enlisted personnel. Alexander had become very aware of this distinction since his first day in the British army.

Sometime around 3:00 A.M. the *Torbay's* crew went into full alert, battle stations being sounded. Alexander glanced apprehensively at Sergeant Feldmann, who appeared calm and unruffled.

"Don't worry, Laddy, we're surfacing. It's only a routine precaution," he added in his odd Anglo-Germanic accent.

The sub's conning tower had broken through the surface of the water of the Cretan Sea and moved slowly into the Gulf of Iraklion. The motors stopped, and all that could be heard were the small waves lapping against the metal of the wet deck. The *Torbay's* captain was on the bridge with Duncan-Moore, looking through their binoculars at the distant, dark shoreline. They waited and waited for the signal as the appointed hour came and passed.

"There, Sir!" shouted the deck officer, pointing to a distant glow that appeared from the beach. Both the *Torbay's* skipper and Duncan-Moore peered into the darkness. There was a flashing beam: three dots, three dashes, followed by three dots. It was repeated two times more. There now followed a five-minute interval of complete darkness, after which the same signal was repeated three times again. Five minutes later the signal flashed again as before. It was the agreed upon sign that all was safe for the landing party to come ashore.

John Alexander and Lieutenant Forrester were already on deck, waiting for the dinghy to be lowered into the water. They were to precede the rest of the group to the beach, make contact with the guerrillas, ascertain that the coast was clear of Germans, and then signal Duncan-Moore to come ashore with the rest of the commandos. Alexander's knowledge of Greek was to prove of utmost importance in this first liaison between the commandos and Cretan guerrillas. It was for this reason that Alexander had been assigned to this mission.

It took approximately twenty minutes for Lieutenant Forrester and John Alexander to row themselves to the beach. When they landed, they came face to face with the muzzles of three guns. In the deep shadows of darkness, it was difficult to see who held the weapons.

"Yu spika Englezika?"—"You speak English?"—It was the raspy voice of a Cretan guerrilla who emphasized his question by aiming his Sten gun at the two commandos.

"Mono dio?" inquired the second guerrilla of the first, shaking his head in disappointment, as he eyed the two arrivals. "They said they were sending a company!"

They were surprised when Alexander replied in Greek. The third guerrilla focused his flashlight momentarily on Alexander's face, long enough to recognize him.

"You are the Alexander boy! Nicholas's son. My name is Aleko. You do not remember me? I was your neighbor on Grigoriou Street when the devils came!"

From that moment forward, a deep camaraderie developed. The tall, burly Aleko hugged Alexander and kissed him on both cheeks. When he tried the same greeting on the lieutenant, the phlegmatic Forrester pushed him away.

Another Morse code signal was now flashed seaward in the direction of the *Torbay*. This time the message was more direct, sent rapidly and without hesitation by Forrester in person. It read: ALL CLEAR TO LAND.

Within a half-hour, although to Alexander and Forrester it seemed like hours, six rubber dinghies broke through the surf onto the beach. The remaining thirteen commandos of the raiding party were now on Cretan soil.

With the dinghies that brought the thirteen commandos to shore were two crewmen from the submarine. Their assignment was to row the rubber boats, in tow, back to the submarine. There was to be no trace left for the Germans to discover that a commando party had landed at this point.

The three guerrillas greeted the new arrivals, surprising them by shaking each man's hand.

"Let's get off the beach before a German guard spots us!" the major commanded sharply, annoyed at the delay caused by all this handshaking.

Aleko and the other Cretan guided the commandos off the beach, inland. Duncan-Moore noticed that the third guerrilla was sweeping the sand with a huge branch of a tree, thus eliminating the footsteps left in the sand by the presence of so many men in one area.

"Clever," commented the commando leader to his second in command. Alexander heard this offhand remark, and added informatively, "These Cretans *are* very clever, Sir. You will find them to be excellent marksmen and good fighters, as you will see, *Sir!*"

Duncan-Moore glanced at Alexander disdainfully, annoyed by his interjection. After all, the remark came from an American "colonial" of Cretan ancestry, even though he was a British serviceman.

He responded with an aloof, "We will see."

The guerrillas guided the commandos stealthily through olive groves and fruit orchards, along goat trails, always keeping distant from the main curving roadway that usually carried motorized German patrols at night. They finally reached the village of Amoudara, located 3 kilometers from the Iraklion airfield.

On the outskirts of the village stood the house that would serve as the raider's temporary shelter. It was the home of Marianthe Marianakis, whose husband had been killed in a skirmish with the Germans. The commandos were to stay at this "safe house" until the hour when they would leave for the airfield.

Once again the privilege of rank manifested itself. The officers were to sleep in the main house, while the enlisted men were relegated to the adjoining barn. John Alexander was to stay in the main house with the officers so that he might be available as an interpreter.

When Duncan-Moore and Forrester first entered the Marianakis house, they were met by a tall, bearded, regal-looking Cretan, dressed all in black with knee-high boots and a huge pistol at his waist. On either side of him were two burly men with bandoleers crisscrossing their chests and machine guns hanging from their shoulders. From the firm steel-grey look of his eyes, one could appreciate that this tall Cretan was a guerrilla leader. He was, in fact, Kapetan Yeorgis Petrakogiorgis—known to the British underground as Kapetan George Petergeorge. It was he who, almost a year earlier, had met in a mountain hideout with other guerrilla leaders such as Bandouvas, Xilouris, and Kapetan Satan to form the Cretan Resistance Movement to fight the Germans. During those months, he had become one of the outstanding guerrilla leaders in the province of Iraklion.

A businessman in peacetime, Petergeorge gave everything up when the Germans came to his beloved island. He fought them during the battle for Crete and lost a son in that bloodbath. When the battle ended, he took to the hills and was soon joined by hundreds of others. In time, he collected a number of Cretans, trained them, and created a formidable guerrilla group that brought fear to the German occupying garrison in the Iraklion area.

When introduced to Alexander, a sympathetic Petergeorge greeted him warmly. Aleko, the guerrilla who had greeted Alexander earlier on the beach and knew John's father, had related the tragic episode of Grigoriou Street to him. The guerrilla leader's cold steel eyes warmed as he embraced the young American. He took an instant liking to the boy, for he reminded him of his dead son.

Duncan-Moore accepted the guerrilla leader's greeting with a curt nod.

While Duncan-Moore, Forrester, and Alexander ate the meal that Mrs. Marianakis had placed before them, the Kapetan sat in a shadowy corner of the room, studying them.

"These two Englishmen are different," he opined in Greek to Alexander. "They are not like Dunbabin, Smith-Hughes, or Xan Fielding. Not even like my friend Paddy Leigh-Fermor," he added as he referred to the British SOE agents that had worked with his guerrilla group.

"These two are not friendly! Too aloof! They do not seem to like us! But we will help them anyway, inasmuch as we are fighting the same enemy."

John Alexander replied, almost apologetically, that those he mentioned were "scholar-soldiers" while Duncan-Moore and Forrester were regular army soldiers through and through.

The Kapetan smiled genially at the apology offered by the young American in British uniform. When told that the commando mission was to enter the German airfield at Iraklion and destroy as many aircraft and supply stores as possible, his smile disappeared.

"That would be suicidal! It would be impossible for anyone to penetrate the heavily guarded airfield," the guerrilla chief exclaimed, rising from his chair in the corner and approaching the two Englishmen.

"There is thick barbed wire all around the perimeter of the airfield in three rows, electrified in some areas, and it is guarded by sentries with dogs. No one can cut through that wire and live to talk about it," he warned. He waved his arms at the two officers to emphasize the danger.

Duncan-Moore and Forrester listened to Alexander's interpretation minus the hand animations.

"In that case, how could we possibly get in without creating a bloody row?" inquired Forrester rather disappointedly.

Kapetan Petergeorge turned to leave, but his parting remark, when translated, stirred the major.

"The only thing that goes into that camp is the motor supply convoy that arrives each Thursday at dusk from Suda Bay. It is always there, on time, and always the same ten trucks in number. Typical of the Germans never to vary their ritual!"

"The only way to get in, then, would be through the main gate!" replied Duncan-Moore tersely, but with the slight presence of a smile that betrayed the excitement that was racing through his mind.

Forrester and Alexander looked at each other incredulously—all except the guerrilla leader. He understood. Petergeorge stopped at the door, his face beaming for he had read the major's mind even before John Alexander had finished speaking.

"We will hijack a German truck for you, Major Duncan-Moore," he said with a smile, as he made an effort to pronounce the commando leader's name.

"Bravo!" replied Duncan-Moore enthusiastically, his aloofness waning. "We will use the truck and follow the convoy into the airfield compound. Tomorrow is Saturday, we must have the truck by Wednesday the latest."

Marianthe Marianakis heard the whole conversation in disbelief, shaking her head at the audacity of the plan. She made the sign of the Cross and, while still rolling her head side to side, rose to clear the table.

Saturday evening, an explosion, like the sharp clap of thunder, was heard throughout the town of Rethimnon. The residents of Rethimnon thought that the Royal Navy was bombarding the harbor. When they looked out, they saw a bright red glow in the sky. The German motor pool had been bombed. The ensuing flames were spreading quickly throughout the compound. The whole German garrison was called out to help fight the conflagration before it got to the main gasoline storage tanks. It took many hours for the flames to be brought under control. When the fire was finally extinguished, one of the German trucks was missing.

The guerrilla underground had purposely set the fire. It was set in Rethimnon to derail any possible thought that the Germans might have about enemy activity in the Iraklion area. In the rush to keep the fire from destroying the whole compound, many of the trucks were driven away from the endangered parking area.

One of the Cretans, who worked for the Germans in the garage during the day and for the underground at night, was picked by Kapetan Petergeorge to hijack the vehicle. Under the guise of removing the truck to safety, he drove it unnoticed through the streets of Rethimnon to the outskirts, and then continued along the main two-lane, curving highway toward Iraklion. Several miles west of Iraklion, a group of Cretans guided the truck off the highway, down a dirt road, and hid it in a barn. All traces of the truck's tracks down the dirt road were expunged.

Late the next afternoon, Aleko, the same Cretan guerrilla who had greeted Alexander and Forrester on the beach, returned to the Marianakis "safe house" to inform Duncan-Moore, through Alexander, that a truck had been stolen from the Germans, and that it was available for use by the commandos. Kapetan Petergeorge would return that night with a street map of Iraklion and the road to the airport.

As they spoke, Marianthe rushed into the main room, breathless and alarmed. Two German officers were approaching the house from the road.

Alexander rushed into the attached barn to tell the men of the danger and to be prepared to kill the Germans if they were discovered. Aleko, Duncan-Moore, and Forrester squeezed through a narrow trapdoor near the ceiling of the kitchen which served as storage space. They all waited breathlessly for whatever might happen.

The Germans, surprisingly, knocked on the door; usually they walked in or sometimes burst in, hoping to discover some illegal indiscretion. Marianthe Marianakis opened the door slowly and fearfully. John Alexander, in the attached barn with the other commandos, listened intently to the conversation. One of the German officers spoke a smattering of Greek, but Alexander could discern nothing.

Duncan-Moore, Forrester, and Aleko tried to keep their breathing as inaudible as possible. It was very hot and uncomfortable in that small storage space. Aleko had his knife ready. If the Germans were to discover them, he would jump on them and kill them. The commandos must not be discovered; the mission must go on. Aleko, representing his Kapetan at this moment, bore the responsibility that they not be discovered.

Within a few minutes, the Germans left. Through a crack in the barn door, Alexander saw the two officers smile amiably at Marianthe and bow curtly before departing.

"What did they want?" Aleko asked anxiously, worming through the trapdoor before the other two, perspiration droplets running down his face. John Alexander and Sergeant Feldmann joined the sweating threesome.

Marianthe replied that the Germans planned to commandeer her house as quarters for two new officers who would arrive next week. "That's why they were so polite," Aleko sneered sarcastically.

A silence prevailed momentarily as Marianthe's words sank in. It was the realization that whatever the commandos planned to do, it had to be done within the next few days. Time was running short.

That night, Kapetan Petergeorge returned to the Marianakis house. His first remarks were directed at Alexander. He was the bearer of good news concerning Alexander's mother and sisters. When he had left the previous night, he made inquiries about Alexander's family. His eyes warmed paternally as he told Alexander that his mother and sisters were safe in a village in the mountains of southern Crete. He added that he had sent a message to the village, through the grapevine, informing Mrs. Alexander that John was alive and safe. He thought best not to mention that Alexander was on Crete as part of a commando team on the verge of attacking the Iraklion airfield.

The young American was so happy to hear the good news that he hugged the Kapetan. The tall Cretan returned the embrace as warmth glowed in his eyes. Duncan-Moore grimaced and turned away at this sign of affection, particularly from a soldier wearing the British uniform.

Kapetan Petergeorge did not miss the major's obvious distaste for his customary show of gratitude, even as a father might have for his son, or what this tall, bearded Cretan felt paternally toward John Alexander.

The warmth that momentarily had glowed in Petergeorge's eyes disappeared, replaced by the steely cold look that was his way of saying "Let us get down to business!"

From his breast pocket, he withdrew a map and spread it across the kitchen table. He pointed to a small side street just outside the eastern gate of the walled city of Iraklion.

"As my man Aleko told you, we have hijacked a truck for you."

Duncan-Moore and Forrester nodded.

The Kapetan continued, "The German truck convoy usually enters Ikaros Street at seven in the evening. This is a long, curving street which is to your advantage. From *this* small side street," the Cretan pointed to the map against, this time using the dagger with which he was peeling an apple, "your truck can break into the convoy without being seen by the vehicle that follows. You can then ride with the convoy into the airfield!"

The Cretan leader sat back and listened as Alexander completed the translation. He carefully observed Duncan-Moore's response from his facial expression. Petergeorge wondered with a tinge of sarcastic thought, "Would this haughty English officer accept such a proposal coming from a Cretan mountaineer who never attended any military school?"

Duncan-Moore studied the map carefully with Forrester, both nodding their heads approvingly, then turned to Petergeorge, "It is brilliant! The only way." The Cretan was surprised, yet happy that the major agreed.

"Tell me Kapetan Petergeorge, how will my men get to that side street near Ikaros?" Duncan-Moore now sounded more respectful.

The Cretan leader had already resolved that problem.

"One of my men will pick you up in the truck late in the afternoon when the supply convoy is due to pass through," he explained. The driver will be dressed in a German uniform and carry official identification, for this driver also worked for the Germans by day and the underground by night. It was the same man who had stolen the truck during the fire at the Rethimnon motor pool.

"Your commandos would be in the back of the enclosed truck, hidden by tarpaulin. Once you have reached the side street, you will park and wait. My driver will leave. From then on, you and your men will be on your own, Mr. Major."

Duncan-Moore and Forrester agreed that this would be the best and only plausible way to be in position to intercept the convoy. They both laughed and slapped each other on the back, much to Petergeorge's surprise. Duncan-Moore rose and faced the Cretan leader, shaking the Kapetan's hand vigorously with both of his. Smiling broadly for the first time, he exclaimed, "Thank you for your help. What you have done will make this mission a success!"

Petergeorge told Marianthe to bring them some wine to toast the success of the mission. He also asked her to take some jugs to the rest of the men in the barn.

Duncan-Moore raised his glass in a toast to the Kapetan's continued good health and thanked him again for his cooperation. For the first time warmth showed on the commando leader's face.

"He is human, after all," the Kapetan remarked to Alexander in an undertone. Then he raised his own glass to Alexander. "Good luck, my boy. If you survive this, I will help you get to Fritz Schubert!"[2]

Chapter 8

Through the
Front Door

"They are coming, Sir," Sergeant Feldmann announced softly with a touch of excitement in his voice.

"Right! Get your engine going, Feldmann. The noise they are making will drown us out . . . be ready to start when I give the word . . . *you* men in the back, keep low and quiet!"

The twelve commandos obeyed quickly, pulling the tarpaulin over themselves, waiting for the moment when they would go into action.

Earlier that afternoon, Aleko had brought word to the Marianakis house that the usual convoy of ten trucks had finished loading supplies destined for the Iraklion airfield, and that they had begun their five-hour trip from the Suda Bay dock.

No sooner had Aleko brought the message to Duncan-Moore and his men, when Kapetan Petergeorge's man—a short, dark Cretan with heavy eyebrows and an equally heavy moustache—arrived with the hijacked truck. His name was Mimi—a diminutive of Dimitri—who wore a German field tunic over black trousers. He explained to John Alexander that he would take the Englishmen in two's and three's to the truck which he had hidden among some dense olive trees in a nearby grove.[1]

It was a slow, tedious process, getting all the men from the "safe house" through narrow back streets, through dense fields of fruit trees to the truck. It took a while, but it was done successfully without being observed by any German or informer. Most of the Cretans were indoors at that hour, which was the time of the habitual afternoon siesta. Even during the occupation, the Cretans observed their daily afternoon hour of relaxation.

Major Duncan-Moore was the last to leave. With John Alexander translating as usual, Duncan-Moore thanked Marianthe Marianakis for her hospitality, for he knew the great risk she ran by hiding them in her house and barn. If she had been discovered by the Germans, or if she had been reported by an informer, it would have meant instant execution for her and her family of two children.

Disciplined into habit, the German supply convoy of ten vehicles appeared on schedule. It had left Suda Bay that afternoon, traveled along the narrow, winding, two-laned, north shore main road, and entered Iraklion at dusk. The convoy crossed the city along Kalokerino Street, down Constantinos, and out the eastern Venetian gate of the city. Once the vehicles had passed the gate, they turned sharply onto Ikaros Street. On a small side street, one block beyond this turn and perpendicular to Ikaros, Major Duncan-Moore and his fourteen commandos were waiting in their truck.

Sergeant Feldmann, who had been a truck driver in peacetime, took over the wheel after Kapetan Petergeorge's driver had brought them to this point. Seated next to him was Duncan-Moore, while Lieutenant Forrester was squeezed in as the third man in the cab. The rest of the commandos sat quietly in the back of the truck. Each man carried a knapsack filled with demolition charges to be used once they reached their objective. John Alexander had little or no training with explosives. His assignment, during the attack, would be to stay with the truck and guard it.

The dimmed driving lights of the first truck swept into view as it negotiated the sharp turn in the road. The major leaned forward, peering into the deepening twilight, just when the first truck raced past the narrow side street.

"They are keeping a hundred-yard interval between them, Sir," came Feldmann's observation as the second truck sped by. "Shall we let all ten trucks go by and fall in at the rear?"

"Definitely not, Sergeant! If we do that," the commando leader pointed out, "the driver of truck *number ten* will undoubtedly become suspicious when another vehicle turns up behind him."

After a moment, he added, "We will break in after the ninth truck. This way *number nine* will think we are *number ten*, while *number ten* will think that we are *number nine*. Understood?"

The sergeant nodded his head understandingly, feeling rather sheepish at the obvious.

"Get ready!" The major began to count: ". . . six . . . seven . . . eight . . . nine . . . NOW!"[2]

The truck lurched forward, turned, and entered Ikaros Street. No sooner had the commando group joined the column of trucks when vehicle number ten came around the turn—barely 40 yards behind!

Through his side-view mirror, Duncan-Moore kept a close watch on the dim lights of the truck to his rear. The German had opened the gap to 60 yards, but it still worried the commando leader. What did the driver of the tenth truck think when he found the truck in front of him less than the prescribed hundred-yard interval? Did he think there was something wrong with the ninth vehicle? The Germans were so methodical at all times that this very thought could cause the driver of the last truck to speed up and investigate.

Slowly, the last vehicle in the convoy began to fall back to the required space interval. Duncan-Moore nodded in relief, satisfied that the danger had passed.

This sense of well-being did not last long. Feldmann's voice echoed anxiously through the dark cab as he reported that the last truck had put on speed. "He is overhauling us, Major!"

Three short blasts from the horn of the rear truck shrieked through the night air, as the gap between the two trucks narrowed. The major responded to the new danger with the cool, calm air of a trained professional soldier, experienced to such unexpected turns in the plan.

"We had best pull up, Sergeant . . . this is your show, Feldmann . . . you do the talking. All of you back there . . . listen . . . if the situation arises, meet it accordingly. And please, Gentlemen, no more noise than necessary!"

The men unsheathed their knives as their vehicle slowed and stopped at the side of the road. Twenty yards to their rear, truck number ten did the same.

The German next to the driver left his truck and came forward. Duncan-Moore had unholstered his pistol and held it firmly between his legs. The German walked up and stood a few feet from Feldmann's side of the cab. Both Feldmann and Duncan-Moore stared straight ahead, hidden by the shadows. Forrester kept out of sight on the far side of the cab, with his revolver already cocked. They all waited for the unexpected.

"What's the matter with you?" the German grumbled. "How do

you expect us to follow you in this darkness with your tail lights off?"

"I am sorry, comrade," Feldmann answered in fluent German. Although born in England, Feldmann had never forgotten the language of his parents. He leaned forward and flicked on his tail lights.

An impatient toot on the horn of his truck hastened the German's departure. He grunted an oath as he headed back to his vehicle.

"Good riddance," Feldmann mumbled inaudibly, thankful that the German had left.[3] Everyone relaxed. Duncan-Moore and Forrester holstered their revolvers, while the rest sheathed their knives.

Feldmann raced his truck through the darkness to catch up with the rest of the convoy. It was difficult to follow the narrow road in the deepening darkness of twilight. Finally, he spotted the tail lights of the truck that preceded him in the convoy.

"We cannot be too far from the airfield," the major commented to no one in particular.

The convoy left the main highway, and after a short ride over a bumpy dirt road, it drove through a broad gap in a triple fence of barbed wire. The sentries at each side of the main gate leaned idly on their rifles, looking with disinterest at the passing vehicles.

"Right through the front door!" Duncan-Moore chuckled.

By the time the last vehicle of the convoy passed through the same gate, the commandos had dispersed to their assigned targets.

No sooner had Feldmann brought his truck to a halt in a dark area of the airfield, when Duncan-Moore issued his orders: "Off you go, everybody! You know what to do. Remember to keep in the dark shadows of the camp . . . make every bomb count! When you are finished do not hang around—leg it to this truck. Now GO!"

They walked quickly but stealthily through the darkness, cautiously making a wide detour around the only building that showed any sign of human life. It must have been the recreation hall, and it was the only building from which voices could be heard. Beyond this building, the commandos could discern the revetments behind which airplanes were parked. Quickly and carefully the men went to work, each to his assigned task.

Behind one revetment were nine Messerschmitts—six ME110s and three ME 109s—all lined up in threes, the wing tips almost touching in typical Germanic attention to symmetry and neatness.

Lieutenant Forrester and Sergeant Feldmann placed a bomb in the center plane of each trio. The same duo discovered two other revetments in the dark. One of the revetments contained three Messerschmitts, while the other had only one. They planted their bombs and moved on to the next objective. It was easier to see now that their eyes had become accustomed to the darkness.

The other commandos in the group placed their explosives with equal care. Lance Corporal Greene and Private Nathan chose a huge building for their target. It turned out to be the ammunition warehouse. Privates Terry and O'Connell attached their missiles to the base of a huge tank in which aviation fuel was stored.

They moved through the dark night like ghostly shadows, going from revetment to revetment, from building to building. All was quiet, until out of the darkness came a loud, harsh challenge in German.

"Halt! Who are you? Who goes there?"

The shout ended in a gasp, but the alarm had been given. One of the doors to the recreation building flew open and some ten Germans raced out. A spotlight flashed from somewhere, and in its beam the Germans saw Lieutenant Forrester yanking a knife from the crumpled body of the German sentry who had given the alarm. Forrester turned and raced for the dark shadows beyond, with several Germans in pursuit.

Once beyond the circle of light, Forrester whipped out his pistol and fired at his nearest pursuer. The German stopped in his tracks, spun, and fell dead. The other Germans instantly dropped to the ground and fired aimlessly into the dark. One single bullet felled Lieutenant Forrester, killing him. Duncan-Moore raced by just as Forrester fell. He picked him up and carried him across his shoulder heading back to the truck. He had not realized that Forrester was already dead.

The whole airfield compound had now come to life with men shouting and cursing amidst searching beams of light and the din of machine guns, rifles, and pistols echoing in the night air. Tracers streaked through the darkness in all directions.

At the main gate, the two sentries had observed the last vehicle enter the compound. An argument prevailed between them. One of the guards insisted that he had counted eleven trucks in the convoy, while the other claimed that he had miscounted. There had been only ten trucks, he argued, as specified in the manifest.

Their debate was disrupted by the shout of alarm followed by the bark of Forrester's revolver. As the two sentries raced to phone guard headquarters and report that there might have been eleven trucks in the supply convoy instead of the expected ten, the first bomb exploded.

The night air was soon rent with repeated blasts of explosions. There followed a whole series of detonations that spewed airplane parts and gasoline into the air, turning night into day, and creating chaos throughout the whole compound of the Iraklion airfield. Then the ammunition warehouse blew up with a tremendous roar.

All that remained, now, was for the surviving commandos to return to their rendezvous point.

John Alexander had remained with the truck, as ordered, firing his Sten gun in the general direction of the recreation hall. In the darkness, it was difficult to see, and he feared that he might shoot or even kill one of his own men by error.

The sky glowed as sheets of flame from the burning gasoline rose like fingers to light that deep darkness that immediately precedes the first crack of dawn. Through this glow, Alexander could make out the figures of the commandos, returning to the truck, one by one.

The first to return was the major, still carrying the dead Forrester across his shoulders. Then came Feldmann. Then the rest: Barlow, Greene, Nathan, Terry, O'Connell, Keely, Stirling, Leech, and Lewis.

Private Ronald Kirk limped through the darkness to the truck with a deep bullet wound in his upper back. He made a desperate grab at the tailgate before collapsing. They picked him up and sat him gently into the truck. The only man who had not returned as yet was Johnny Keyes. Kirk gasped painfully that he had seen him go down.

Feldmann had already revved up the truck's motor, waiting for the order to move out. When he heard that his good friend Keyes had been hit and was lying somewhere out there in the darkness, he decided to go after him. Duncan-Moore stopped him.

"Stay with the truck . . . keep it running . . . *I* am going after Keyes!" He pointed to his watch: "If I am not back in five minutes . . . leave! That's an order!"

Lance Corporal Barlow yelled over the deafening roar of explosions that *John Alexander had already gone back to get Keyes*.

The major, surprised, remained momentarily silent but pleased.

"Brave lad," he uttered.[4]

In a few minutes, Alexander returned, dragging the body of Keyes behind him. Keyes was dead.

Duncan-Moore nodded and patted the American on the back for his heroic feat. "I could make a good commando out of you, young man!" he yelled over the roar of the truck's motor and the constant noise of explosions and machine-gun fire.

The Germans were closing in on the truck, and the snap of bullets cracked closer and closer. The commando leader leaped into the cab. "Let's get out of here!" he ordered.

The truck raced toward the same gate through which it had entered. At the sound of the alarm, the guards had lowered the boom, and standing before it, kept a constant fire on the approaching truck. The bullets smashed the windshield, hit the front and sides of the vehicle, but miraculously missed the occupants. With a loud crack, the truck smashed through the boom and disappeared down the dirt road into the darkness.

The surviving raiders sat silently in the rear of the truck. They sat quietly, breathing hard, perspired and dirty, totally fatigued from this evening's venture. No matter how well trained they were for this type of work, the tension and anticipation that usually preceded an attack always brought on this letdown.

Alexander sat at the open end of the truck. At his feet were the dead bodies of Forrester and Keyes. He looked out into the darkness, and over the hill he could discern the red glow of the flames that still consumed the facilities of the Iraklion airfield. Occasionally, the sound of exploding ammunition rumbled through the otherwise silent night.

These commandos, who had come to this island with one prime purpose, had successfully fulfilled that mission. *Colonel Laycock had avenged the defeat that his commandos of Layforce had been dealt in the battle of Crete.* However, one thought bothered him: what reprisals would the Germans exact against the Cretan population for this night's raid?

At the point where the dirt road meets the main highway, a blinking light focused on the approaching truck. Feldmann slowed temporarily to see if the light source emanated from friend or foe. He intended to smash through any German roadblock. When they got closer to the light, they recognized the tall, burly form of Aleko, his smiling face beaming through the darkness, signaling thumbs up. With him at this rendezvous point were three other well-armed Cretans.

The Cretans had seen the glow in the sky, heard the roar of detonations, and waited at this crossroad for the commandos to return, if any survived the attack. At the side of the road was an overturned German jeep; its former passengers of two officers and a sergeant were sprawled on the ground, dead. The guerrillas had obviously intercepted this German response to the alarm from the airfield.

The same moustached, heavy-eyebrowed Cretan, Mimi, who had driven the commandos to the side street off Ikaros earlier that same evening appeared out of the shadows, leaped into the cab, and took over the wheel. The other three guerrillas jumped into the rear of the truck. Once again, Aleko went to each man shaking his hand in delight, balancing himself agilely for a big man, as the truck bumped through a plowed field toward the Marianakis "safe house."⁵

The Cretan driver looked at Duncan-Moore, and even though it was dark recognized the commando leader. He then looked at Feldmann and pointed to the seat next to the passenger door where Forrester had sat earlier that evening. With a hand motion, turning the palm of his hand upward, he animatedly asked, "Where was Forrester?"

Feldmann did not understand and did not reply, only wrinkling his dirty, sweaty brow. Duncan-Moore *did* understand and ran the forefinger of his hand across his throat. The Cretan shook his head sadly.

Surprisingly, there was no commotion or stir evident in the immediate area from the catastrophic event that had occurred at the Iraklion airfield. In the distance, groping fingers of headlights clearly indicated that truckloads of Germans were heading out of Iraklion for the airfield. But the road to the Marianakis house was quiet and devoid of any traffic.

After a dusty and bumpy ride, the truck stopped in a field of olive trees. The commandos jumped from the truck and, guided by Aleko and his fellow Cretans, headed toward the Marianakis house. They entered through the rear of the barn and threw themselves onto the dirt floor, totally exhausted.

Marianthe Marianakis had been advised by Kapetan George Petergeorge to leave the village and visit her cousin some ten miles away. If the commandos were discovered now, after the raid, he did not want Marianthe and her children to suffer execution for giving them refuge.

Within the hour, with fatigue still gnawing at their muscles, Duncan-Moore and Alexander, guided by Aleko, left for the beach.

In the shadows where the grassy dunes roll into the sands of the beach, the commando leader signaled seaward. It was the same signal that the Cretans had beamed to them almost a week earlier, telling them to come ashore. Now the commandos were signaling the submarine to take them aboard. There was no response from the darkness at sea.

All the next day the commandos rested, waiting for night to come to depart from Crete. They knew that they could not stay here too long, for the villagers in the area were becoming restive.

On the second night, Duncan-Moore's signal was seen by the *Torbay* and answered. Within the hour, crew members from the submarine appeared through the darkness with rubber boats ready to take the commandos aboard. Quickly and quietly, Duncan-Moore's men were led to the beach by Aleko and his group. They seemed relieved and happy, relieved that they were going home and happy that they had succeeded in carrying out a dangerous raid—with the help of the guerrillas—having lost only two dead on what had been rated a suicidal mission.

As the commandos got into the rubber boats for the trip to the *Torbay*, Kapetan Petergeorge appeared out of the darkness. He had come to see them off, wish them well, and congratulate them for what they had done to the hated Germans.

The last to embark was the commando leader, Major Duncan-Moore.

He turned to the Kapetan and thanked him again for his assistance in making it possible for the mission to succeed. He shook the tall Cretan's hand with such a sincere flow of friendliness that the guerrilla leader was taken aback by Duncan-Moore's warmth. The commando leader was not as cold and phlegmatic on his departure as he had been in the first days of his arrival to the Marianakis house. Cretan hospitality had thawed him.

Then turning to Alexander, he remarked, "You are a good and brave soldier, Lad. You showed me something back there that I did not expect from a youth untrained in Laycock's Special Forces."

Alexander stood at attention, blushing in the darkness.

"I am told," the major continued, "that you are to remain behind and work with our agents of the SOE . . . that you have a special mission of your own . . . well, then good luck!"[6]

Alexander watched as the commando leader, with a final wave of his arm, disappeared into the darkness. He wondered if they were ever destined to meet again.

As the submarine HMS *Torbay* slowly submerged below the surface of the Cretan Sea, Alexander stared into that darkness. In seconds, his mind flashed back over what had happened these past days, from the moment they had landed on this beach to this very moment of departure by Major Duncan-Moore and his brave commandos. Alexander felt proud to have served with these men, the best of the elite. He murmured to himself, "Good show!"[7]

His reverie was disrupted when Aleko's voice echoed a warning. "Let us leave, before a devil spots us!"

"Come my boy," Kapetan Petergeorge said paternally, placing his arm across Alexander's shoulder, "we have work to do, and you have a rendezvous with a certain German Gestapo sergeant in Rethimnon."

Chapter 9

The Cavemen
of Crete

After the commandos had departed, John Alexander went to stay with Kapetan George Petergeorge in his village of Margarikari, located deep in the rugged escarpments of the central mountain range of Crete, where some mountain peaks reach the near Alpine heights of 8,000 feet.

It was a location that the Germans seldom dared approach, even in force, without being confronted by Petergeorge's band of guerrillas who occupied that sector. The tall, regal-looking Petergeorge felt that the young American would be safe here with him until the storm that was certain to follow the Iraklion airfield raid had diminished.

The success of the commando raid had caused a furor at German headquarters.

On the local level, squads of Gestapo troopers, seeking retribution, went about the city arresting any unfortunate person who happened to be caught on the street. Other squads of garrison soldiers went out into the surrounding villages collecting hostages. All these hostages were fated for the same end, the execution wall.

This is what Alexander had feared *would* happen to the local inhabitants in reprisal for the commando raid. He wondered if those twenty-one aircraft that were destroyed during the raid were worth the lives of these hostages. Colonel Laycock had mollified his pride by avenging the defeat of his Layforce battalions in the battle for Crete back in May 1941, but at great heartrending cost in human life.[1]

On the command level, the success of the British raiding party was blamed on the German garrison commander of Crete, General Alexander Andre. The German General Staff claimed that Andre's amnesty agreement with the civilian population was a sign of command weakness that had sent a misinterpreted message to them. The German Army High Command felt that it was the laxity in Andre's authority that allowed the creation of the Resistance Movement and encouraged the local population of Iraklion to render assistance to these commando raiders. The German military mind did not and would not accept the fact that the strength of the Cretan resistance derived from the Gestapo's wanton executions.

General Andre was summarily relieved of his command and replaced by a new garrison commander whose name, like that of Sergeant Fritz Schubert, would soon become an anathema to the Cretan people. His name was General Walter Mueller, commander of the XXII Bremen Panzer Grenadier Division whose headquarters was to be based at Iraklion. Within days of his assignment to this new command, he issued orders for the resumption of the mass executions of hostages, the indiscriminate burning of villages, and the formation of labor gangs, all of which were to mark the appalling harshness of his rule.[2]

The bloodbath that followed in the fall of 1942 was reminiscent of the early days of the German occupation that began back in June 1941. There was one major difference, however, between the days of June 1941 and the fall of 1942. By now, the spirit of the Cretan Resistance Movement had become deeply rooted within the hearts of the Cretans, having spread across the rugged mountains and into the verdant valleys of the island, and was an organized response to the renewal of these atrocities under General Mueller's new command. Guerrilla leaders like Kapetans Petergeorge and Bandouvas, together with others, met to formulate plans with which they would counter Mueller's pogroms. Also present to advise and assist them in this continuous struggle against the German occupation force were "their friends"—the secret agents of the SOE.

Throughout the tall mountains of the island, farmhouses of mountaintop villages, stone huts, caves, and even sheepfolds became, at some time or other, the headquarters hideouts for the strange men of the SOE who had come to this foreign land to help the native population in their struggle against the Nazis.

For these men who came from comfortable homes in England and from the scholarly halls of universities, their daily existence in these mountains had become the life of hermitic cavemen. With the exception of enemy activity which was more energetic and more prevalent in summer, life in the mountains during the warm season was inspiringly beautiful, albeit dangerous. However, in the winter it was a life of bitter hardship.

During the extreme cold of winter, fires with which to cook and warm themselves could never be lit outdoors, for the smoke would be a telltale signal to enemy patrols. Nor could they venture far outside their lair, for footprints in the snow would mark the path to their location which enemy patrols could easily follow.

Most of their time was spent in deep mountain caves, where stalactites dripped irritatingly on their heads and the dampness of the winter cold penetrated into the very marrow of their bones. These cave dwellers padded the wet rocks with brushwood and built a hearth, the fire of which would cook whatever food was available, while its smoke irritated their reddened bleary eyes. They sat around the warming flames for hours on end, even days, and talked and waited for their runners to bring them messages of German troop movements that would be sent by wireless to Cairo, or to bring them orders from Cairo. And while they sat, waited, and talked, they passed between them the fiery native liquor *raki* or a gourd full of wine that warmed their spirits and made the time pass more quickly.

The English officers, by habit, washed as often as convenience allowed, usually by melting snow to provide water in winter and wading in mountain streams in summer. They always managed to look clean. The others usually waited until the spring thaw.

They had one additional pastime during those long hours of waiting in which all the cave dwellers participated. They sat around the warming fire picking *pediculus humanus* off their clothing. Lice! Lice crawled in abundance everywhere. On one occasion, Leigh Fermor and Psychoundakis shared a clean white bedsheet during an overnight stay in a farmhouse. When they awakened the next morning, the sheet was covered with tiny crablike crawling bloodsuckers. The men took this in stride, for this was part of life to these cave dwellers.

While they sat in these caves, they were always alert to the danger from enemy probes. Their security depended on white-cloaked shepherds from the guerrilla bands that tenanted that sector who had been assigned to assist these English "friends." These shepherds took turns as lookouts, sitting in the snow with their guns across their laps and with the flask of raki next to them, ever watchful for the approach of enemy patrols.

These mountain cave dwellers did not remain long in their hideouts, for the enemy was always on the prowl, and the danger of discovery and capture was always present. So they moved from cave to cave, from hut to hut, and from sheepfold to sheepfold, always on the run, one step ahead of the bothersome German patrols.

The shepherds and villagers were usually reliable in maintaining the secrecy of the location and identity of the Resistance forces, even in the face of immediate execution. But there were some traitors (they were called "bad Greeks") who served in the employ of the Gestapo. When such informants disclosed their discovery, the Germans would follow in force, compelling the guerrillas and the SOE agents to flee to another hideout. Before departing, depending on the haste and urgency of their departure, they would hide the explosives, supplies, and wireless transmitters in the depths of the cave, or carry them on their backs over the rugged escarpments to another cave on another mountain miles away.

Such was the day-to-day life of these guerrilla fighters of Force 133 of the Cretan resistance movement and the British secret agents of the Special Operations Executive–the SOE.[3]

From the day when Lieutenant Patrick Leigh Fermor assumed command of the western part of Crete from Captain Xan Fielding, he immediately set out to conform with one of the dicta set forth in the field manual of the SOE–to fade into the environment and become one of the local inhabitants.

When George Psychoundakis, the small-statured Cretan runner, first met Leigh Fermor, he gazed upon the tall Englishman with wonder and admiration. "Mr. Michali"–the sobriquet which the Cretans had given him–was wearing Cretan breeches, a black shirt, an equally black fringed turban, and boots that reached almost to his knees. He had dyed his blondish moustache and curly brown hair to a deep natural-looking shade of black. The very fact that he spoke Greek and had introduced into his speech elements of the Cretan dialect, transformed him into the exact image of a local inhabitant.

Leigh Fermor and his runner Psychoundakis became close friends from the very first moment they met in July 1942 in the headquarters cave above the village of Vaphe deep in the White Mountains. Leigh Fermor enjoyed his runner's humor and was enchanted with his homespun philosophy.

George Psychoundakis was from the village of Asi Gonia, south of Rethimnon, on the ascending slopes of the island's central mountain range. The village inhabitants were poor, and George's family was perhaps the poorest of them all. But George had an inquisitive mind, and in the weeks that Fermor and Psychoundakis worked together on various missions, he constantly pestered Fermor with questions of the outside world. Leigh Fermor took great delight in answering these questions about life in England, the world religions, the various political systems, and Churchill. Psychoundakis's curious mind wondered how trains stayed on track, or how whiskey was made, or why the Scots wore kilts.

Fermor marveled at Psychoundakis's innate intelligence. Here was a 21-year-old mountain youth with no formal schooling, who had taught himself to read, had devoured what few books he could lay his hands on, and remembered everything his large olive-black eyes read.

During one mission that required a continuous trek which began before dawn and continued well past sundown, Psychoundakis narrated the plot of a novel that depicted life during the Byzantine Empire. While on another mission that brought Psychoundakis and Fermor to a mountain cave high above George's home village to inspect a cache of explosives, Psychoundakis spent the hours of the march reciting an epic poem he had written in the traditional fifteen-syllable Cretan line about the war, beginning with the invasion of Poland, the fall of France, the Greek triumph in Albania, and the tragedy of the German invasion of Greece that followed. At the conclusion of his tale, he always exhibited a youthful exuberance of what the Cretans would do to the Germans on Crete by taking a pistol and firing it into the sky, until, laughingly, Fermor would stop him lest the Germans be alerted of their presence.

Like most mountain youths of that period, Psychoundakis had never traveled beyond his island; in fact, he had journeyed to Rethimnon and to the capital of Khania only two or three times. He had never gone as far as Iraklion, which was considered too distant. Now, as a runner for the British underground agents of the SOE and the guerrilla forces, he ranged far and wide, mile after treacherous mile from mountain to mountain, over stony trails and meandering goat paths.[4]

Like all those youths who carried messages for the men of Force 133, Psychoundakis's work as a runner for the underground was fraught with danger. He hiked on foot at an immense pace, sometimes covering as much as twenty to thirty miles in one day over the precarious mountain trails, bringing messages to the various lairs that secreted the wireless stations of the SOE. He carried batteries and radio transmitters hidden in saddlebags on the backs of donkeys or mules, just like those he carried for Father Lagouvardos and Commander Frank Pool to the Monastery of St. John at Preveli. Similarly, he carried arms and explosives through German garrisoned towns and past outposts, knowing that, if caught, it would mean instant death. Yet he never wavered in the face of this danger.

On one occasion, he was stopped at a German outpost near the village of Kouphi. Nonchalantly, Psychoundakis strode past the guard, but he was seen. The guard whistled and shouted for him to approach.

"Komm!" the guard repeated.

"Kalimera—Good day—Kamerad."

"Kalimera," the sentry replied, "Gut papier?"

"Ja, Kamerad," Psychoundakis answered, showing the German his identification papers. "Gut papier."

"Gut!" The sentry gave the identification papers back without looking at them.

It was the first time that Psychoundakis had been stopped and his ID papers inspected. Had the guard searched him, he would have found SOE maps hidden in his boots. The youth waved to the German with a smile and walked away.[5]

His missions also involved guiding British and civilian stragglers to the southern coast for evacuation, or safety—as when he brought John Alexander to the safety of the monastery at Preveli. Other times he greeted newly arrived SOE agents on the beach and then guided them over mountain trails, past German outposts to the secret mountain hideouts. Each mission was as dangerous as the one preceding it, yet, he was always willing to go, never demurring. He enjoyed the excitement of being a member of Force 133. This work was his life, his contribution to the fight against the Nazis.

When the battle for Crete began back on May 20, 1941, George left his home and promised his father that he was going to fight the invader and "bury some German officer!" He never fulfilled that promise during the battle, but his work as a runner for the underground during the hard years of the occupation more than made up for that unfulfilled wartime promise.

In the early days of the occupation, there were only twelve runners, like Psychoundakis, who daily faced the danger of capture and death through execution. Three were captured early in the occupation, all of whom were shot after excruciating torture. George Psychoundakis was luckier than the rest.

Besides the danger of capture and death in his service to the men of the SOE, this poor shepherd's son encountered other problems of a more personal nature.

Returning to his home one evening after a particularly difficult mission, he found that thieves had stolen all the sheep that his family possessed. These sheep represented the sustenance of life for this impoverished family, for the sheep would have provided food and clothing for them during the winter months. Psychoundakis raced from village to village in the hope of finding them but without success. He later discovered that the culprits were some of his neighbors. He could not press any formal charges against them, for there were no civil courts functioning, and the Germans exhibited little or no concern for people with such problems.

There was no possible way to mete out justice to the perpetrators of this theft, except by finding and killing them. In the past, such deeds had resulted in bloody feuds that lasted many years. But this was wartime, and Psychoundakis was not a killer of his own people, even if they rightfully deserved such a fate. He let it pass, hoping that justice would be served to these thieves from another source. He cried for his parents and this misfortune which would bring hunger to a poor family facing the onset of a hard Cretan winter.[6]

Like his parents, most of the people of Crete faced starvation during the winter of 1942, for the Germans had seized all available foodstuffs, homegrown produce, and cattle for themselves. Surprisingly, food was also scarce among the guerrilla members of Force 133 and the SOE operational groups.

Patrick Leigh Fermor and Xan Fielding decided to ask Cairo to send them a supply drop by airplane. They radioed the coordinates of the DZ (the drop zone) and the type of signals that would mark the landing spot. In the meantime, while they waited for a reply to their signal, they starved, for they had not eaten for three days. Nothing that was edible was available in the deep snows of the mountains. Even the raki and wine supply had dwindled. Fielding and Fermor learned, like all the rest, that the pangs of an empty stomach are soon overcome by the shivers of the cold.

Psychoundakis, ever resourceful, scrambled out of the cave like a rabbit and went scrounging for food. He found nothing but a basketful of vetch which was used only as fodder for sheep. Vetch is a legume, a common broad-faced bean the seed of which contains an alkaloid poisonous to humans.

"What you bring here is poisonous," he was warned by a fellow cave dweller.

Psychoundakis acknowledged that to be true, but hunger makes you do strange things to fill an empty stomach. George knew that it was poisonous, but he also knew, from his mother's teachings, that if you boiled the vetch over a strong fire, and each time poured off the water, repeating the process seven times in all, you would have an edible nontoxic end-product. With the ample addition of salt and olive oil to make it palatable, they grabbed the paste with their hands, eating it with the delight of the starved. It was their first taste of solid food in many days.[7]

Winston Churchill has written that "The Greeks rival the Jews in being the most politically minded race in the world. No matter how forlorn their circumstances or how grave the peril to their country, they are always divided . . . with many leaders to fight among themselves."

He continues: "Both have shown a capacity for survival, in spite of unending perils and sufferings from external oppressors, matched only by their own ceaseless feuds, quarrels, and convulsions."[8]

Some leaders of the Cretan Resistance Movement were no exception to this concept.

The supply drop that had been requested, and for which the men of the SOE anxiously awaited—considering that the canisters would contain foodstuffs among other needed items—finally arrived a few nights later. However, Lieutenant Colonel Andreas Papadakis, a self-appointed leader who felt that rightfully he should be the commander of the Resistance Movement on Crete, was furious with the British of the SOE for not supporting his claim to the leadership of the Resistance. To avenge this "insulting" lack of support by the British, he decided to act independently and against the SOE and the other guerrilla leaders.

When Papadakis received word through the grapevine that a drop was scheduled for that night, he summoned some of his own people and ordered them to go to the drop zone and collect all the supplies that landed by parachute. The people involved were simple villagers who knew nothing of the strife that existed between Papadakis and the others of the Resistance Movement. They looked on Andreas Papadakis as their respected village elder whose wishes had to be fulfilled. These people had no relationship with the other members of the underground. In their eyes, Papadakis was the commander of the Resistance. At least that is what *he* told them.

Colonel Papadakis took the supplies that the villagers delivered to him and hid them. He craftily felt that he was not obligated to distribute any of these supplies to his villagers; instead he hid them for his own purposes. When he was asked to share the supplies with the other guerrilla leaders of Force 133, and with the British agents of the SOE, he refused, claiming that the supplies had been lost or destroyed. He fooled no one by this fabrication.[9]

Even his relative, who was Papadakis's God-brother, Kapetan Petrakas Papadopetrakis—one of the most reliable and courageous underground leaders in the Resistance—was angered by his relative's deceptive act.

"God-brother," he remarked angrily to Papadakis, "if everyone thinks of his own interests, we will never get on together. From now on, we go our own ways."[10]

Ironically, one day, the Germans came to the Papadakis home to arrest him. They had heard of his claim that he was the leader of the Resistance and believed him. They did not find him or his family, for he had been forewarned by friends in the Cretan constabulary and had fled to the mountains seeking assistance from the very people he had deceived and despised. The Germans did not find Papadakis, but they did find the storage place where he had hidden the supplies, and confiscated them.

A second airdrop also failed when the supplies fell among villagers who were out during that night searching for snails to eat. The barrels of flour shattered among the rocks. The rest were lost. Only some cartons filled with boots fell into the hands of villagers. Soon, many villagers sported brand-new boots, while the mountain fighters of the Resistance and the agents of the SOE, some of whom were almost barefoot in the snow, walked with shredded boots.

There was one successful airdrop that took place several nights later, which came from two aircraft instead of one, and provided an ample amount for all to share. This supply drop included tins of bully beef, ham, bacon, sausages, chocolates, rum, tea, and the sweet smelling aroma of cigarettes and tins of tobacco. It was manna from heaven for these deprived cave dwellers of the mountains. Included in the drop were twelve long-barreled Smith & Wesson .32 caliber revolvers.

At last, George Psychoundakis received his first army revolver.

Patrick Leigh Fermor and another SOE officer, Captain Tom Dunbabin, who had arrived in Crete in May 1942, requested assistance in gathering these supplies from Kapetans George Petergeorge and Manoli Bandouvas and their men. After the supplies had been collected and placed in piles and listed, Dunbabin stated that he was going to put them into storage for the present and make the distribution at a later date.

Manoli Bandouvas objected strenuously to Dunbabin's plan. He insisted that the whole supply drop should be turned over to him and his men, claiming that these supplies were meant for his group, and only his group. Dunbabin stared incredulously at Bandouvas and then argued adamantly that only he had that responsibility and that he would make the distribution when *he* saw fit.

Bandouvas strode forward, placing his massive body between Dunbabin and the pile of supplies. His heavily whiskered face and forceful personality bristled at Dunbabin's resistance. Bandouvas threatened to seize the whole lot, and turning to his men ordered, "Sta opla, paidia!"—"Stand to arms, men!"

Bandouvas's men raised their weapons, ready to fire. Kapetan Petergeorge glanced at his own men, outnumbered by Bandouvas's band three to one, and signaled them to stand still. It was an electrifying tense moment.

Captain Dunbabin was determined that Bandouvas was not going to take possession of the supplies. These were English supplies that were meant for the SOE, and he was going to take the responsibility of seeing it done his way. Without further delay, Dunbabin surprised everyone by climbing up and sitting on top of the pile.

Opening his arms wide, he addressed Bandouvas's men, "Alright! Go ahead then, gentlemen, and shoot an unarmed man!"

Bandouvas, dumbfounded by Dunbabin's action, glanced at his men and then broke into a hearty laugh. He ordered his men to lower their weapons. The rebellious Kapetan admired Dunbabin's courage in the face of so many muzzles. The SOE captain would have his way after all.[11]

On the outer perimeter of the near-revolt by such a dominant powerful guerrilla leader as Bandouvas was a young man in British uniform who had accompanied Kapetan Petergeorge to the drop zone. Watching this whole dramatic scene was Corporal John Alexander.[12]

For many weeks thereafter, the officers of the SOE teased Psychoundakis and the other men of Force 133 by freely using the expression, "Stand to arms, men!" The expression was followed by a smile or a mischievous snicker.

It was obvious to all that Patrick Leigh Fermor, Xan Fielding, and the other officers had lost respect for Bandouvas as a result of that incident, and henceforth had little regard for him. On the other hand, they held the regal Kapetan George Petergeorge in very high esteem.

George Psychoundakis found it very difficult to continue as a runner for Leigh Fermor or Xan Fielding. The sharp mountain rocks had torn his boots to shreds, rendering them useless. One day, he complained to Captain Fielding.

"Mr. Aleko," he remarked, addressing Fielding as always by his Cretan nickname, "it is difficult to walk with torn boots. I am almost barefoot."

"Don't worry, George," Fielding consoled him. "Someday we'll be lucky with these drops, and then we'll be all set."

"I'm afraid, Mr. Aleko, that will never happen if Colonel Papadakis has charge of the supplies. They are stolen every time, and what remains is hardly enough for anyone."

Thereupon, Psychoundakis explained what happened to the first airdrop, as confirmed by Kapetan Petrakas, Papadakis's God-brother. Xan Fielding was shocked by this revelation. He shook his head, remembering the Bandouvas incident earlier, and now this.

"I thought we were all on the same side and suffered together in this fight against the Hun." He was silent for a moment, then added inquiringly, "Is he selling these supplies to someone?"

Fielding sat down and immediately wrote a memo to Papadakis demanding an explanation.

"Take this as fast as your feet will carry you to Papadakis's hideout. I want him to answer my note—and you must wait for an answer. Wait, if you have to, even if it takes three days."

It was late at night when George Psychoundakis arrived at the Papadakis hideout and handed the message to his aide. When Colonel Papadakis read it, he turned livid with anger at the sharpness of Fielding's letter and furious at Psychoundakis for revealing what happened to the supplies.

"What's all this you have been telling Mr. Aleko, you wretch?"

"What have I been telling Mr. Aleko?" Psychoundakis replied, feigning ignorance of the note's contents.

"That I hide the supplies dropped by parachute and steal them, and give nothing to anyone—and who knows what else!" he replied angrily, shaking the letter before George's face.

"I told him the truth," George answered and then added, "I'm not going to run barefoot and naked and remain silent for an eternity while you hide the supplies and allow them to fall into the hands of the enemy!"

"Listen to him!" Papadakis shouted in the shrill voice of a person who is losing control of his emotions. He pointed a shaking finger at Psychoundakis and continued unabated, "Listen to the pig—daring to speak to me like that!" He was red-faced with furor, getting angrier at the intensity of his own words.

"Get out of here!" he ordered. "Your service with the English has come to an end!"

"If the English depended on you," George replied sarcastically, "the service would have come to an end a long time ago!"

"I am the leader of the Resistance here in Crete, remember that! I give the orders! And I say to you never set foot here again!" With that, the old man struck Psychoundakis across the face.

Everyone in the cave rose to their feet.

"I have orders to wait here for a reply to Mr. Aleko's letter. You can't turn me out! You can hit me over and over again, and I will not raise my hand against you out of respect for your age—but I'm not leaving here just because you want me to go. I have to answer to others!"

"If you don't leave this minute, I'll kill you!" Papadakis screamed at the top of his voice and rushed to find a pistol.

The colonel's radio operator stepped in and ushered Psychoundakis out of the cave for his own safety, until the enraged Papadakis's temper cooled.

The next morning, Psychoundakis returned to Xan Fielding's cave, exhausted by the previous night's episode.

"Welcome back, George," Fielding greeted him, "anything for me?"

"Absolutely nothing, Mr. Aleko."

"Then why did you leave so soon?" Fielding inquired, intuitively guessing what had happened.

"I did not leave, I was thrown out!"

"By whom?"

"By the so-called leader of the Cretan Resistance Movement," Psychoundakis replied and then explained what had happened at the Papadakis hideout.

"Who appointed *him* the leader of the Resistance?" Fielding commented. Then shaking his head added, "What arrogance!"

An angry Xan Fielding rose, threw his haversack over his shoulder, reached for his walking stick, and beckoned Psychoundakis to follow.

"Off we go, George. We'll go to Papadakis's straight away and I will tell him that he can quarrel with you every day, but he can't sack you unless *I* give the order."

While on the trail to the Papadakis house, Fielding confided, "I saw from the start, George, that we could not work with this man. He kept repeating that *he* was the boss of this whole thing. He even tried to give orders to me!"

When they finally reached the Papadakis hideout, Xan Fielding sat and talked with the colonel for almost two hours, while Psychoundakis waited outside the cave. When the conference had ended, Fielding summoned George and in front of Papadakis stated in strong terms, "You are to stay, George. He can't turn you out. *I* give the orders here!"

The question as to who was the leader of the Resistance was settled for the moment. The old colonel stood silent and humiliated, but rage was evident in his eyes.

Captain Xan Fielding decided at that moment that it would be best for all concerned if Colonel Andreas Papadakis and his family were evacuated from the island. "You can't put two heads into one hat." he commented to Patrick Leigh Fermor when he announced his decision.[13]

George Psychoundakis returned to his village of Asi Gonia, arriving at night during a heavy rainstorm. Tired and wet, he decided to stay at home instead of seeking a safer refuge in a cave. Having slept very little for the past few nights, he quickly fell into the deep slumber of the weary.

Early the next morning, he was awakened abruptly by his mother. Alarmed, she shook him excitedly, warning him that "The Germans are here!"

"Never mind, mother," he replied, quickly squirming into his wet pants and boots. "Don't be afraid, and above all, don't look frightened!

George went into the main room while his mother wakened his father, brother, and sisters.

Three Germans entered the dirt-floored main room of the house shouting and whistling in pidgin Greek, "Oli apano, parti!"—"All get up to leave!"

George heard them and wondered what "parti" meant. Obviously, these soldiers had served in France, but George was quick to grasp the word.

"Tempo, tempo!"—"Quickly, quickly!" the Germans kept repeating.

"Where parti?" George asked.

"Klissia, klissia"—"The church," the Germans replied, brusquely pushing them out the door.

While the Germans marched them down the path to the church, George, who led the group, cautioned his family to dawdle. The slow pace extended the line of march to some 40 yards. When George looked back at the rear of the column, he saw that the Germans had been distracted and were looking in the other direction. That is all George needed to flee from the trap.

His mercurial feet propelled him down an embankment into a nearby stream. Once out of sight, the two Germans did not even notice his absence. He waded downstream, leaving the narrow waterway at the site of the Chapel of St. George, after whom he had been named. As he climbed up the bank, he ran into two other Germans on the other side. He remained hidden below the bank until the guards went into a garden in search of fruit. Taking advantage of their departure, he turned and ran along the embankment until he reached the safety of a nearby mountain.

The next day, he returned to his home. Fortunately for George, he met his aunt on the path. "Run! Run!" she warned, "Don't go home or they'll get you! They're waiting for you!"

A platoon of garrison soldiers had returned to the village and asked for everyone's identification papers. One of the Germans asked, "Is anyone here called Psychoundakis?"

One of George's cousins replied, "Which one? There are lots of them!" The villagers sensed that the Germans were looking for young George, the runner who was working with the British agents of the SOE, but they feigned ignorance. The Germans left empty-handed.

Two days later, a patrol of twenty Gestapo troopers returned to Asi Gonia again asking for the whereabouts of George Psychoundakis. The leader of the patrol was a short, dark-complexioned German who looked more Greek than German. It was Fritz Schubert. He was anxious to capture George Psychoundakis alive and in person.

Several Germans served as outposts at the approach to the village, standing at the far end of the road with an informer, who was there to identify George Psychoundakis should he be apprehended.

Schubert stopped one of the villagers and asked him to point out George Psychoundakis's house.

"Which George?" he asked. "There are several of them by the same name."

"The son of Nicholas," Schubert persisted.

"Oh, I don't know that one," the villager lied.

Schubert struck the villager with his stick. Then the other troopers hit him blow upon blow with their rifle butts.

"I'll kill you here and now if you don't tell me!" Schubert threatened.

Frightened, the villager yielded and took them to George's house.

They found George's mother standing in the doorway of her home. Again they asked, "Are you the mother of George Psychoundakis?" And again they received the same response, "Which one? There are several."

Frustrated Schubert asked more emphatically this time, "The son of Nicholas Psychoundakis!"

"Yes, I am," she confessed, trying to mask her fear.

"Then where is your son?" Schubert sneered.

George's mother replied deceptively that she had not seen her son for three months. The last she heard of him was that he had gone to work for the Germans in Khania. She looked unflinchingly straight into Schubert's eyes when she spoke. Her son's safety depended on the conviction of her lie.

Schubert ordered that the house be searched thoroughly. They looked everywhere, but there was no George Psychoundakis to be found. Had they looked beyond the house, they might have found him in an irrigation ditch hiding under several layers of bamboo.

Before departing, Schubert had the last word. He threatened that if George Psychoundakis did not report to the Rethimnon headquarters of the Gestapo by January 17, the Gestapo would return and burn the whole village.

George Psychoundakis was never able to discover who had betrayed him to the Gestapo. Was it someone acting on behalf of Colonel Papadakis, or was it one of the thieves who had rustled the family sheep?

When Psychoundakis finally reached the safety of the cave which was the latest hideout for Mr. Aleko and Mr. Michali, both Xan Fielding and Patrick Leigh Fermor agreed that George had been betrayed to the Gestapo and that next time he might not be as lucky to escape their dragnet.

"I think the time has come, George, for you to leave the island until your trail cools down," Xan Fielding advised.[14]

Psychoundakis's evacuation from Crete did not take place for several weeks. In the interval, the whole Fermor-Fielding operational group was almost captured by the Germans during a skirmish at a hideout that bore the name of "the beehive hut." Flight from the area of the skirmish and seeking the safety of another mountain cave was one reason for the George's delayed departure.

Psychoundakis finally left Crete for the safety of Egypt on the night of February 14-15, 1943, aboard one of the Royal Navy's trawlers with Lieutenant John Campbell at the helm. It was the first time George had left the island of his birth. After many months of sight seeing in the free lands of the Middle East, he returned on the night of July 29, 1943, to resume his duties as the runner for the cavemen of Crete.[15]

Chapter 10

The Moment
of Truth

While life on Crete in the fall of 1942 and spring 1943 worsened under General Mueller's despotic regime, and while the agents of the Special Operations Executive with the guerrilla forces of the Resistance continued their subversive activities, events elsewhere beyond the island began to tip the scale of war against the Germans.

For the first time since the invasion of Russia on June 21-22, 1941, the German army was facing the reality of defeat. Russian troops advancing southeast of Stalingrad began to close a steel ring around the German Sixth Army in that city. On October 14, 1942, the ferocious battle for Stalingrad had begun. It was destined to become the graveyard of over half a million German soldiers when Field Marshal Friedrich Von Paulus eventually surrendered his army on January 31, 1943.

In North Africa, the Germans fared even worse. On November 2, 1942, General Bernard Montgomery and the XXX Corps of his Eighth Army struck hard at Erwin Rommel and his vaunted Afrika Korps. On November 4, the British army made a major break-through at the battle for El Alamein, routing the Afrika Korps and sending them back in headlong retreat into Libya.

A week later, on November 8, General Dwight D. Eisenhower, the Allied commander for Operation Torch sent U.S. and British troops ashore in North Africa in the biggest amphibious operation in human history up to that time. The landings were made at Algiers, Oran, and Casablanca. Rommel's Afrika Korps was now trapped between two Allied armies, the British coming westward from Egypt through Libya and the Americans advancing eastward toward Tunisia. The two armies eventually linked up in April 1943. North Africa was cleared of German troops by May 1943.

With this defeat in North Africa and the loss of hundreds of thousands of troops in that campaign, Adolf Hitler now had to send all available troops to hold back the advancing Russians in the east and to reinforce Italy and the coast of France from the possibility of an Allied invasion.

There would be no more troops available to reinforce the garrison on Crete, even if their numbers diminished under the constant harassment of the Cretan guerrilla bands.

The creation of the Cretan Resistance Movement and the success of their incessant spirited attacks on the German garrison, aided by the agents of the SOE, soon reached the ears and hearts of other peoples of German-occupied nations. Spurred by humankind's natural desire to be free, these people formed plans that emulated the Cretan Resistance.

Yugoslavia and France set the prime example of such resistance. It began on Crete and then spread to the Partisans of Yugoslavia and to the French Forces of the Interior. Like those on Crete, the Partisans and the Free French Resistance forces were to suffer similar reprisals. Thousands were executed in the mountain villages and cities of Yugoslavia, and on August 11, 1942, the Gestapo executed ninety-nine hostages in Paris in retaliation for Resistance attacks on German soldiers and their installations.[1]

What had begun on the island of Crete in June 1941 and continued through 1942 into 1943 had now spread to the continent of Europe.

It had snowed all night, and by morning the mountain trails were covered by a three-foot blanket of white. The day dawned with the sun shining brightly in a sparkling blue sky that contrasted sharply with the ferocity of the previous night's storm. The air was bitter cold and the wind cut like a Cretan dagger, spraying snow into the faces of the guards who served as outposts at Kapetan George Petergeorge's headquarters cave, situated on a mountain above the village of Kamares, some forty miles southwest of Iraklion.

Inside the huge cave, flames from several fires cast warm shadows against the rocky walls reflecting grotesquely the figures of the men grouped in the center. Kapetan Petergeorge and several of his lieutenants sat together around a huge flat boulder that served as their table. Pieces of bread and cheese were pushed to one side of the table, while the group periodically savored gourds of wine and raki, adding an inner warmth that the surrounding fires could not affect.

In the center of this rock-hewn table was a rudimentary map of the immediate area covering the city of Iraklion on the north coast, through the central mountains of Mount Ida, to the southern coast of Timbaki on the Gulf of Mesaras. The elder Kapetan was discussing plans for a surprise foray against a nearby German garrison. He spoke convincingly that the Germans would never expect such an attack now in midwinter with the trails and landscape covered by heavy snows.

"That element of surprise would give us the perfect opportunity for success . . . we could do much damage to them . . . for they would not expect us."[2]

His lieutenants nodded agreement.

The guerrilla leader sat back satisfied with the plan. He paused, took a swig of raki, wiped his lips with the sleeve of his jacket, rubbed his hands together to warm them, and then resumed with the logistics of the plan. He knew, of course, that before undertaking such an attack he would have to review it with the SOE agents in the area, in this case Captain Tom Dunbabin.

At the far end of the table, John Alexander sat listening to his host. John was in a dilemma. He wanted to participate in the forays that Petergeorge's men carried out against the Germans, but the guerrilla leader would not allow it.

"I would have to clear it with our friends of the SOE," Petergeorge would say each time. Then he would remind Alexander that "you are here on a special mission that could serve the people of Crete to a greater purpose." Each time he made that comment he followed it with a mischievous smile. It was a sly smile that had but one meaning—the disposal of Fritz Schubert.

A runner from a nearby SOE hideout brought Petergeorge a message that, during the night of November 8, Allied forces had invaded North Africa. Petergeorge offered a toast to the success of the invasion and expressed the opinion that "the weather was changing." Alexander, familiar with Cretan proverbs, understood it to mean that the allies were at last on the march to victory.

"Soon they will come here to Crete!" Petergeorge added hopefully.

The invasion of North Africa by U.S. and British forces

bothered Alexander. It bothered him because he was an American in the service of the British, in a British uniform, while the land of his birth, the United States, was sending Americans to fight in North Africa and probably later in Europe. His conscience nudged him that he should be there with the American troops as an American soldier.

The first time this thought entered his mind was when he was in Cairo before being attached to Laycock's commando group. It was then that he heard, for the first time, about the Japanese attack on Pearl Harbor and found out that the United States had been thrust into the war. Dispatches about the war thereafter were scattered and scarce, for as far as the men of the SOE and of the Resistance were concerned, the day-to-day war against the Germans centered on Crete.

When on one occasion Alexander voiced his feelings to his host about serving in the American armed forces, Kapetan Petergeorge responded with words of gentle reproof, "You are doing your share against these devils—the Nazis. What you and the others did at Iraklion was magnificent and heroic! You'll get your chance with your own kind." In time, Petergeorge's words proved to be prophetic.

But the young American had another worry. It concerned his widowed mother and his two sisters. The Kapetan, who felt very paternal toward this youth with a mission, this youth who reminded him so much of his own son killed in the battle for Crete, understood that concern and tried to alleviate it. Periodically, he inquired through the grapevine about John's family and passed the reports on to him. But John had not seen his family in almost two years, not since the day of his father's murder.[3]

A signal from an outpost above the headquarters cave passed from sentry to sentry that a runner was approaching the lair. It turned out to be Petergeorge's able assistant, Aleko—the same burly guerrilla who had first greeted Alexander on the beach prior to the airfield raid.

Petergeorge took Aleko aside and conversed with him at length, periodically casting side glances at Alexander. Then the guerrilla leader announced that Aleko was to lead a patrol and that he needed ten men. He turned to Alexander and smiled. "My boy, you have hounded me to go on one of our missions. Now I *want* you to go on this patrol with Aleko."

The patrol set out early the next morning and struggled through the deep snow of the mountain trails. When prodded to reveal the purpose of the patrol and its destination, Aleko only smiled and repeated, "You'll see soon enough, when we get there." Alexander could not understand the secrecy concerning the mission, particularly when he remembered the lengthy and detailed planning that Petergeorge had discussed with his lieutenants the previous day in the cave. He just shrugged his shoulders, accepting the fact that this was how these mountain people conducted their patrols.

From the position of the sun, John observed that they were traveling southwestward. Late in the afternoon, they entered the village of Magarikari, Kapetan Petergeorge's home village. It had not been a long trip, but it was an exhausting one maneuvering through the waist-high snow.

The mountain villages of Crete were never built on hilltops or mountaintops that would make them vulnerable to a siege, but rather on the ledges of the mountain. This was a throwback to the days of the Ottoman occupation. Magarikari was no different from the rest.

Aleko sent two scouts ahead into the village to make certain that there were no Germans in the area. Then he posted lookouts, while he and John approached a house on the far edge of the village, near the base of a huge mountain. A trail came down from the mountain and passed adjacent to this house. "Good for a fast escape, if deemed necessary," John noted.

An elderly couple greeted John and Aleko at the entrance to the house. They smiled when Aleko introduced Alexander and mentioned who he was. "Let's go inside, John, there is someone I want you to meet."

John entered the primitive, dirt-packed main room of the house. This house was no different from any other Cretan village home, austere, primitive, yet clean. But what he saw inside made his heart skip and his eyes tear. Sitting at a table in the center of the room were his mother and two sisters.

Not since that frightful day on Grigoriou Street had he seen them, when his mother lay in a faint on the floor next to his dead father with his two sisters crying hysterically, while he was dragged out by Gestapo troopers. With a yell of joy, he ran to her and hugged her while she sobbed the tears of a mother's love and happiness at seeing her son again. They sat together, saying not a word, only holding hands and looking at each other. The words would not come; they just sat in joyful silence. Then they spoke simultaneously, each trying to outdo the other.

From the door of the room, Aleko and the elderly residents of the house witnessed the reunion. Aleko tried to hide the tears that glistened in his eyes, a sight unusual for a hard, burly mountaineer like him. "Too bad the Kapetan isn't here in his own village to see this with his own eyes. After all, he arranged it," he whispered softly to the old couple as he led them from the room.

"You have until tomorrow night, John," Aleko remarked closing the door.

It was not to be. At noon the next day, Aleko returned. He spoke hurriedly with a hint of alarm in his voice. "Germans have been spotted coming through the pass approaching the village. We have to leave immediately!"

They left within minutes from the rear of the house using the trail that passed nearby to climb the mountain and safety, heading back to the hideout. John's mother and sisters remained behind in seclusion.[4]

* * * *

The Germans pursued with a greater intensity their drive to find the caves that sequestered the men of Force 133 and of the SOE. "These damned cavemen must be caught!" Mueller demanded of his staff.

Germans, dressed as English soldiers, filtered into villages asking the mayor and the villagers for refuge and assistance in contacting the leaders of the Resistance or with English officers who might help them be evacuated from the island.

Most villagers warily denied knowledge of any British officers or guerrillas in the area. The human grapevine had forewarned them that these "English soldiers" were Germans in disguise. Quite a few villagers, however, in all innocence, fell prey to the German trap and were eventually arrested, imprisoned, and some executed. This deceptive ploy by the Germans continued over a period of many weeks.

One day, in the early months of 1943, three Germans in British uniform entered a village and again pleaded with the villagers to "save them from the Germans." One of Patrick Leigh Fermor's runners, a young Cretan named Petro who had temporarily replaced George Psychoundakis during the latter's absence in Egypt, was staying at the home of a relative in the same village. The village elders came to him requesting his assistance in putting these straggling "Englishmen" in touch with a representative of the SOE.

Petro went with them to meet the "Englishmen." Unseen by the German spies, he eyed them from a distance.

"You idiots!" he roared, scolding them. "Can't you see they're wearing German boots! They're Germans!" The revelation angered the villagers.

"We'll kill them and return them on the back of a mule!"

"No!" interrupted Petro, "I've got a better idea."

Upon his suggestion, the villagers seized the German spies, tied them securely, and dragged them to the headquarters of the local garrison commander.

"Look, Mr. Commander, look what we bring you," they exclaimed with artificial enthusiasm pointing to the three Germans, "English stragglers!"

Someone in the crowd added sarcastically, "See how we cooperate with you Germans." There were a few audible snickers and an exchange of knowing looks among the villagers.

The garrison commander smiled weakly, eschewing any knowledge of this German deception by ordering the three "Englishmen" thrown into the garrison prison. It was his way of saving German integrity, assuring the villagers that these three would be treated as spies and worse. The villagers nodded and smiled, happy that they had turned the tables on the Germans.[5]

At the village of Sfakia on the southern coast of the island, a German patrol found a dead soldier lying in the stinking filth of an outhouse.

The next day, a platoon of German garrison soldiers led by a Gestapo officer entered the village and demanded to know who was responsible for the killing. Since not a single villager confessed or expressed knowledge of the killing, the Germans selected ten men at random and shot them in the village square in front of their kin. Then they dumped the bodies down the well in the center of the village.

On the following day, one of the villagers appeared before the local garrison commander complaining that during the search of the village by his soldiers, one of them had raped his daughter. The company commander—a dignified Wehrmacht Hauptmann—courteously and sympathetically listened to the girl's father and requested that he return the next day at 8:00 a.m. with his daughter.

John Adamakis was cautioned by his fellow villagers not to go back, advising him to drop the charge of rape against the German soldier. His niece argued that it was a trap and that if her uncle appeared the next day he would be arrested and shot. "God only knows what would happen to your daughter!" she added. But Adamakis was stubborn in spite of the existing danger, for his daughter's honor was at stake.

"What would the German captain care if one of his soldiers *did* rape your daughter," Adamakis's sister philosophized, persistently trying to change her brother's mind. She was wearing her mother's black dress for the first time in her life, grieving for her husband who was one of the ten hostages executed the previous day. "After all, yesterday these soldiers executed without trial ten of our innocent men like animals. What makes you or your daughter different in their eyes?"

John Adamakis listened with turmoil in his heart, but turned a deaf ear to all their cautions and entreaties. He decided to go, whatever the danger.

Promptly the next morning, Adamakis and his daughter appeared before the garrison commander. They noted that the whole garrison was standing in formation in the field beside the captain's headquarters.

"Come with me!" the captain beckoned politely to Adamakis and his daughter. He took them in front of the formation and, through an interpreter, asked the girl to go through the ranks and identify her rapist.

She walked down the lane between the first and second ranks, finally stopping before a tall trooper. She uttered a strange sound of revulsion and burst into hysterical tears, pointing an accusatory finger at the German.

"Are you certain?" the captain asked.

"Look at the scratches on his face! That's the bastard!" she screamed, spitting at the soldier.

The captain thanked her and ordered the company sergeant to dismiss the formation. The rapist was immediately arrested and after court-martial was executed. The village priest brought the news of this strange form of German justice.

"Justice has been served," John Adamakis remarked while comforting his daughter and his own pride. "But I must admit, these Germans are a paradox!"[6]

When John Alexander returned to the Petergeorge hideout, he felt a deep warmth of happiness that he had finally seen his mother and sisters after all these months, even though the reunion had been cut short by the approach of the German patrol. He owed a depth of gratitude to the Kapetan for his kindness in arranging the reunion.

A week late, the Kapetan summoned Alexander to his quarters.

"Are you still interested in fulfilling a certain vow you had taken relative to your father's demise?" he asked.

Alexander's eyes lit up. "Of course!" he uttered, and leaned forward eagerly. From the tone of the Kapetan's question, he sensed what was to follow.

"The house that Fritz Schubert is presently occupying in Rethimnon was formerly the home of one of Aleko's cousins." Kapetan Petergeorge continued, "If you are still willing, Aleko can take you north to Rethimnon and introduce you to his cousin, Yanni. He can give you the layout of the house, and you can develop your plan of approach. I have asked Yanni to help you."

They set out two days later, Alexander, together with Aleko and an escort of three men. On their backs, they carried provisions for several days, knowing full well that they could always replenish their needs at the homes of friendly villagers along the way.

When Alexander left the headquarters lair, he was accompanied for a short distance by Kapetan Petergeorge. The tall guerrilla leader walked slowly with John, his arm placed paternally on the youth's shoulder.

"By the way," Petergeorge remarked suddenly, "I do not approve of this mission." Perplexed, Alexander turned to him. Ignoring the young American's glance, the Kapetan continued, "This mission will be dangerous, and Schubert is not a man to be trifled with. But you have made a vow, and in Crete, we Cretans keep our vows. As long as you are in my care, I must let you have a go at him."

Petergeorge paused, a trace of a smile on his face. "After all, I promised you, didn't I, back on the beach at Iraklion!"

After the traditional embrace of departing friends, John and the rest began the trek down the trail. At the first turn, John looked back. The elder Kapetan was still there watching them. With a final wave, he turned and headed back to the cave.

The journey north from the cave above Kamares was strenuous and lengthy, taking many days of hiking over mountain escarpments and through deep gorges, made more difficult by the varying depths of snow.

The Cretans usually determined distance by counting the number of suns it took to reach a distant destination, or by the number of hours traveled. Short distances were measured by the number of smoked cigarettes, but they saw no value in the estimate of mileage. John Alexander's journey was gauged by counting the many suns it took to reach Rethimnon.

They traveled in a northwest direction, hiking all day and resting at night, usually settling in some secluded sheepfold or cave. Most villages were bypassed except when they ran short of provisions. It was a trip that took many days, until finally they stood on a height from which they could see the ceramic roofs of the houses of Rethimnon.

Carefully avoiding German outposts or patrols, Aleko guided the group to the home of his cousin, Yanni Vandoukakis. "That bastard, Schubert, moved into our house a month ago," Yanni explained. "His original residence was commandeered by a Gestapo officer, which made Schubert so furious that he threw us out of our house without giving us the opportunity to take anything. That's how we came to live here with my uncle—my mother's brother!" He added that everyone in Rethimnon hated this devil, Schubert.

The group remained secluded indoors for two days, sleeping, eating and relaxing from the rigors of the trip. They did not waste time, however, for during those two days they discussed a plan by which John Alexander could gain entrance to the Schubert residence.

In that same interval, Alexander prepared himself psychologically for the moment when he would face his nemesis. He still wore the regulation British army trousers and shirt, and his boots were those he wore during the commando raid on the airfield. Although scuffed badly, they had somehow survived the cutting sharpness of the mountain rocks. His only deviation from the official army dress was his black jacket and fringed turban. Tucked into his belt was a revolver that he hoped to use on Schubert when he at last confronted him, now that he was within reach.

Yanni drew a simple road map to the Schubert residence, the floor plan of the house, and most important of tall, the location of the secret entrance into the tunnel that would bring Alexander into the main room. It was not unusual for many of these houses to have such hidden tunnels. The houses were old, built during the Turkish occupation of the island in the years before 1912 when Crete finally threw off the yoke of the Ottomans. The tunnels represented a rapid rear exit of escape from marauding Turkish soldiers who often entered Christian homes and pillaged, raped, and murdered. Over the years, some of these tunnels were filled in with soil or became storage spaces for provisions, while others became wine cellars. In the Yanni Vandoukakis family home, the tunnel was still there as it was from the day it was built late in the 1880s.

On the third night of their stay, Yanni's uncle predicted that it would be a moonless one. It would be an ideal night for clandestine movement since without a moon there would be no shadows. By 7:00 P.M., the moon had dropped below the horizon, casting the whole area into deep darkness. It was time for Alexander to go. He had committed the road map and floor plan to memory, and he checked his revolver for the first time since the raid at Iraklion airfield.

A little before midnight, Alexander left the Vandoukakis house. He approached the Schubert residence slowly and carefully, stealthily moving from building to building. Fortunately, there were no Germans in the streets of Rethimnon that night.

He found the house easily, and he smiled at the accuracy of Yanni's crude map. The rear of the house was surrounded by a wall composed of overlying layers of bamboo, placed there to protect the fruit trees from northerly winter winds. Between the second and third section of the bamboo wall was a separation, just as Yanni had described, that led to an opening. That opening was the entrance to the tunnel.

Alexander squirmed through the narrow opening and entered the tunnel. He bellied along the dirt floor, wiping thick layers of cobwebs from this face along the way. Several times he felt rats run past him. He ignored them, took a deep breath, and continued to crawl forward toward the end of the tunnel. Then he came to a wooden panel. He pushed it gently, carefully, so as not to make any noise. The trapdoor moved and fell inward with a dull, low decibeled sound.

He paused a few minutes, waiting to see if anyone had heard the noise. It remained still and quiet, and so Alexander squeezed through the opening and entered the room. The room was dark, and his eyes, already accustomed to the darkness of the tunnel, scanned around quickly. He realized that he was in Schubert's bedroom.

The bed was empty.

A bright shaft of light emanated from the main room down the short hall that connected it to the bedroom. Alexander drew a deep breath, cocked his revolver, and tiptoed down the hall. He moved forward slowly, careful to avoid making any sound. With each step he drew closer to that moment of truth when he would confront the murderer of his father.

He reached the door to the main room and passed through. Seated at a desk on the near side of the room close to the door, with his back to him, was the object of Alexander's mission, the subject of his vow, Gestapo Sergeant Fritz Schubert.

The German was leaning over the desk, writing. He never heard Alexander enter the room, nor was he aware of his presence. Alexander took a deep breath, grabbed the chair, and spun the German around. The moment of truth had come!

The German and his intruder were both surprised. The German was startled by the intrusion and frightened by the look of hate on the face of his intruder. Alexander was surprised and greatly dismayed. The German seated in front of him was *not* Fritz Schubert!

"Where is he?" Alexander demanded, prodding the German's belly with his revolver.

The startled and now totally frightened Gestapo officer stammered half in pidgin Greek and half in German that he was Schubert's replacement. That Fritz Schubert had been transferred and reassigned to Gestapo headquarters in Iraklion.

In a fury created by frustration, Alexander struck the German a full hard blow across his face with the barrel of his revolver, knocking him senseless. Breathing heavily as he looked down at the unconscious, bleeding German, Alexander listened for the sound of anyone approaching in response to the noise. He was ready to kill anyone who walked through that door. But no one came.

Alexander left the same way he had entered. When he arrived safely at Yanni's house, he had tears of frustration in his eyes. His prey had gotten away. He vowed anew that there would be another time some other day; he was determined to get Fritz Schubert, even if it was destined to be the last act of his life.[7]

Chapter 11

The Hinge
of Fate

With the German defeat in North Africa, the Allies turned their attention to the mainland of Europe.

On July 10, 1943, the Allied armies invaded Sicily. Over 160,000 U.S. and British troops invaded the southern coast of that island, the Americans under General George Patton going ashore at Gela and the British under General Bernard Montgomery landing at Cape Passaro.

By July 12, the British had captured Syracuse, and ten days later, Patton's Seventh Army captured Palermo. In the briefest period conceivable, the Allied armies rushed to complete the seizure of Sicily, with Italy eyed as the next target. Meanwhile, Allied aircraft raided Naples and bombarded military objectives in Rome.

On July 25, fifteen days after the invasion of Sicily had begun, the Fascist Grand Council of Italy forced dictator Benito Mussolini to resign. It was Mussolini who in 1940—to prove to his Axis ally, Adolf Hitler, that he was as successful a conqueror as Hitler— invaded Greece and failed. This failure had compelled Hitler to come to Mussolini's assistance, which led to the invasion of Crete and the subsequent occupation. It had taken this "modern-day Caesar" twenty-one years to build his Pax Romana, only to lose it in fifteen days. No sooner had Mussolini resigned when he was arrested by his successor.

Marshal Pietro Badoglio was appointed by King Victor Emmanuel III to become the new head of the Italian government. Three days later—July 28—Badoglio declared that the Fascist party of Italy was dissolved and subsequently opened negotiations for an armistice with the Allies. This armistice was soon to affect all Italian troops on the island of Crete.

Crete is divided geographically into four provinces: Khania in the western part of the island; Rethimnon in which Psychoundakis's village of Asi Gonia was located, as was Father Lagouvardos's Monastery of St. John at Preveli; Iraklion where the British commandos raided the airfield; and the easternmost province of Lasithi with Neapolis as its capital.

During the occupation of Crete, the Germans controlled the provinces of Khania, Rethimnon, and Iraklion, while the eastern province of Lasithi was placed in the hands of Hitler's ally, Mussolini. Lasithi was occupied by the Sienna Division under the command of General Angelo Carta. When Marshal Badoglio requested an armistice with the Allies, General Carta passed the word to the British that he was ready to surrender his division with all its equipment to the British rather than allow it to be taken by the Germans. He requested a conference with a British representative to discuss terms.

The British Mediterranean Command in Cairo sent a wireless to Patrick Leigh Fermor—now promoted to the rank of captain—advising him to proceed to the city of Neapolis, which was the headquarters of the Italian division, and negotiate with General Carta.

Accompanied by a guerrilla escort from Kapetan Petergeorge's group, Leigh Fermor force-marched through the mountainous trails, starting below the village of Vaphe in the province of Khania, hiked on a course parallel to the southern coast, past Rhodakinon Beach, to the village of Saktouria, then to Timbaki. At the village of Timbaki, his escort changed hands. The Petergeorge men were replaced by an escort from Manoli Bandouvas's band, inasmuch as Fermor was now in Bandouvas's territory.

From Timbaki, Fermor and his new escort followed the guerrilla trail across the central spine of mountains past Mount Ida—the highest peak at 9,000 feet—past the ancient Minoan archaeological site at Knossos, skirted south of Iraklion, and then eastward to Neapolis in Lasithi province. It was an exhausting journey that took many days. As the crow flies, it was approximately 100 miles, but when the ascending and descending trails are measured, added to the deviations around German outposts and German patrols, it would be safe to state that the trip covered almost 375 miles.

The fierce-looking, burly Manoli Bandouvas, while escorting

Leigh Fermor during the latter part of his trip, was superficially friendlier with Fermor than with any other British officer. He should have been, for Fermor had earlier arranged a special airdrop that provided ample arms and supplies distributed only to Bandouvas and his men. In return, Captain Fermor asked Bandouvas to guard the Lasithi mountain passes with his men to keep the Germans from passing through and occupying Lasithi and confiscating the weapons of the surrendered Italian division.[1]

Dimitrios Kokkinis, a cafe owner in Neapolis, was surprised to see a British officer enter the city with an armed band of guerrillas while the Italian soldiers sat around listlessly.[2]

Over many cups of Italian coffee–distasteful to an Englishman with a preference for tea but more used to the heavier Turkish-Greek coffee–Fermor began the negotiations with Carta. The Italian general agreed to turn over all his division's pistols, rifles, machine guns, mortars, and related ammunition to the guerrillas. The artillery, too bulky for use in the mountains, was to be destroyed. Fermor went one step further in his negotiations by convincing Carta to leave Crete for the safety of Egypt, as a prisoner of war, to be given the courtesy and honors due general officers. The Italian agreed but wanted to take his whole officer staff with him. When told that such a large complement of men would pose a problem on board a trawler with a limited capacity, he agreed to take only his executive officers.

With the final terms accepted, military protocol stipulated that the official surrender of the Italian division take place in Cairo where Carta, a general officer, would surrender to a British general. After all, Patrick Leigh Fermor was only a negotiator holding the rank of a captain.

The trip south to Rhodakinon Beach for eventual evacuation to Egypt began some days later. For General Angelo Carta, the war was over.[3]

Once John Alexander returned to the home of Yanni's uncle and told them what happened at the former Fritz Schubert residence, it was decided to depart immediately–within minutes–before the alarm was given and a search for them begun.

The trip back to the Petergeorge hideout in the cave above Kamares village seemed longer and more arduous to Alexander than when they traveled north to Rethimnon. The exuberance and anticipation of confronting Fritz Schubert had turned to disappointment and frustration. It was a frustration that brought tears to his eyes. Few words escaped his lips during the trip south, even during the short pauses to rest their weary bodies. Aleko understood and left him alone in the silence of his feelings.

It would have been a greater frustration for Alexander had he known that he missed Schubert by just one day. The Gestapo sergeant had left for his new assignment in Iraklion the previous day.

The ability of any local civilian to enter unobserved the residence of a senior Gestapo officer did not speak well for German security in Rethimnon. Everyone buzzed in the headquarters offices and mess about the previous night's occurrence. After that shocker, every Gestapo and headquarters officer looked back over his shoulder or kept out of the shadows at night. Alexander's intrepid act had put fear into the hearts of the masters of fear.

They reminded themselves of the raid at Iraklion and that the vehicle that carried the British commandos onto the airfield came from the Rethimnon motor pool following the great fire set by a Cretan arsonist. First that and now this! So the Gestapo tightened the noose, took in hostages for questioning, tortured some of them, shot a few, and released the rest.

Fritz Schubert, now in Iraklion, heard the news and wondered who wanted to kill him. He did not know that the young American had taken such a vow.

Manoli Bandouvas—Emmanuel was his baptismal name, but everyone on Crete referred to all Emmanuels as Manoli—was perhaps the most powerful guerrilla chieftain on Crete. He was not as respected as Kapetan George Petergeorge, but he was an important leader with over a hundred well-armed men in his group. He was a person to be taken seriously.

Captain Fermor's earlier effort to supply him with a large arms drop was a mistake in view of Bandouvas's rebellious attitude exhibited earlier against the British. When the additional Italian weapons surrendered by General Carta's Sienna Division were turned over to him, he became all-powerful. For a proud, self-centered, and illiterate guerrilla leader, who bore a strong resentment of the British, such power was like a lit powder keg ready to explode.

With all this power in his hands, he exploded! Without consulting anyone, he decided to carry the war to the Germans in the district of Vianos on the border between the provinces of Iraklion and Lasithi. He consulted neither with his fellow guerrilla chieftains nor with Fermor, and never with Captain Dunbabin, the SOE officer in his sector, whom he disliked most of all.

Bandouvas launched his campaign on the misapprehension that the Allies were ready to invade Crete. He planned to pave the road for them and emerge a national hero. Wireless messages had informed him of the Allied armies' successes in North Africa, and of Sicily's invasion and occupation. Bandouvas had also heard, through the grapevine, of military operations taking place in the Aegean on the islands of Kos and Leros. In his misdirected mind, that meant that Crete would be next on the Allied agenda. Had he conferred with Fermor or Dunbabin, he would have learned that the battle for Kos on October 4, 1943 and for Leros on November 16 were defeats for the British garrisons on those islands.

His spies informed him that a German supply column was heading south along the narrow road that snaked through the western portion of the Lasithi mountain range. Bandouvas decided to ambush the column at a pass that ran below the village of Apano Siphi.

Like the wily mountain fighter that he was, he set his trap and the Germans fell into it. In the skirmish that followed, Bandouvas's men, mountaineers who had grown into manhood with a hunting rifle in their hands, made each shot count. The weaponry that had been supplied to these men by Fermor's airdrop, as well as the Italian arms, overwhelmed the German column. Over a hundred Germans were killed in the heat of battle with all their vehicles set afire.

Before the brief battle had concluded, a new motorized column of reinforcements raced to the rescue of the decimated Germans. It was a battalion of half-tracks, light tanks, and self-propelled artillery that immediately salvaged victory out of defeat and put the guerrillas to flight. A strafing sortie by a flight of Messerschmitts made the rout complete. Bandouvas pulled his band back after suffering heavy casualties.

The German commander, General Mueller, furious that any guerrilla band would dare attack German troops in strength, decided to retaliate. Like a flaming scythe, he sent his troops through the district of Vianos, bringing with them death and desolation. His troopers executed men, women, and children—those who had not fled the villages earlier—and set fire to their houses. Whole villages went up in flames. When the fires diminished, they dynamited the remnants and then plowed the debris into the soil. Mueller's fury had no end.

When he learned through his spies that Manoli Bandouvas had led the guerrilla band that had ambushed the German column, Mueller placed a bounty on his head. When Bandouvas was told that the Germans were out to get him at all costs, he sought assistance from the one person he despised most of all, Captain Tom Dunbabin. Although Dunbabin distrusted Bandouvas, particularly after the affair of the third airdrop, he agreed to take Bandouvas and his lieutenants to the beach for evacuation to Egypt until such time when his trail would cool and the Germans would relax their vigil.[4]

When Dunbabin, Bandouvas, and Bandouvas's lieutenants finally reached the southern coast in the sector between Saktouria and Rhodakinon Beach, they were surprised to meet Leigh Fermor who had arrived at the same destination earlier with General Carta and general's staff officers. Arriving within hours of the Leigh Fermor-Dunbabin entourage was Kapetan Petergeorge and his lieutenant Aleko with John Alexander.

They greeted each other warmly and remarked on the circumstance of their meeting within hours of each other at the same site as if it were prearranged. One of Petergeorge's scouts came down from the cliff to report that there was an enemy guard post less than one-half mile distant manned by three German sentries. Petergeorge suggested to Dunbabin and Leigh Fermor that they cut the telephone wires to the guard post, capture the Germans, and take them to Egypt as prisoners of war.

At the crest of a nearby hill, Dunbabin saw some shepherds, whom he recognized as friends from a previous occasion, and went to speak to them. When the shepherds heard what the group was planning to do with the guard post, they pleaded with Dunbabin not to attack the Germans. They explained that it would not be worth the aftermath that would assuredly follow. From their past experience of similar situations, the shepherds knew that the Germans would commandeer all their goats and sheep in reprisal. Dunbabin consented to leave the Germans alone. In appreciation, the shepherds guided the group to a safer sector of the beach far from any chance of German observation.

They waited all afternoon in a cave on the mountainside facing the sea. When the first shadows of dusk began to spread across the landscape, Leigh Fermor, Dunbabin, and their signalman left the group and descended to the beach to begin the series of signals seaward that would alert the boat of their readiness to be evacuated.

Leigh Fermor had brought with him his own radio operator whom the Cretans had named Siphi. Siphi's arrival on Crete differed from that of the other British, for he was not an SOE agent. He was an airman whose bomber had been shot down over Iraklion. His actual name was Flight-Sergeant Jo Bradley from Wales. There had been six crewmen aboard the bomber when it was hit by German antiaircraft fire. Three of them, the pilot, co-pilot, and chief engineer, perished when the bomber crashed, while the remaining three parachuted to safety. The Germans captured one of the three, but the other two were rescued and hidden by the Cretan villagers who eventually brought them to Dunbabin and Leigh Fermor.

Jo Bradley was the radioman aboard the ill-fated bomber, and since Leigh Fermor's original signaler had been captured and executed by the Germans, he decided to retain Bradley to fill the void. Bradley turned out to be a charming person with a beautiful singing voice. Fermor enjoyed his company; each night they sat in the hideout and sang together, much to the delight of the Cretans.[5]

The signaling began, with the same signal repeated each hour until a response was received from the sea. The response would be the boat's appearance offshore.

It was quiet where the three men stood and watched; all that was audible were the slap of waves breaking on the beach and the roar of a sea beyond. Suddenly, out amidst the inky blackness of the sea, there came a sound heard above the roar of the sea. It sounded like the motor of an airplane, at first, until the noise increased in volume and tempo. Then out in the darkness beyond the cove loomed the shadow of a huge monster. It was a large trawler, apparently larger than the previous boats. In this case, it was the *Fairmile* captained by John Campbell, as usual.

A flashing Morse Code light from the trawler signaled that the sea beyond the cove was too rough to launch boats for the evacuation. Both Leigh Fermor and Dunbabin were surprised that Campbell would breach security and signal from the dark background of the sea which could be seen by the Germans, and alert them to the evacuation that was to take place. Siphi signaled in response that the waters were calmer within the cove, and the decision was made to launch the boats.

The first rowboat came ashore with two sailors aboard, who immediately tied the end of a cable around a huge rock that was well embedded in the sand. They left another cable which the shore crew were to use as a pulley to haul the rowboats back and forth. This method worked better and faster than the use of oars.

Patrick Leigh Fermor was the first to go aboard the trawler together with General Carta. He introduced him to Campbell, saw to the General's needs, and then returned to the beach. John Alexander, Kapetan Petergeorge, Aleko, and some of the Italian officers were the next to leave the beach.

Once the rowboats were hauled by the attached cable past the calm waters of the cove, the sea was running so high that it made embarkation difficult. Each time the rowboats made the run from the trawler to beach and back they ran the risk of being swamped. On one of the trips, the rowboat was picked up by a huge wave and slammed against the bulkhead of the trawler, nearly overturning it, soaking the frightened evacuees with cold seawater. Campbell, as master of the ship, decided to cancel any further embarkation, and prohibited Leigh Fermor from returning to shore.

When Campbell put his trawler in reverse and hastily departed to prevent the huge waves from driving the boat onto the nearby rocks, Leigh Fermor was stranded on board. Fermor's orders dictated that he remain on shore and continue SOE operations, but fate had willed otherwise.

One of the persons left behind because of the trawler's departure was Tom Dunbabin, who actually had been ordered to embark for Egypt. Stranded with him on the beach was his antagonist, Manoli Bandouvas, the one man the Germans ranked on top of their list for capture. With Bandouvas were the men he had brought along for evacuation.

The guerrilla chieftain from Asites was furious that he had been left behind. He shouted and gesticulated angrily, blaming Fermor and Dunbabin for conspiring to leave him on the beach so that he could be captured by the Germans. In his fury, Bandouvas ignored Dunbabin's reply that he *also* was scheduled for departure. Dunbabin just shook his head and walked away. There would be another boat on another day.[6]

The hinge of fate plays tricks with the lives of men.

Chapter 12

A Change
in Allegiance

The Allied campaign against Nazi Germany was progressing well. On September 3, 1943, the British Eighth Army invaded Italy, sending its troops across the Straits of Messina from the newly occupied island of Sicily. On September 7, General Maxwell Taylor, the American airborne commander, made a clandestine trip into Rome to study German strength. His evaluation indicated that Rome was too well fortified by German troops to allow a successful Allied air invasion of that city.

Six days later, General Mark Clark and the men of this Fifth U.S. Army landed at Salerno, thirty miles below Naples, and captured Naples by October 1.

The Eighth Army on the east coast of Italy and the Fifth Army on the west swept up the boot slowly over difficult terrain in a hard-fought campaign. The British liberated the heel of Italy up to a line above the city of Bari, while the Americans entered the town of Monte Cassino on December 7, 1943.

With military success continuing in Italy up to the approaching battle for Monte Cassino in early 1944, the military leaders of the Greek army-in-exile headquartered in Cairo, as well as the leaders of the Cretan Resistance Movement, hoped that an Allied invasion would soon take place to liberate Crete.

The Allied High Command, however, decided not to invade and liberate that island. It was a decision made at the insistence of the British who promulgated an official policy that was more political than military. British political policy toward Greece at that time favored the restoration of the Greek monarchy. Inasmuch as the captive Greeks on the mainland and on Crete, and the spokesmen for the free Greeks in exile in Egypt, expressed various opinions on this subject, it was determined to hold a plebiscite on the subject once Greece and Crete had been liberated from the German occupation.

In the meantime, the British persisted in the policy that the people of Crete fend for themselves, the only assistance coming through the SOE's activities.

The sea voyage from Crete across the Mediterranean to Egypt was a stormy one. Although the sun shone brightly in a cloudless sky, the sea ran high with huge 20-foot swells that shook the trawler violently forward to aft and then starboard to port.

John Campbell and his crew, as expected, were the only men on board who carried on with their duties as if it were a smooth crossing. Patrick Leigh Fermor took the voyage well but did not exhibit his characteristic smile and jocular manner. Alexander sat in his bunk unfazed by the boat's rocking response to the sea, but reminisced of a smooth sea voyage he had taken with his parents and sisters across the Atlantic in June 1940, almost four years earlier. When they sailed from the Port of New York for Greece, which now seemed to him a lifetime ago, no one ever envisaged what fate had in store for them.[1]

General Carta lay in his bunk, moaning. Kapetan Petergeorge teased the deathly ill Aleko, until he also joined the majority at the trawler's rail. All the other passengers clung desperately to the rail retching into the sea. In fact, there was not enough room for everyone, and soon the wet deck became slimy with vomit, a condition that made standing on a heaving deck almost impossible.

Since it was a bright sunny day, the crew maintained a constant vigil for enemy aircraft. On one occasion, all the passengers were ordered below deck when one of the crew sighted a black speck in the western sky. It turned out to be a friendly aircraft, but forcing the seasick passengers below made a bad situation worse. Now they could only use pans or the deck to bear the exudate that came from their upheaved stomachs. It did not take long for the stench to become unbearable. Fermor and Alexander decided to spend the rest of the stormy trip breathing fresh air topside.

By nightfall of the next day, the sea had calmed and the *Fairmile* pulled into the harbor of Mersa Matrüh in Egypt. Even in the dark, they could see a harbor filled with many ships moored around hulks of derelicts sunk during the earlier days of battle and bombardment.[2]

Once the boat docked, several large trucks were on the quay waiting to transport the newly arrived evacuees from Crete to their respective destinations. Quickly loaded with the healthy, the recovering, and the still queasy passengers, the vehicles departed for Alexandria. They drove through the desert all night into the afternoon of the next day, an uncomfortable ride in tarpaulin-covered trucks. Everyone agreed that, as stifling as this leg of the journey turned out to be, it was better than what they had experienced during the recent sea voyage. Once in Alexandria, they stopped at a British army camp for food, rest, and medical care.

Two days later, a smaller vehicle left Alexandria for Cairo with Fermor, Alexander, and General Carta aboard. They drove southward through the desert along a narrow strip of blacktop highway that paralleled the Nile, finally arriving at the Egyptian capital early the next day. Once in Cairo, the three went their separate directions.

Patrick Leigh Fermor, dressed informally in a British officer's uniform that bore only the three pips of a captain on his shoulders, escorted the Italian general to British Command Headquarters. There, the general officially surrendered to a British general as protocol dictated. With that obligation completed, Fermor departed for the SOE safe house that he shared with five others in the Cairo suburb of Zamalek.

He was happy once again to be driven through the bustling streets of Cairo and to view the familiar sights of the carts (the gharris) and the customary flowing white robes (the galabias), topped by the red fez (the tarbouch). There were also the other sights so inevitable in a city filled with military uniforms. There were many colorful figures: the old whiskered man outside the Shepheard Hotel who offered to elevate anyone to peerage for a price; the man who stood outside British Army headquarters shouting "Chocolates . . . cigarettes . . . O.B.E.'s"; and the young pimp in a city filled with prostitutes who offered his sister for a price with the revelation that "she is clean and white inside like Queen Victoria."[3] Fermor laughed at all these sights, for they were part of Cairo life; Cairo would be home to him for the duration of the war.

His vehicle crossed the Nile to Gezira Island, down the Sharia Fouad el Awal to Zamalek, and then to the familiar street of Sharia Abou el Feda. Fermor ran up the steps of the sprawling safe house that bore the name of Tara. It was named not after Scarlett O'Hara's family home but rather after the ancient wooden stronghold of the High Kings of Ireland. Fermor pounded energetically on the wooden door, which was soon opened by the ever-smiling houseboy, Abdul. When he entered the front foyer, the household pet, Pixie, came up, licked his hand, and ran off with his hat. Moments later, the five other occupants of the residence came down to greet him.

Fermor shared this residence with a diverse group of people, all of whom were involved with the Special Operations Executive. There were Sophia Tarnowska, a Polish countess who had fled to Egypt through the Balkans just two steps ahead of the advancing German armies; William MacLean of the Scots Greys Regiment whose war exploits carried him from Ethiopia, to Turkey, and into Albania; David Smiley of the Horse Guards Regiment who had just returned from a parachute expedition into German-occupied Greece; William Stanley Moss, a tall six-foot-plus officer from the Coldstream Guards who had an early background as varied as Patrick Leigh Fermor's. The fifth member of the six-residence household was Xan Fielding—Aleko to the Cretans—who had returned some weeks earlier from that island.

Fermor was happy to see all five of his friends, for it was seldom that all of them gathered together under the same roof at the same time. Their duties carried them to different countries, and their return to Tara was seldom synchronized. They were so happy to be together that they planned to celebrate the event.[4]

Alexander did not share the same joy Fermor felt, for Cairo was not home to him. He had no home in this big city, no friends to greet him. Everything that was dear to him was located in some cave or village in the mountains of Crete where his mother and sisters had sought refuge, or back home in Wheeling, West Virginia.

Cairo only called up sad emotions for this young refugee who had arrived lonely and penniless from the Monastery of St. John at Preveli, three years earlier in 1941. Much water had flowed up the Nile in those three years. Now he was back as a corporal in the British army who had seen service with a commando group in a raid on the airfield at Iraklion and with the SOE in the rugged mountains of Crete. Nonetheless, he felt alone and lonely, an American in a British uniform in a foreign land.

Once billeted, he reported to the Cretan Section of the SOE for assignment. But Alexander was not officially a member of the Special Operations Executive. Thus, it was recommended that he report to the headquarters personnel office in Cairo for reassignment to official duty.

The summons came unexpectedly the next day. An army messenger arrived at Alexander's quarters with orders to escort him to British Army Headquarters on official business. The messenger—a private—had no answers in response to Corporal Alexander's questions. The trip to the headquarters building was direct, and in less than an hour of his summons, Alexander stood at attention before the desk of the senior officer commanding the personnel section of the British army in Cairo.

The officer—a major—was seated behind his desk with his eyes glued to a folder open before him. It contained Alexander's army service record. Occasionally, he made a weird exhalation, looked up at Alexander through wire-rimmed glasses, but offered no comment.

All the while, the young corporal remained at attention.

From the corner of his eye, Alexander noticed the presence of another person sitting cross-legged in an armchair in the far corner of the room. He wore a uniform that was unfamiliar to Alexander. He soon discovered that the officer was an American.

"Very well, Corporal," the round-faced personnel officer finally remarked. "Your request has merit and has been approved. After all, you *are* an American by birth, and we are all brothers-in-arms!"

"My request, Sir?" Alexander asked, puzzled.

The British officer ignored the question. Instead, he introduced the American, who finally came forward.

"This is Major Sebastian Braun of the United States Army contingent here in Cairo. He wishes to speak with you." Alexander clicked his heels in salute.

The British major gave Alexander's service record to the American and left the room. The American officer took his place behind the desk, opened the folder, and began reading. He had already gone through it once, but he wanted to review its contents a second time.

In that interval of silence that it took for the major to go through the file, Alexander studied him. The American was tall, rugged faced, well-built, and wore a neat beribboned tunic. What caught his eye was the unit patch the major wore on his left shoulder. It was diamond-shaped, blue with yellow lettering that spelled "RANGER." Alexander recognized the unit, for it was the American version of the British commandos.

Finally, Major Braun looked up.

"Why are you, an American, serving in the uniform of the British army?"

Alexander was taken aback by the question, but explained quickly and briefly the circumstances of June 1941 and his subsequent enlistment in the British army, before the United States entered the war. Braun nodded. It was all there in the service record.

"I see you graduated high school; you were a three-letter man in football, baseball, and wrestling; graduated at the top of your class; and you speak Greek besides English."

"Yes, Sir." Alexander was amazed at the information in his file.

"You served with Laycock's commandos and with the SOE on Crete."

Again, "Yes, Sir." Alexander was getting tired standing at attention.

The major seemed impressed with what he read in the file. He closed the folder and stood up to his full height of six feet. He looked sternly at Alexander and asked suddenly, "How would you like to transfer to the United States Army?"

The major's remark was uttered in the tone of a command rather than a question. His eyes dared John Alexander to say, "No!" Alexander thought, "Do I have a choice?" Openly, he replied as before, "Yes, Sir!"

Major Braun reacted as if he did not expect a negative response from this young corporal. "Good! As of this date your file will be transferred to us. I'll arrange it with the Limeys."

"Of course," the major added as an afterthought, "You will have to take an oath of allegiance and undergo the army examinations, the AGCTs, and appear before an interview board. But all that will be arranged!"

The next day, John Alexander, formerly a corporal in the British army was sworn in as a private in the United States army. He took the AGCTs and later appeared for his interview before the army review board.

The board was comprised of a lieutenant colonel and two majors, one of whom was Major Sebastian Braun, the Ranger officer. A first lieutenant, sitting at a side desk, was taking notes.

Private John Alexander, U.S. Army, had scored well on the AGCTs; in fact, his score placed him in the top percentile. His service with the commandos and the SOE impressed the board, just as it had impressed Major Braun at the initial interview.

The review board wanted select men like Alexander to serve in a special duty assignment in the Mediterranean. The Mediterranean theater of operations had been a British affair from the beginning of the war until 1942. With the joint American-British invasion of North Africa and the subsequent Allied operations in Sicily and Italy, the American command wanted an equal share in all phases of military operations in the Mediterranean, overt and covert.

The interview board asked Alexander to wait outside. In his absence, they conferred and then recalled him. Alexander entered, snapped to attention, and saluted smartly for the first time as an American soldier.

The senior officer spoke first. "You have passed your tests and the interview with flying colors. Upon Major Braun's recommendation, we are assigning you to serve with the OSS."

"What's that, Sir?" Alexander asked innocently.

"The Office of Strategic Services!" Major Braun interjected. The OSS, as a covert operation, was not familiar to too many in the American armed services.

"You have served in clandestine operations with the SOE on Crete, have you not!" Again it was not a question but rather a statement of fact. The colonel eyed the young private and concluded, "Now you will serve in the OSS—the American version of the SOE."

Thus, John Alexander, formerly a corporal in the British army, was promoted the next day to the six stripes of a master sergeant in the United States army and ordered to report to Bari, Italy, for duty with the OSS.[5]

The Office of Strategic Services (OSS), the organization to which Master Sergeant John Alexander was now attached, was created on June 13, 1942 by executive proclamation of the president of the United States, Franklin Delano Roosevelt.

The proclamation directed that the OSS "collect and analyze such strategic information as may be required by the United States Joint Chiefs of Staff." It also stated that it was to "plan and operate such special services as may be required." This was the paragraph that gave clearance for the formation of a specialized unit of select personnel who would carry covert operations behind enemy controlled territory. The president had rendered to himself the authority of selecting the director of this new organization. Paragraph four of the proclamation appointed William J. Donovan as the director of the Office of Strategic Services.[6]

Long before the war came to Europe and to the rest of the world, Franklin Roosevelt prophetically recognized the need for information that would keep him abreast of the rapid changes that were taking place in the capitals of the world. To achieve this purpose, he asked his trusted friend, William J. Donovan, to be his personal emissary to the various capitals to gather the many tidbits of political and military information for evaluation. Thus, the American hero of the First World War—holder of the Congressional Medal of Honor—William J. "Wild Bill" Donovan, became Roosevelt's intelligence agent without portfolio.

Donovan had once been an assistant attorney general with the Justice Department and was comfortable with the political scene of the nation's capital. At one time, he had even been considered for appointment as secretary of war. As a result of his service to the president in the capacity as the unofficial U.S. intelligence representative, Donovan must be given credit as the man who laid the foundation for creating the American intelligence community in the period before the United States entered World War II.[7]

Up to June 1941, there existed no United States agency to collect, coordinate, and evaluate intelligence information in order to help the president develop a sound military and foreign policy. In fact, seven different federal agencies functioned as separate entities, each collecting intelligence for its own respective organization. This information was never shared with any other agency because of internal rivalries.

No greater rivalry existed than that between the U.S. army's G-2 section—army intelligence—and the navy's Office of Naval Intelligence, the ONI. The State Department entered into this rivalry with its diplomatic corps of elitists who reported their information to their own superiors with an eye to personal promotion and advancement. The Treasury Department with its Secret Service collected information about counterfeiters and about those who threatened the life of the president of the United States. The Department of Immigration and Naturalization, which was under the

Labor Department, collected its information on the thousands of immigrants and refugees who sought asylum in this country, but had no information of enemy spies who sneaked past the borders of this nation under the guise of refugees or immigrants.

The Federal Communications Commission monitored foreign shortwave radio broadcasts from which little intelligence was discernible, for they had no method of deciphering encoded broadcasts. Finally, the Federal Bureau of Investigation, the FBI, had duties to prohibit infiltration into this country of foreign enemies and to observe any anti-American activities.[8]

It was obvious that these multiple governmental intelligence agencies needed a central control for proper coordination. It was so bad that the government of Nazi Germany made derogatory comments on the United States "intelligence service" by describing it on Radio Berlin as "fifty professors, twelve monkeys, ten goats, twelve guinea pigs, and a staff of Jewish scribblers."[9]

On June 18, 1941, President Roosevelt summoned William Donovan to the White House for breakfast, after which he gave his friend the assignment to organize a national intelligence agency whose purpose would be to coordinate all the information gathered by these federal agencies and to collect this material and evaluate its relationship to American national security and policy. Roosevelt went one step further by adding that Donovan include in this agency a plan for espionage activity behind enemy borders. The president appointed Donovan to be the director of this new agency and gave him the title of coordinator of information (the COI).

Thus, on July 11, 1941, Roosevelt formally announced the creation of this new agency by issuing Executive Order 8826 in which he designated a coordinator of information to "collect and analyze all information and data which may bear upon national security." Paragraph two of the directive stipulated that "all governmental agencies would make all their intelligence information available to the COI."[10]

When J. Edgar Hoover, the director of the Federal Bureau of Investigation, heard of the COI, he protested loudly, claiming that the COI's overall espionage activity represented an infringement on his department's authority. The matter was settled by directing that the COI utilize its intelligence information in dealing with espionage *outside* the United States, while the FBI would conduct espionage vigilance *within* the borders of the United States.

During his travels to European capitals, Donovan had developed a close affiliation and friendship with the leaders of Great Britain's intelligence community. He admired the work of England's Special Intelligence Service (the SIS) and the sabotage subversive activities of the Special Operations Executive. When he returned to Washington, he described these agencies to Roosevelt and recommended that the United States create a similar form of intelligence service.

When the United States found itself thrust into the war overnight by the Japanese attack on Pearl Harbor on December 7, 1941, Roosevelt remembered Donovan's memorandum. He disbanded the existing agency and in its place created the Office of Strategic Services—the OSS.

Donovan continued his work as director of America's intelligence service. Working out of the cramped office in the National Health Institute in Washington, he issued his directives to his specially trained agents.

Under his directorship, the OSS was not a tidy bureaucracy. It did not function with military precision or efficiency. As a matter of fact, insubordination became a way of life for OSS officers, but Donovan was unconcerned. He often said, "I'd rather have a young lieutenant with guts enough to disobey an order than a colonel too regimented to think and act for himself."[11]

OSS policies and operations were often contradictory and improvised. Orders were given and forgotten or ignored. The agency was racked with ideological conflict. Millions of dollars were spent without budgetary control. But in spite of all these shortcomings, there were also many espionage coups. OSS officers and enlisted men were typically young and brilliant amateurs who dared the patience of the enemy. They left their mark on the outcome of the war.

The excitement inherent in serving with the OSS attracted such diverse individuals as Stewart Alsop, John Birch, Julia Child, Allen Dulles, Arthur Goldberg, and Arthur Schlesinger, Jr. These are just a few of the famous and well-known members; there were more who were not as famous, among them, Master Sergeant John Alexander.

Operating out of Cairo, OSS staffs began to organize their resources and enlist selected personnel for duty within the ranks of the organization.

Master Sergeant John Alexander received his orders for Bari the very next day, signed by Colonel John Tuhlman, the OSS chief in

Cairo. He was driven by jeep to Alexandria, where he boarded a U.S. army transport for the crossing to Sicily. During that sailing, he compared the smooth flow of this large ship with his rough and unsettling voyage from Crete to Mersa Matrüh.

When Alexander disembarked in Sicily, he reported to the Air Transport Command at the nearest airfield where a special OSS C-47 flew him to Brindisi, a port halfway up the heel of the Italian boot. From Brindisi, he was driven the approximate sixty-mile trip north to the city of Bari and OSS headquarters.

The next day, he reported to his new unit, the 2677 Regiment (Provisional) OSS for assignment to his new duties.[12]

The party held by the residents of the Tara safe house on Sharia Abou el Feda in Cairo continued into early evening, finally ending by 9:00 P.M. Four of the six party participants had retired to their rooms, happy in the thought that they had given Patrick Leigh Fermor a warm welcome for his return from Crete. They were very proud of his latest exploit in escorting General Angelo Carta safely out of the German-occupied island.

The only two still sitting in the main lounge of the residence were the guest of honor, Leigh Fermor, and his friend from the Coldstream Guards, William Stanley Moss. These two found they had much in common in that they both had shared unique adventures in the early years of their lives.

Moss was born during the Japanese earthquake in Tokyo in 1923. The outbreak of the war in 1939 found him living in Stockholm. He crossed the U-boat infested waters of the North Sea to England by private yacht. After some months as a volunteer guardsman, he was commissioned in the Coldstream Guards Regiment. The next few months found him serving guard duty at the Court of St. James and at Churchill's country estate at Chequers.

During the British breakout at Alamein, the Third Battalion of the Coldstream Guards had suffered heavy casualties. Among the rein-forcements sent to Africa to supplement that famous battalion's ranks was Lieutenant William Stanley Moss. After the North African campaign ended, he was returned to Cairo. There, he was posted to the SOE because he spoke Russian. In typical army fashion of assigning the right man to the wrong place, he was scheduled for duty on Crete, inasmuch as he spoke neither Greek nor German. Now he sat with Leigh Fermor and talked late into the evening about the Germans and Crete, and waited for his eventual call to duty.

There glasses were empty and so was the bottle on the table. Moss examined his empty glass and broke out in the devilish smile so typical of the roguish six-footer.

"What say we go to the club, Paddy, for another round?"

Fermor liked Moss's suggestion, and within minutes they were in a car heading for the starlit Club de Chasse in the center of Cairo. After several drinks, Moss turned to Fermor and teasingly remarked, "You know, ol' chap, that episode was really a piece of cake!"

"What episode?" Fermor mumbled, looking at him through half-shut eyes.

"Well, after all, Paddy, the Italian general didn't resist. Now, did he?"

"And so?" Fermor mumbled a second time, a fixed smile on his face, while trying to place his empty glass on the table but missing.

"Well, it was no great challenge! Carta surrendered willingly," Moss teased. "Tell me, Paddy," Moss continued, his speech beginning to slur, "Wouldn't it rather unsettle the Hun if we go in and steal their general? Take him out as a prisoner? Now, that *would* be a challenge, wouldn't it?"

Fermor's eyes opened wide, his frozen smile turned into a mischievous snicker, and excitement rang in his voice.

"Yes, Billy, it *would*! Let's do it!"[13]

They staggered to their feet and clinked their glasses, spilling the liquid over their unsteady hands. They toasted the success of this irrational suggestion agreed upon by two tipsy Englishmen.

What began as a humorous challenge was soon to develop into an adventure that would startle the world with its audacity.

Chapter 13

The Kidnapping of
a German General

Patrick Leigh Fermor and William Stanley Moss may have had one drink too many at the Club de Chasse the night before, but when they awakened the next morning, they remembered. They were up early, and by midmorning they appeared at the Cretan Section of the Special Operations Executive with their proposal.

"And who would you have in mind for this abduction scheme?" they were asked by the chief of operations.

"Why Walter Mueller, of course!" came Fermor's reply. "The anathema of Crete!"

The plan was rejected outright as being "absurd, outlandish, too theatrical." But neither Fermor nor Moss accepted the rejection as final. They went to Major Jack Smith-Hughes, director of the Cretan Desk, for having served on Crete he would probably be more sympathetic to the proposal. Smith-Hughes listened at length and agreed with the others in the Cretan Section that it *was* somewhat "theatrical," but he felt that properly planned and executed it had a fair chance for success.

The British, after all, had a reputation for such irregular forms of warfare. It would be in the same tradition as the commando raids in Europe, Colonel Laycock's raid to capture General Erwin Rommel in North Africa earlier in the war, and more recent raid on Iraklion airfield.

"If this succeeds," Smith-Hughes confided, "it would demean the German and shatter his prestige and self-confidence." The very scope of the plan's audacity brought a smile to his face. Approval for the operation was finally granted.[1]

From the beginning of the planning period, it was decided that the quickest way to return to Crete would be by parachute. In the days that followed, the initial phase of the operation developed: the SOE agents on Crete were told of the pending arrival; they were notified to select a landing site, arrange a pattern of signals to guide the aircraft to the drop zone, and obtain the cooperation of the local guerrilla leader and his men.

This first phase of the plan also involved equipment, supplies, and personnel. The equipment would be minimal because of the manner chosen for their return. Supplies would follow in parachuted canisters. Because of the space limitations posed by the airdrop, the personnel involved would be kept to four agents. These four would include the originators of the plan, Fermor and Moss, and two Cretan guerrillas who had previously been evacuated from the island. These Cretans had just completed a course in demolitions and had recently graduated from a parachute training program. Their names were Manoli Paterakis and George Tyrakis.

George Tyrakis, from the village of Amari, was 24 when he was assigned to this operation. His effervescent personality made him a likable addition from the first moment he joined the team. He was a lighthearted youth with twinkling eyes and a smile that was always ready to burst into laughter.

Manoli Paterakis, on the other hand, was more serious, his aquiline features rarely creasing into a hearty laugh as George's. Paterakis only smiled. His pointed nose, jutting jaw, and penetrating eyes underscored the intensity and strength of his personality. The only facial features common to both were their dark complexion and the thin moustache that adorned their upper lip.

Manoli Paterakis was from the village of Koustogeriko, the highest mountaintop village in the Khania province of the White Mountains. When the Germans invaded Crete, he was already in the uniform of a field gendarme. He made good use of his rifle during the battle, and many enemy parachutists fell victim to his marksmanship. When the fiercely fought battle for Crete had concluded, Paterakis could not and would not accept defeat. Instead, like hundreds of others, he fled to the mountains, and from there he continued the struggle to remain free.

George Tyrakis was also in uniform at the time of the German airborne invasion, but it was the uniform of a Greek army straggler returned from the Albanian campaign against Mussolini's legions.

Like Paterakis, he also took to the mountains and joined the guerrilla movement.

This was the first time that Paterakis and Tyrakis had been called upon to serve together in an SOE operation. They made a fine pair, for their lively frivolities chased boredom away. If they were not pulling jokes on each other, then they would select some unwary victim to be the object of their amusement. However, once involved in the serious business of the pending operation, they were the classical models of cooperation, patience, and good humor.[2]

Finally, when every arrangement had been completed, the target date for the parachute descent into Crete was selected. It was to be the night of February 6, 1944.

It was a normal takeoff, and the flight to the drop zone was smooth. When they arrived over Crete there was a heavy overcast, but through a break in the clouds they spotted the lights of the ground signals. The landing area was very small—a narrow plateau between two of the Lasithi Mountain peaks—too narrow a site for all four men to jump simultaneously. After a studied glance, the pilot advised that only one of the four should jump each time the aircraft flew over the drop zone; otherwise, they could miss the target and land into a snowdrift, if not worse.

Leigh Fermor was the first to jump, landing directly in the center of the drop zone, where he was greeted by an SOE agent and some guerrillas. The transport circled and returned for the second run over the target so that Moss could jump. By the time the aircraft completed its circle, the clouds thickened, making it impossible to locate the drop zone. The pilot took his aircraft over the area several times but could not see the ground signals through the heavy overcast. Fermor and the others on the ground could hear the motors and stoked the fires for better illumination, but it was useless. The clouds hung low and heavy through which not the slightest glimmer of a signal fire could be discerned, and the danger of striking the side of a mountain prevented the pilot from flying below the clouds.

For one full hour, the aircraft circled over the landing zone, its pilot looking for an opening in the cloud cover. With fuel running low, he decided to fly on to Brindisi, to the overwhelming disappointment of Moss, Paterakis, and Tyrakis, not to say of Fermor who waited for them anxiously on the ground.[3]

The three members of the team made twelve additional sorties over the same area on twelve other nights, all unsuccessful. During the second flight to the same area in the Lasithi Mountains, some nights later, the clouds were again so thick that they were forced to abort the mission. On another night, the sky was crystal-clear, but there were no signal fires from the ground, so the transport returned to base. Then, on another flight one of the motors overheated leaving a trail of smoke, forcing them to return long before they reached the target zone. Finally, after the twelfth such unsuccessful flight, it was decided to go to Crete by boat.[4]

When Fermor received the radio message that the other members of the kidnapping team would arrive by sea rather than by air, he made plans to travel to the southern shore to greet them.

During the trip through the mountain passes southward, Fermor arrived at a small monastery run by an archimandrite—a clerical rank above a priest but below a bishop—who directed the edifice together with a nun who bore the adopted name of Porphyria and an acolyte named Stelio.

The day before, another SOE agent had arrived at the same monastery to meet Fermor. It was Lieutenant John Stanley, nicknamed Yanni by the Cretans. Stanley had not seen Fermor for many months and in the interval had grown a luxurious, well-cultivated beard. With that overgrowth of hair, he looked so much like a cleric that the archimandrite draped him in the frock of a monk for disguise.

When Fermor arrived the next day, the archimandrite introduced the "monk" as a visitor from another monastery. Fermor did not recognize Stanley through the disguise. The archimandrite, trying not to laugh, took Fermor aside and whispered a warning that he did not trust this robed visitor from another monastery.

While everyone kept a straight face, Leigh Fermor approached Stanley, bowed, kissed his hand, and said irreverently, "Death to the enemies of Crete!" Afterward, Fermor sat in a darkened corner of the main room but kept his pistol handily available, periodically casting furtive glares at the "monk." The priest could not carry the joke any further, so that he and all the rest soon burst into paroxysms of laughter. Once the jest was revealed, they all sat down to a memorable repast of good food with wine and raki flowing amply.

Fermor had declared his intention to depart the next day, but the availability of so much good wine and raki caused him to sleep through the morning hours. It was not until the archimandrite, at

Stanley's playful suggestion, held an old portable phonograph to Fermor's ear, playing it full blast, that Fermor stirred from his deep sleep.

After the customary embraces with his newfound friends and blessings from the archimandrite, Fermor left that same evening for his rendezvous with Moss, Paterakis, and Tyrakis.[5]

It was strange, thought Billy Moss, that everything hinged on the number four. The abduction team had departed from Cairo to begin its mission on January 4, 1944; Leigh Fermor parachuted into Crete on February 4; the closest the rest of the team came to parachuting into Crete successfully was on the night of March 4; and now the boat arrived off the southern coast of Crete on April 4.

It was on the clear starlit night of April 4, with the high mountain peaks towering like dark turrets over the beach, that the motorized Royal Navy trawler slowed and stopped just outside the cove and waited for the all-clear signal from shore.

Lieutenant Brian Coleman, instead of the more familiar person of John Campbell, was at the helm on this trip, and he stood at the bow peering into the inky darkness. Next to him, crouched over the rail, was one of his crew watching for underwater rocks. The moon shimmered on the low waves of the cove, and the night was so quiet that it was possible to hear their lapping on the distant shore. Then the signal came, a pinpoint flash in the dark, repeated several times. Was it friendly or was it an enemy trap? Coleman had to be certain. The light kept blinking, and he summoned the radio operator to report to the bridge to read the signals.

"That's them alright, Sir. Signal's correct," the radioman reported.

The boat crept slowly into the cove, while the crewman at the bow kept repeating his periodic soundings, "Five fathoms, Sir."

The trawler drifted landward and finally dropped anchor at 150 feet from shore. Through his field glasses focused on the darkness of the beach, Coleman could distinguish the movements of the reception committee.

"All right, off you go!" he ordered, and Moss, Paterakis, and Tyrakis slipped carefully into the dinghy that was to take them to the beach.

As soon as the small craft ground to a gentle stop on the sandy bottom, Paterakis and Tyrakis jumped into the water and raced up the beach. They had spotted Leigh Fermor in the darkness and embraced him in the Cretan tradition of good friends. Standing off to one side of this reunion were four German soldiers which the reception committee had taken prisoner while on their way to the beach and now intended to send them off to Egypt as prisoners of war.

Leigh Fermor and Sandy Rendel, who had come to the beach for the occasion, greeted Billy Moss when he finally waded to shore. Moss remarked on seeing Fermor that his cheeks had filled out during the two months that he had waited for the rest of the team to arrive, but with his newly grown moustache and Cretan garb he looked every bit like a local native.[6]

All told, Brian Coleman had brought twelve other Cretans to shore who had been evacuated earlier. When the last dinghy disappeared into the night, the trawler turned and sailed away leaving behind a reunited team of abductors with mischief on their mind.

Now began the perennial trek over the mountains to Kasta-monitsa, a village chosen for its proximity to Iraklion, where they were to settle for the night. As usual on Crete, it was a march over a huge conglomeration of rocks that comprised the mountain trails. Each time they reached the top of a peak, another appeared beyond. After many months of duty on Crete, Fermor was accustomed to this terrain, as were the other native Cretans, Paterakis, Tyrakis, and the rest. But for Billy Moss, this was his first exposure to the rugged escarpments of the island.

"How much further?" Moss inquired.

"Only ten more minutes!" came the reply from their guide, Zahari. It was the same reply every time Moss made that inquiry, and he had the occasion to ask that question at least once every hour for the rest of the night, well into the next day.

After struggling across one particularly difficult pass from one peak to another, Moss asked with exasperation, "Are they all as high as this?" Whereupon everyone burst into laughter.

Once they reached their destination and relaxed in the home of their guide, Fermor inquired about his friends back at the safe house in Cairo. It was then that Fermor revealed to the members of the team that the subject of their planned abduction, General Mueller, had been relieved of his command and assigned elsewhere. Their quarry had gotten away! The man who in the short period of command on Crete had governed with a reign of terror, the general whom the Cretans had come to despise more than any other, including Fritz Schubert, had been taken out of their reach. Disappointment was visibly etched on the faces of Moss, Paterakis, and Tyrakis.

"Does that mean we abort the mission?" inquired Moss. They waited anxiously for Fermor's reply.

"As far as the ultimate effect of our plan is concerned," Fermor analyzed, "I suppose one general is as good as another."

Everyone nodded agreement and smiled happily.

In Mueller's place came a stolid general officer who wore the Knight's Cross and had been a divisional commander in the German campaign against Leningrad. His name was Major General Heinrich Kreipe, and he had been sent to command the division occupying the Iraklion-Lasithi sector.

The Cretans had no grievance against this new German garrison commander. The man they wanted was Walter Mueller, but now he was out of their reach. Nevertheless, Fermor felt that, although the kidnapping of General Mueller would have had a greater impact on the Cretan population, still, the abduction of any German general would go far to soothe the Cretan outcry for revenge. Besides, it would be a deed that, if successful, offered the opportunity of embarrassing the Germans in the eyes of the world, and that was the main purpose of this mission.

The abduction team was joined by several other Cretans who came to assist them with their plan. They all possessed long Cretan names, as usual—for example, Andoni (Anthony) Papaleonidas, Gregory Xnarakis, and Mixali Akoumianakis, whom Fermor called Mickey. Akoumianakis was to be an invaluable addition to the team in that his home was situated across the road from the new general's residence—the villa Ariadne, in the village of Knossos, site of the Minoan archaeological ruins.

During their stay in the Zahari home, there was a continuous flow of visitors. Having heard through the grapevine that English officers were present, they wanted to see what they looked like. There was one visitor, a wizened 74-year-old man dressed in the somber robes of a Russian priest, although he was neither a priest nor Russian, who came for lunch with the group. When he saw an English newspaper that Moss had brought with him from Cairo, he sat there for the rest of the afternoon reading *The Times*. It was strange, thought Billy Moss, to see this old man reading the society page.

Another visitor, even older than the former, explained that he had been evicted from his home in Khania and had come to stay with relatives in the nearby village. He added that at one time in his long life he had worked as a waiter in Los Angeles, where he had learned and adopted two favorite American expressions that he repeated over and over again. For something that he liked, he would say "Hot dog!" When referring to the Nazis in general, he would reply with a smile, "Those Goddamned sonofabitches!" That was the extent of his knowledge of the English language.

Perhaps the most impressive visitor of all was a tall, paunchy Cretan with massive shoulders, who looked older than his 50 years. He was the leader of a guerrilla band who had arrived to protect Fermor and his group from the Germans. His name was Athanasios Bourdzalis.

The mannerisms of this self-styled guerrilla chieftain reminded Moss of Shakespeare's Falstaff. When Bourdzalis sat down to eat with them at their first meal together, he crossed himself and burped loudly at the same time. Instead of a fork, he dug the point of his Cretan dagger into a large piece of mutton and commenced to tear it apart with his hands and teeth. Fermor was accustomed to this lack of table manners by the nature of his many months in these mountains, whereas for Moss it was a new experience. He just sat and stared at Bourdzalis with a mirthful curiosity.

When Bourdzalis became aware that Moss was staring oddly, he spiked a sheep's eyeball from the platter with his dagger and offered it to him. Moss refused, horrified at the thought of munching on this gelatinous mass, whereupon Bourdzalis shrugged and popped this Cretan delicacy into his mouth. Moss continued to stare, watching the sheep's eyeball riding up and down like a golfball in Bourdzalis's cheek.[7]

The days passed, and Fermor and Moss made their plans for the kidnapping. Piece by piece, like a puzzle, the strategy and logistics fell into place as details were developed and finalized. The site of the ambush was selected, the escape route charted, a communication system established and all necessary supplies furnished.

Disguised as Cretan peasants, Fermor and Moss joined Mickey Akoumianakis at his house from where they could study General Kreipe's movements. From the window of Mickey's house, they were able to look out upon the Villa Ariadne, a beautiful structure that was built by Sir Arthur Evans during the period of his Minoan excavations at Knossos.

Watching from this secluded vantage point, they noted that the general commuted twice daily from his residence at Knossos to his headquarters at the village of Ano Archanes. Usually, he left for his headquarters office by 9:00 A.M., returned at 1:00 P.M. for lunch and siesta, and went back at 4:00 P.M., remaining until 8:00 P.M. Sometimes he stayed later, the reason being, as they learned later, that he played Bridge with his staff.

From these observations, it became evident that the best time to abduct the general would be during his last trip of the day at 8:00 P.M., when darkness would hide the obvious—since sunset would be at 7:45 P.M. This latter consideration also presented the probability that the general's house staff would assume that he was delayed at his headquarters by his penchant for periodically staying late and playing Bridge.

The best location for the ambush would be at a point where the secondary road from Ano Archanes intersected at a T-junction that main Iraklion road. This intersection was at such a sharp angle that all vehicles had to come to a full stop. Once on the Iraklion road, the kidnappers would flee northward to Iraklion through the Fortetza Gate of the walled city. It was reasoned that when the abduction was discovered and the alarm sounded, the Germans would never expect to find their abducted commander in their midst, but logically would extend their attention southward into the mountains.

The night of April 24 was selected for the operation to begin. Thus, the plans were completed, and the die was cast for the kidnapping of the German general.[8]

April 24 proved to be a disappointment. Late in the afternoon, the grapevine brought word to Fermor and Moss that the general had left his office for the Villa Ariadne late in the afternoon, before dusk. Since there was too much daylight at that hour and not enough time to position the men, the operation for that evening had to be postponed.

Some of the superstitious Cretans surmised that the delay was an ill omen, that by the time the actual date would come to carry out the deed, the Germans would be forewarned. Fermor disregarded such thinking as nonsense, but he was concerned that Bourdzalis's men had been observed strolling the nearby fields in daylight instead of hiding. That posed the danger that an informer might report

them and jeopardize the whole operation. It was decided, reluctantly, to ask the old chieftain Bourdzalis to leave. Bourdzalis was
upset by this request, but his men appeared happy to oblige. Each
was given a gold sovereign for their trouble, which made them even
happier.

Early in the afternoon of April 25, when word reached them that
German patrols had been seen in the area, Fermor and Moss began
to wonder whether the plot had been exposed. They decided to
proceed with the operation that same night, in spite of the earlier
reports. However, by 5:00 P.M. fate again took a hand.

A runner arrived with a message from the Akoumianakis house
that the general had not left his villa all day and obviously did not
intend to travel to his headquarters that day. The report struck the
group like a bombshell. The Cretans who spoke of bad omens
shook their heads. Fermor worried that by now too many local
villagers had heard of the plan, and *that* knowledge was dangerous.
One wrong word at the wrong time, overheard by a Gestapo
informant, could bring the Germans into the area. There was
another danger of greater import: a local communist band had
threatened to expose the plot to the Germans and list the names of
each participant.

The decision was made to proceed with the plan on the night of
April 26—come what may. Fermor and Moss agreed that if there
were any further delays, they would cancel the entire operation.
Everyone directly involved in the abduction was warned to remain
secluded until nightfall.

Although the day of April 26 dawned with the sun shining, it
began to rain by afternoon, which created the additional problem
that snail-hunters would be all over the ambush site that night,
gathering snails for food. Fermor gave momentary thought to this
possibility, but then shrugged his shoulders and continued to read.
He had spent the whole morning reciting Shakespeare in German,
while Moss read, and Paterakis and Tyrakis relaxed. By late
afternoon, the rain had stopped so that the problem of the snail-
hunters diminished. At 6:00 P.M., Elias Athanassakis, who worked
with Akoumianakis, returned to the hideout to inform Fermor and
Moss that General Kreipe had left the residence for his headquarters.

The hour had finally arrived for the Fermor team to go to work.
Word was passed to the others to gather at the abduction site no
later than 8:00 P.M.

That evening an indescribable calm settled over the men involved in the operation. At last they were going to do what they had come to Crete to do, in spite of the two earlier delays and the tensions that these delays had engendered.

Elias Athanassakis and Mickey Akoumianakis positioned themselves on a hillock approximately 900 feet up the Archanes road as lookouts for the general's limousine. An extended roll of wire was laid along the roadside that reached the T-junction where Fermor and Moss were located. This end of the wire was connected to a buzzer.

By 8:00 P.M., Fermor and Moss had reached the T-junction. They were both dressed in stolen field-grey summer uniforms of the Feldpolizei—the German military police. Along the way, they had encountered a few local villagers whom they greeted gruffly in the typical manner of the conqueror—anything to dispel the real purpose of their presence. Once at the intersection, they took cover and waited. All the others were already in position.[9]

There were several false alarms during their wait, all of which increased anxieties. Two army trucks, two staff Volkswagens, and a motorcyclist trundled past on five different occasions in that one hour. It felt awkward to be crouching by the shoulder of the road in the deep darkness and see steel-helmeted enemy soldiers drive past, just beyond arms reach, with no inkling that nine men were watching from the shadows with the intention of seizing their commanding general.

At 8:30 P.M., General Heinrich Kreipe left his army head-quarters, which was situated in a schoolhouse on Odos Martiriou (Martyrs Street) in the village of Ano Archanes, and seated himself in the passenger side of his staff limousine next to his chauffeur, as was his daily custom. The limousine turned down the Archanes road and headed for the T-junction where it intersected the road to Iraklion.

From their hidden position on the hillcock that overlooked the Archanes road, Athanassakis and Akoumianakis saw the limousine drive past and recognized the general's silhouette in the front seat. They pressed the signal button. The electrical impulse traveled along the full length of the wire to its terminal, and the buzzer on the other end croaked noisily.

A late addition to the abduction team was Dimitri Tsatsos—nicknamed Mitso by Fermor—whose duty was to signal Fermor and

Moss when the buzzer sounded. It was 9:30 P.M. when Mitso's flashlight blinked three times. Each blink had a prearranged significance. It implied: GENERAL'S CAR; UNESCORTED; ACTION!

Fermor turned to Moss, tapped him on the shoulder and said, "Here we go!"[10]

Across the road from Fermor's position, Manoli Paterakis and George Tyrakis also observed Mitso's signal and waited, wetting their lips in excited anticipation of what they were about to do. Paterakis checked his pistol and smiled, for the very thought amused him.

"I would like to see those German faces when they discover that we have taken their general," he whispered to Tyrakis.

At that moment, General Kreipe's powerful and sleek Opel limousine approached, its light beams flooding the road ahead. When it reached the intersection, it slowed for the customary stop before turning north onto the Iraklion road.

Fermor and Moss stood in the middle of the road in their German uniforms, well illuminated by the Opel's headlights. Moss waved a traffic disc, while Fermor, signaling with his red-lit flashlight, shouted the command, "HALT!"

The general's limousine came to a full stop.

Fermor and Moss avoided the glare of the headlights and walked into the shadows along either side of the vehicle, Fermor on the passenger's side and Moss on the other. Fermor clicked his heels in salute, inquiring in flawless German, "Ist dies das General's Wagen?"

"Ja, Ja," came the response from inside the limousine.

"Papiere, bitte schoen!" Fermor replied, requesting their identification papers.

The general's gold braid was visible in the dim light, as was his Knight's Cross suspended at the throat below his beefy face. He smiled at Fermor and reached into an inside pocket for his identification papers.

At that moment, Fermor pulled open the passenger door with a quick movement, shouting, "Hände hoch!"—"Hands up!"

Simultaneous with Fermor's movement, Moss opened the door on the chauffeur's side. Startled, the German driver groped for his weapon, forcing Moss to hit him hard across the head with his pistol. The driver slumped senseless over the wheel, blood flowing from the gaping wound. Stepping in quickly, Tyrakis hauled the hapless German out of the vehicle and threw him to the ground. Just as quickly, Moss jumped into the driver's seat, checked the gauge, and revved up the motor.

On the other side of the limousine, the general was struggling furiously, lashing out with his arms and kicking with his feet. Paterakis had his powerful arms around Kreipe's waist in a tight grip, immobilizing his movements.

"Was zum Teufel ist denn das?"—"What the hell is this?" the general screamed, cursing his abductors.

Kreipe finally stopped struggling when he realized that he was not going to be shot outright. Paterakis tied the general's arms behind him, while Fermor still kept his pistol firmly pointed at Kreipe's chest.

"What is the meaning of this Hussar-like stunt?" Kreipe inquired in a more subdued voice, still dazed by this rash escapade on his person.

"I am a British officer," Fermor explained, "and I am taking you to Egypt as a prisoner of war!"

General Kreipe stared at Fermor, glanced momentarily at Paterakis, and then continued staring in utter disbelief.

Without further delay, Paterakis roughly dragged the general into the back seat of the limousine, forcing him to sit on the floor, while he kept a pistol to Kreipe's head. Tyrakis and another Cretan tried to raise the stricken chauffeur to his feet unsuccessfully, for he was still unconscious and bleeding profusely from his wound. Tyrakis left him and jumped into the back seat with Paterakis and the general. Also joining them in the back of the Opel was another new member of the abduction team, a former policeman, Stratis Saviolakis, who kept the sharp point of his Cretan dagger pinching the general's throat to keep him quiet.

In spite of the knife at his throat, the general kept asking for his officer's cap. His cap was now being worn by Leigh Fermor, sitting up front in the passenger's seat.

Moss put the vehicle into gear and the Opel limousine sped off, turned left on the Iraklion road, and disappeared into the darkness. The other Cretans of the abduction team remained behind in order to erase any evidence of the ambush. When the Cretans finally left the intersection, they took the now-semiconscious chauffeur with them. The whole kidnapping episode had taken *less than 90 seconds!*

No sooner had the abductors disappeared into the night, when a convoy of troop-filled army trucks rumbled past the same intersection. Only minutes had separated that slender interval between success and failure.[11]

Chapter 14

The Flight
to Safety

The first part of the plan had gone well, despite the problems that nearly caused the mission to be canceled. However, the abduction was only the beginning, for ahead lay the most dangerous aspect of the whole mission: slipping the kidnapped general past the many German roadblocks that lay ahead and eventually shipping him off the island successfully.

The Opel limousine raced through the night with Fermor and Moss straining their eyes peering into the darkness beyond. The three other members of the team sitting in the back with the general were chattering enthusiastically among themselves about their accomplishment. General Kreipe remained bound on the floor of the sedan, crammed into an uncomfortable position with Saviolakis sitting on top of him. He was still dazed by the daring impossibility of the episode that had just occurred. At first, he mumbled incoherently to himself, but later he kept asking for his hat. Fermor assured him that he would soon get it back, to which he responded with a dry, "Danke, Danke."

Fermor looked imposing wearing the cap of a general officer. Satisfied with the success of this phase of the plot, he lit a cigarette, the fragrance of which whiffed backward past the general's nostrils.

"How long do you expect to keep me in this undignified position?" the general asked.

"If you give me your word that you would neither shout nor try to escape, we shall treat you not as a prisoner of war but as one of us," Fermor responded in German. Kreipe agreed.

Moss asked him if he spoke English at all. "Nein!" came the reply.

"Russian?" inquired Moss again, the one foreign language with which he was conversant.

The reply was the same, "Nein!"

"Parlez-vous français?" Moss and Fermor inquired simultaneously, searching for a common ground of communication.

"Un petit peu."

Thus, for the rest of the days that they were to be together, Kreipe and Moss, Moss in particular since Fermor spoke German fluently, communicated in French, a language in which both were poorly versed.[1]

"Checkpoint ahead," cautioned Moss, slowing the limousine ever so slightly. The men tensed as a German voice boomed out of the night the command to "Halt!"

When the guards noticed the general's emblematic flags on the front fenders, they snapped to attention and saluted. Obscured in the shadows of the Opel's interior, Leigh Fermor returned the salute.

"Marvelous," murmured Moss, as they all let out a sigh of relief. The first obstacle had been passed, but they knew that there would be other sentry posts ahead.

A few miles beyond, another red flashlight signaled their approach to a second roadblock. Again the command to "Halt!" echoed through the dark, and again it was followed by a salute, as the guard, recognizing the general's flags, waved the limousine onward. This was followed by a third and a forth checkpoint, all with the same result. Fermor, Moss, and the rest felt the tension easing, while the general's consternation increased. Kreipe silently cursed the duped guards for their laxity in not examining the limousine and its passengers more thoroughly.

Even at the Fortetza Gate, which was the eastern entrance to the Venetian-walled city of Iraklion, the flags on the Opel's fenders were sufficient to raise the red-striped barrier without the slightest hesitation. Once inside Iraklion, they drove westward toward the Khania Gate, the only western exit out of the city.

The streets of Iraklion were filled with soldiers who made passage slow and difficult. The Opel crawled along at an alarmingly slow pace, trying to break through a swarm of German soldiers who had just exited from a local movie theater. Moss blew the horn but feared making too great a commotion which might attract attention to them. Any one of the soldiers taking a more than casual glance into the limousine as it passed below the dim street lights, might discover that the passengers were not German, and give the alarm.

The moments were tense. All five men in the Opel strained, ever alert, taking short, shallow breaths as the soldiers stepped aside to let the vehicle pass.

"If we are trapped," Fermor directed, "use the grenades and guns to blast them back . . . make for the alleys . . . and leave the general tied in the back seat!"

Luckily, the crowd gradually thinned, and the limousine picked up speed as it approached the Khania Gate and the final checkpoint. For some reason, the guard at the Khania Gate did not respond in the same manner as had the guards at the previous checkpoints. This sentry persistently waved the flashlight and refused to budge from the Opel's path. Moss was forced to stop a few feet from the barrier that remained closed. Fermor noted that excluding the four guards at the gate, there were a dozen additional soldiers standing nearby, all well-armed, with their watchful eyes drawn to the limousine.

Fermor and Moss looked at each other. They did not utter a single word, but they knew what the other was thinking. *Had the kidnapping been discovered? Had the alarm reached these guards: Were these soldiers waiting for them?* Everyone in the vehicle tensed. Sharp clicks were heard as Paterakis, Tyrakis, and Saviolakis cocked their weapons. Strati unsheathed his knife and placed it against the general's throat once again as a reminder that he remain silent.

"Steady! Everyone, steady!" cautioned Fermor.

The three guards remained at the wooden gate, while the fourth approached the vehicle. If this guard so much as looked in, all would be lost.

Quick-minded, Fermor lowered the window on his side and shouted in a loud, apparently annoyed tone, "Achtung! Generals Wagen!"[2]

The words had an immediate effect. The guard jumped back and snapped to attention, the soldiers saluted, and the wooden barrier was raised. The limousine edged slowly through the Khania Gate and, gradually picking up speed, raced westward into the darkness and safety. All in all, they had passed through twenty-two checkpoints from the moment they left the abduction site.

For the first time that evening, the audacious kidnappers felt the weight of anxiety lift from their chests. Fermor smiled; Moss laughed; Tyrakis and Saviolakis broke into song, soon joined by Paterakis. Only the subdued general remained silent. Cigarettes were distributed to all, including the prisoner. Fermor even complied with the general's repeated requests and returned his hat to him.

The Opel limousine sped through the night, its headlights stabbing like two white fingers into the darkness, striking the rocks and olive trees that lined the highway. Once the immediate danger had passed, monotony set in, and after several hours of continuous driving, the smooth hum of the powerful motor lulled the passengers into silence.

Many hours passed before Fermor announced that they had at last reached their destination. The Opel stopped on the main road at the bottom of a goat trail that tortuously ascended along a path that led to the mountaintop village of Anoghia, located halfway between Iraklion and Rethimnon.

When they got out of the limousine, the general protested, alarmed by the thought that he was to be abandoned by the two British officers and turned over to the Cretans. He feared that the Cretans would slit his throat in retribution for Mueller's atrocities. Fermor assured him that they had other plans for him.

Moss started up the dirt trail, followed by General Kreipe, with Paterakis bringing up the rear. Their orders were to climb up to the village and wait on the outskirts for Fermor's arrival. In the meantime, Fermor and Tyrakis were to dispose of the vehicle. After Moss and Paterakis had departed with the general, it occurred to Fermor that he did not know how to drive this vehicle, not having driven for over five years; nor did Tyrakis. That did not stymie them, however. After a series of stalls and pushes, they managed to steer the Opel onto a dirt road that led to a cove opposite the island of Peristeri—so named because pigeons often roosted there.

Before leaving the vehicle, Fermor left the limousine's floor littered with Players cigarette butts, a British commando beret, and a Cadbury chocolate wrapper. To the back seat of the Opel, he pinned a previously prepared note written in German and addressed to the German authorities in Crete:

Gentlemen:

Your Division Commander, General Kreipe, was captured a short time ago by a British raiding force under

our command. By the time you read this, both he and we
will be on our way to Cairo.

We would like to point out most emphatically that this
operation has been carried out without the help of the
Cretans or Cretan partisans, and the only guides used were
serving soldiers of his Hellenic Majesty's forces in the
Middle East, who came with us.

Your general is an honorable prisoner of war and will be
treated with all the consideration owing to his rank.

Any reprisals against the local population will be wholly
unwarranted and unjust.

Auf Baldiges Wiedersehen![3]

Both Fermor and Moss had signed the letter before the kidnapping with their ranks indicated, and they even had waxed seals
added and impressed by their army signet rings to give the note an
air of officialdom. Moss in his devilish sense of humor had added
the postscript:

"We are very sorry to have to leave this beautiful car behind!"[4]

Tyrakis and Fermor hiked all night under a bright new moon to
join Moss, Paterakis, and the general. They crossed ravines,
climbed cliffs, scrambled over boulders, and pushed through heavy
underbrush of cacti and tall grass to reach Anoghia. By dawn, they
arrived at the outskirts of the village where the rest of the group was
waiting for them.

Anoghia was the largest village in Crete in 1944, with a 900-
year history. It was so remote and isolated that the Germans did not
garrison it permanently. As the sun rose over the eastern mountain
peaks, the village women came to the water troughs in the center of
the village to do their laundry. In the traditional manner of the day,
they wet the clothes and pounded the dirt out of them amidst gossip,
chatter, and laughter—until Leigh Fermor appeared, with Stanley
Moss and the general trailing behind.

The energetic Fermor, tired as he was from his all-night hike,
led the others briskly through the center of the village. When the
women saw them their laughter and conversation stopped abruptly.
They stared coldly at the interlopers; many women even turned their
backs to them. Fermor glanced inquiringly at Moss, who being just
as bewildered, shrugged his shoulders. The cold reception surprised
them. When Paterakis and Tyrakis, who brought up the rear,
arrived on the scene, they solved the mystery.

The general, of course, was in the uniform of the enemy, but so were Fermor and Moss. They were still wearing the purloined outfits of the Feldpolizei which they wore at the time of the abduction. When Paterakis explained to the villagers who they were and what they had accomplished, the villagers could not do enough in offering these visitors their hospitality. They kissed them, embraced them, fondly slapped their backs, and brought out what little food and wine they had to feed the hungry group.

Fermor dispatched two messages which he gave to Stratis Saviolakis. One message was to be carried to Sandy Rendel in the eastern range of the Lasithi Mountains, and the other to Tom Dunbabin, instructing him to inform Cairo that the abduction had been successful. He was to request Cairo to make the announcement over the radio as previously arranged and to drop leaflets to the Cretans announcing the event.

The original plan dictated that as soon as the kidnapping had been accomplished, Cairo was to send aircraft to drop pamphlets written in both Greek and German explaining that the operation had been the work of British commandos. It was felt that this would prevent unnecessary reprisals against the local population in that sector. The plan also included an announcement by Cairo Radio that General Kreipe *was already on his way to Cairo*; thus, they hoped to allay German pursuit of the abductors.

As in all matters of this type, negligence superseded intelligence. No pamphlets were dropped because of "bad flying conditions" and the radio announcement erred by saying that the general "was *being* taken off the island."

The group remained in Anoghia to rest. The general, tired from the trek up the trail to the village, promptly fell asleep. For the first time since the moment of the kidnapping, Fermor had an opportunity to study his prisoner. Heinrich Kreipe was a thick-set man with the typical Germanic countenance of thin lips, bull neck, and blue eyes. He was greying at the temples, so Fermor judged him to be in his early fifties.

Before falling asleep, Fermor chatted briefly with the general. Kreipe related that he had been sent to Crete on a "rest cure" after his service on the Russian Front. Ironically, he reflected, the previous day he had ordered that a guard post be mounted at the exact T-intersection where he was seized. Even more ironic was the fact that he had a premonition that "something was going to happen" on his trip home that night! Kreipe did not learn until after the war that the day before his abduction the German High Army Command had promoted him to the rank of lieutenant general. He never received official word of his promotion before the hour of his kidnapping. Finally, Kreipe inquired about his chauffeur. The general was assured that his driver would arrive later. Fermor had no way of knowing at that time that the hapless chauffeur never survived the blow to his head. He died of the injury and was buried by the guerrillas in a nearby field.

It did not take long for the Germans to discover that their general had been kidnapped. The house staff in his residence became concerned about Kreipe's delay in arriving home that evening of April 26, and phoned the general's headquarters, only to be told that he had left at the usual hour. A motor patrol traveled the entire route from Villa Ariadne to headquarters and back with no sign of the general or of anything unusual along the way. The limousine was sighted the next day by a Fieseler-Storch observation plane, and when a patrol arrived later, they found Fermor's note.

That same afternoon, low-flying aircraft circled over the villages of eastern Crete dropping leaflets with threats of reprisals:

TO ALL CRETANS:
LAST NIGHT THE GERMAN GENERAL KREIPE WAS ABDUCTED BY BANDITS. HE IS NOW BEING CONCEALED IN THE CRETAN MOUNTAINS AND HIS WHEREABOUTS CANNOT BE UNKNOWN TO THE POPULACE.
IF THE GENERAL IS NOT RETURNED WITHIN THREE DAYS, ALL VILLAGES IN THE IRAKLION DISTRICT WILL BE RAZED TO THE GROUND AND THE SEVEREST MEASURES OF REPRISAL WILL BE BROUGHT TO BEAR ON THE CIVILIAN POPULA-TION.[5]

All over Crete, the abduction of the German general elicited hilarity and jubilation among the people. Its very audacity drew their admiration. One villager expressed the feelings of all: "Imagine," he remarked gleefully to another, "taking their general right out of his headquarters!"

Even the personnel at British headquarters in Cairo smiled phlegmatically at the success of the operation. The director of the

Cretan Desk of the SOE, Major Jack Smith-Hughes, released a sigh of relief, commenting happily that "it looks as if Fermor and Moss did it!" After all, it had been Smith-Hughes who had granted permission for Fermor and Moss to proceed with the operation, over the objections of the operations chief of the Cretan Section.

General Bruno Brauer, who was the overall commanding general of the Fortress of Crete with headquarters in Khania, while Kreipe was the divisional commander in the Iraklion-Lasithi district, reacted immediately to the abduction episode. As a colonel during the battle for Crete back on May 20, 1941, he commanded the First Parachute Regiment and had parachuted with his troops into Iraklion. Now, he strengthened his headquarters guard and increased his personal escort. He was taking no chances of being kidnapped like Kreipe by British commandos or by Cretan guerrillas.

The next morning, the alarm spread that Germans were in the area. Paterakis awakened Fermor abruptly, shaking him out of his dreams. Manoli's face was visibly excited.

"Germans coming!" he warned. "Plenty Germans in village!"

Everyone scrambled into their clothes and left hastily for the security of a cave in the nearby mountains. Light, slow-moving aircraft like the Fieseler-Storch observation plane flew over the sector looking for signs of the general and his abductors. From the camouflaged opening of the cave, Fermor and the rest looked up and could see the observation aircraft flying back and forth overhead.[6]

With nightfall, Fermor, Moss, Paterakis, and Tyrakis, with the general in tow, left the cave for the long, hard trek southward to the beach and eventual evacuation. The movement was at a snail's pace because the general, being unaccustomed to such physical exertion, was slow-moving, slowed further by his complaint of a pain in his leg.

"Pain my—!" Paterakis shouted angrily. "He moves slowly purposely to delay us, that's what!" And with that, he prodded the German with his weapon.[7]

Before dawn, they approached a mountain peak where they were greeted on the trail by an old, toothless, white-haired shepherd who, offered them the hospitality of his sheepfold. With the first rays of daylight dawning, it was well that they hide from enemy observation. The old shepherd fed them goat cheese, bread, and wine, which they ate ravenously. He sat off to the side of his stone hut and watched them, telling them how honored he felt to have them share his food and simple shelter with him. He offered to guide them along the trail southward to another sheepfold and another shepherd.

No cave, track, or hiding lair was unknown to these shepherds, and the Germans knew it. They also knew of the assistance these shepherds gave to the guerrillas and to the agents of the SOE. The Germans soon discovered that this particular shepherd had assisted the abduction team in its trip through the mountains. A few days later, a German patrol captured this old white-haired shepherd and shot him in the back as he scurried off. They gathered his few sheep for the German mess hall and left his corpse to rot among the mountain escarpments where he had spent all his life.[8]

Because of the kidnapping, reprisals now began against the local population even though Fermor's note denied their involvement. The Germans burned and dynamited every house in Anoghia and in other villages in the Anoghia district. They even divebombed these villages. The inhabitants, accustomed to such barbarous acts, fled to the mountains. The few who remained were summarily executed with no regard for age or sex. It was reported that, in several instances, the Gestapo threw tied villagers into the flames of their burning homes, while they stood around and laughed. It was the shadow of June 1941 all over again.

After many hours of travel over the rugged mountains—now traveling in daylight but always keeping in the shadows and hiding from overflying aircraft that appeared periodically—Fermor and the rest climbed the heights of Mount Ida, the tallest mountain in Crete. From this elevation they could see the southern waters of the Mediterranean, so close yet so far.

As they traveled through the mountain passes, they noted guerrilla lookouts, positioned intermittently on rocky outcrops, who whistled from one to another signaling their approach. Finally, at one point on the trail, a host of guerrillas appeared, greeting Fermor, Moss, and the rest with kisses and embraces. There to greet them personally and congratulate them heartily for their heroic action was the leader of the band, the handsome, white-haired Michali Xilouris. With him were three other SOE agents led by a Lieutenant John Houseman. One of the trio was Captain Tom Dunbabin's wireless operator.

Sadly, Fermor was to learn that Tom Dunbabin was in hiding, suffering from malaria, and could not be located. Furthermore,

Houseman's radioman reported that his wireless was not operating because of an irreplaceable broken tube. Much to Fermor's chagrin, this news meant that Dunbabin had not communicated the schedule as to time and date for evacuation to Cairo, nor could it be from this mountain lair. Fermor decided to send runners with written instructions to Captain Sandy Rendel, the SOE agent stationed in the Lasithi Mountains area, and to Captain Dick Barnes, a recent SOE arrival working in the western part of Crete, telling them to transmit the message to Cairo and set the date and place for evacuation.

When they finally departed from Xilouris's hideout, the Fermor-Moss team was escorted through the mountain passes by the Xilouris guerrillas until they left that sector and entered that of Kapetan George Petergeorge. There they were met by the tall, bearded, aristocratic-looking guerrilla chieftain whose warlike apparel gave the assurance of security. He was the same guerrilla leader who had shown such paternal affection for the American, John Alexander, during his stay in the mountains. Fermor and Moss respectfully referred to him as "P.G." and could not forget that he, a merchant before the war, maintained his band of followers in his personal war with the Nazis at his own expense until the British began to subsidize his group.

They waited anxiously for several days at Petergeorge's hideout for receipt of any message from Cairo, but none came. Meanwhile, the Germans tightened the noose in the area as they searched relentlessly for their general. At last, on May 2, they received a message by runner from Sandy Rendel. A boat would meet them at the inlet near the village of Sakhtouria on the southern coast that night. If Fermor and the rest were delayed, the boat would return for four consecutive nights. This schedule gave them several days to reach the embarkation point. Unfortunately for them, fate willed otherwise.

The very next day, over 200 Panzer Grenadiers entered Sakhtouria, which they demolished together with many surrounding villages including Margarikari, Kapetan Petergeorge's home village where John Alexander had spent a few hours with his mother and sisters. At the time, the Germans did not know that their intervention had blocked the kidnapper's plan to escape with their prisoner. Simultaneously, other German units entered the southern villages of Timbaki, Melambes, Akoumia, and Spilia, thus forming an arc of strong points that interdicted access to the southern coastal waters of the Mesaras Gulf. The Fermor-Moss team was cut off to the south.

On May 3, Mickey Akoumianakis and Elias Athanassakis—the two members of the original abduction team that had remained behind—arrived from Iraklion. Akoumianakis mentioned the prevailing rumor that the general's A.D.C. and the sentries at the Villa Ariadne had been arrested by the Gestapo. The general shrugged his shoulders indifferently when told, commenting that "he did not care what the Gestapo did to his sycophantic aide-de-camp, who was nothing but an idiot, but felt sorry for the guards who were good men."[9]

The only possible route that remained open to the Fermor-Moss team was westward to the village of Kerames on the western side of the 5,800-foot Mount Kedros. But before they had begun this arduous journey, word was received via the reliable guerrilla grapevine that German troops had already seized the village. So the days passed slowly and anxiously.

Another message received by runner on May 5 related that a commando unit, under the famed George Jellicoe, would land at the coastal village of Limni on May 9 with orders to contact the Fermor team and help disembark them. The very next day, Limni was occupied by the Germans, and the plan had to be abandoned. The Fermor-Moss team was isolated together with their valuable prize.

Things were getting desperate, and for the first time since the kidnapping, Fermor was beginning to worry. Wherever he turned, German detachments appeared ahead of them, while other enemy units followed close on their heels. At one point, a German patrol entered a village searching for Kreipe. Through loudspeakers they called for him by name, the sound of which bounced repeatedly against the canyonlike walls of the surrounding mountains, echoing over and over again. From a cave high up on one of those mountains, Fermor, Moss, Paterakis, and Tyrakis watched the Germans move like ants below them. they were getting closer and closer, but as Moss expressed it best, "they were not close enough!"

Several explosions echoed beyond the mountains, indicating that the Germans were dynamiting villages and setting the area afire. Throughout the long arduous trek, General Kreipe continuously complained of poor food, fatigue, and his constant leg pain. But when Kreipe heard the explosions, he shook his head and smiled for the first time since his capture, smiling at the thought of what tribute his troops were exacting from the local population for this kidnapping.

"It is so easy and so practical for us to kill Cretans and destroy their villages in reprisal for what you British do!" he commented.

The words stunned Moss, who admonished the general sharply with strong words. Later, Kreipe apologized for his behavior, attributing his words to his lack of familiarity with the French language, the medium with which he communicated his thoughts to Moss. With each passing day, Kreipe's hopes·for rescue by his troops diminished. Daily, he observed Cretan guerrillas coming and going over the mountain passes, fearlessly ignoring the presence of German patrols. It seemed that a strong line of guerrillas was always present to protect the Fermor-Moss team. He was amazed at the hundreds of these mountain fighters who came out of their hideouts, escorted them a short distance, and then disappeared like shadows, only to be replaced by others who flitted like ghosts out of nowhere. It was reassuring for Fermor and his team, yet mystifying and dismaying to Kreipe, who as a general of a conquering army thought of Crete as a German-occupied land.

Kreipe seemed to have accepted his fate as a prisoner. He thought it an insult to his military honor that the troops under his command did not make a greater effort to rescue him. Who had every heard of a German general officer being kidnapped by his enemies? What an embarrassment, he must have thought, to the whole occupation force in Crete. These very thoughts were enough to bring forth sighs of despair from an otherwise silent captive. Fermor and Moss heard these signs and understood their significance.

Life in the mountain hideouts continued until word came from Cairo. One day, Moss decided to bathe, a rare event for these mountaineers. He had spent the earlier part of the morning stripped to the waist and picking fleas and lice from his clothing. He eventually collected quite a colony of live ones which he carefully dropped one by one into a sock. Then he took off the rest of his clothes and stood under a waterfall entirely nude, enjoying the refreshing flow of water on his body. The Cretans were shocked by his nudity in front of them. Their pattern of washing was first to take off the top clothes, wash to the waist, put the clothes back on, and then do the rest. They would never appear totally in the nude. When they saw Moss standing before them in his birthday suit, the

Cretan onlookers looked in another direction, and then scampered away. Moss and Fermor laughed at their reaction.[10]

The next night, they departed for a new hideout. One of the guerrillas liberated a donkey from a nearby village especially for the general, to relieve him from walking on his aching leg. After Kreipe mounted the animal and moved along the trail, the donkey stumbled. The resulting jolt broke the saddle-strap, throwing the general onto the rocks. He fell heavily on his shoulder, injuring it severely, Kreipe lay there writhing in pain and cursing in fashionable army language, spewing a multitude of invectives at the donkey, the Cretans, the mountains, and, of course, Fermor and Moss.

They made an improvised sling for him and slipped it onto his shoulder, easing his discomfort. Without further delay, they continued on the trail to their next hideout. One of the Cretan guerrilla escorts was assigned to hold onto the animal's strap to prevent a reoccurrence of any similar mishap to their captive. On another occasion, while on foot, the general slipped on some loose rocks and rolled upright into a hollow. From the sound of his surprised scream, everyone thought he had fallen over the precipice. When they reached him, they found him sitting comfortably on his derriere, uninjured, with a boyish smile on his face.[11]

On May 12, they met Captain Denis Ciclitiras, another SOE agent, a British officer of Grecian ancestry. He had arrived at the hideout the previous day and waited for Fermor and Moss. It was this same officer who back in early 1942 had recommended that John Alexander be posted with Colonel Laycock's commando force for the Iraklion airfield raid.

Ciclitiras, nicknamed Dionysios by the Cretans, informed Fermor and Moss that his wireless set was at George Psychoundakis's village of Asi Gonia, which was now totally under German control. It would be very difficult, he pointed out, to send a message to Cairo from his transmitter, in view of the German presence. Fermor felt stymied again, and time was running out. In spite of the danger involved, Ciclitiras left the next day for Asi Gonia, with the promise that he would try to make contact with Cairo to set a new date for a boat to come and evacuate the group. They waited hopefully throughout the day of May 13 for confirmation that he had indeed made contact with Cairo, but none came.[12]

That night, they had a nocturnal visitor in the person of Captain

Dick Barnes (Pavlo) who had received Fermor's letter some days earlier. He had contacted Cairo successfully, and now had arrived at this hideout above Yerikari village to bring the message in person.

He shook Fermor and Moss vigorously, trying to waken them from the deep sleep that fatigue and wine had induced. Fermor stirred, blinking his eyes to get used to this rude awakening. "What the hell is it this time?" he grumbled.

When Dick Barnes's baritone voice echoed in the darkness, both Fermor and Moss jumped up.

"A boat is coming to fetch you at Rhodakinon Beach tomorrow night," he said. "You had better hurry up if you want to get there on time!"

They held a hasty conference and made an equally hasty departure. Before setting off, Barnes gave them the map coordinates of the beach site where the boat would meet them, and the coded signals for identification.

A half day's march westward, near the boundary that separated the province of Rethimnon from that of Khania, stood the southern village of Rhodakinon with its coastal beach. The village had a deep water cove, and most important of all, it was still free of Germans. As Barnes had reported, the boat was going to be at that site at 10:00 P.M. on the night of May 14. The race was on! The Fermor-Moss team with their prisoner had to reach that beach before the Germans could block that last avenue of escape. It was a thought that feverishly raced through the mind of each man as they began what they hoped would be the final leg of this circuitous journey to safety.

Fermor, Paterakis, and Kreipe took the longer thirteen-hour trail to the beach, which was safer and less arduous for the general to maintain. Moss, Tyrakis, and the others traveled the more difficult one which took only five hours. They met on the heights above the beach by 11:00 A.M. of May 14, nineteen days since the day of the abduction.

At nightfall, about 9:00 P.M., they descended to the beach and waited for the ten o'clock rendezvous hour to approach. Exactly on the hour, Fermor handed Moss a flashlight from his knapsack. Moss climbed a rock and prepared to give the signal.

"What are the code letters?" Moss asked, having forgotten Barnes's instructions.

"S.B.," Fermor replied.

"How do you spell S.B. in dots and dashes?"

"Haven't a clue. I thought *you* knew how to do it."

"Not I."

"Sure?"

"I know how to do S.O.S."

"God forbid!" responded Fermor, horror-struck.

They looked at each other for a few minutes and said nothing. Then they decided to give the "S.O.S." signal, omitting the "O" which left it only partially correct.

"After all," Fermor argued, trying to excuse the fact that neither of them knew Morse code, "we are not regular soldiers—Coleman knows that!"[13]

Moss blinked the signal repeatedly: "S-S-S-S." Then he waited anxiously for a reply. None was forthcoming. Nothing was seen; nothing was heard. There was utter silence. Even the lapping waves were quiet.

Paterakis *did* hear something. Touching Fermor on the shoulder, he pointed to his ear. From the inky blackness where the sea blended with the darkness of night, the sound of a boat's engine was audible. It lasted a few minutes, then faded away.

Tyrakis murmured worriedly, "I think she go away!"

Fermor agreed, remarking disappointedly, "They have missed us!"

They sat there on the rock, disconsolate, almost to the point of tears.

Then out of the darkness, they heard a familiar voice hailing them: "Paddy, Billy!" It was Denis Ciclitiras, who did not go back to Asi Gonia as he had planned, but hiked to the beach instead via a detour to avoid German patrols.

"Do you know the Morse code?" Fermor and Moss inquired simultaneously, hoping that he did. He did, indeed!

Ciclitiras took the flashlight, mounted the rock, and began flashing the correct signal, "S.B.-S.B.-S.B." as quickly as his finger could press the button.

It took time, but soon the throb of engines was audible again, getting louder and louder. Then a huge black shadow loomed out of the darkness. It was the rescue boat. Everyone jumped with excitement and relief at the sight. Even the general smiled, for his ordeal was almost over.

In a short time, several dinghies reached the beach, and well-armed men with blackened faces and wearing berets came ashore. They were British commandos who came to safeguard the rescue. Additional dinghies arrived moments later, bringing more commandos who appeared anxious for a fight with hate in their hearts and murder in their eyes.

"Where are the Germans? We'll kill them!"

"There are no Germans here," Fermor replied.

"Then we'll go find some and shoot the bastards!"[14]

After much debate, Fermor finally succeeded in dissuading them from such rash action, which would delay and jeopardize the evacuation. The commando leader, Robert Bury, eventually relented, and disembarkation began when the landing officer interjected, "Excuse me, Gentlemen, but we ought to get a move on!"

Farewells were said with hugs and kisses, and the Cretan escorts invited them to return to the island soon. Then Fermor, Moss, Paterakis Tyrakis, and the general were rowed out to the waiting motor launch. Brian Coleman, the boat's commander, greeted them when they came on deck.

As the motorized Royal Navy boat pulled away from Rhodakinon Beach, they all stood by the rail peering into the darkness at the rapidly disappearing coastline of Crete. Only the dark-shaped mass of mountains, soaring up against the star-filled sky, could be discerned as the boat turned and cut through the waves for Egypt.

It was safety at last for these gallant men of the abduction team and a prisoner-of-war camp for their captive, General Heinrich Kreipe. The daring abduction of a German general was over.

Chapter 15

Politics Is the Object;
Battle Is the Means

The voyage from Rhodakinon Beach on Crete to North Africa began well. Everyone was below deck celebrating the success of the mission. Although fatigued from the strain of anticipation that prevailed in the last hour before sailing, no one considered the thought of sleeping. They just sat, crammed in the boat's small ward room, and talked, and laughed, and talked some more. Everyone chattered happily and loudly in a Babylonic crescendo of Greek and English—everyone, except Heinrich Kreipe. The general sat in the corner, silent and morose, like a defeated gladiator.

Halfway across the Mediterranean, the north wind (they call it the Boreas) increased in velocity, churning the sea into huge waves with deep troughs that rocked the large motor launch violently enough to slow its speed. Surprisingly, no one on board noticed or cared.

It was not until after midnight that Brian Coleman nosed his craft through the dark harbor waters of Mersa Matrüh, past sunken hulks and anchored ships, until it reached the dock. Then everyone went on deck, waiting for the word to go ashore. The motors finally stopped, the mooring lines were cast, and the gangplank was set into place.

"Off you go!" Coleman shouted from the bridge. They did not have to be told a second time.

There was a reception committee on the quay led by a general officer. Leigh Fermor and William Moss led Kreipe down the gangplank to the wharf. For the first time in his military career, General Kreipe's feet stood on English territory. The British brigadier approached the German, saluted him respectfully, and much to Kreipe's surprise, greeted him in perfect Viennese German.

Kreipe smiled—it was only his second smile since the abduction—and returned the salute with his uninjured arm.

The brigadier greeted Fermor and Moss warmly. "You've given me grey hairs, old chaps, with your delay in leaving the island. However, it was a good show!" Thereupon, he informed both of them of their promotion—Fermor to major, Moss to captain—with the recommendation that both be awarded the DSO, the Distinguished Service Order.[1]

The next day, the brigadier flew with General Kreipe, Fermor, and Moss to Heliopolis airport outside Cairo. After some routine formalities, Fermor and Moss bade a final, sad farewell to General Kreipe, having become somewhat attached to him during the past three weeks. They exchanged last salutes, the general smiling—for the third time—a rueful smile tinged with a kind expression. Then he entered the staff car to be driven to his new home as a prisoner of war. Without further delay, Fermor and Moss clambered into another vehicle for the joyful ride home to their safe house, Tara, on Sharia Abou El Feda.

Press photographers had taken pictures of General Kreipe during his arrival in Cairo. The BBC subsequently announced to the free world that "the German garrison commander of Crete had been abducted from his headquarters and escorted to Cairo as a prisoner of war . . . an effort made possible by the valor of two British officers, Patrick Leigh Fermor and William Stanley Moss.

British newspapers carried a brief, albeit undetailed, account of the kidnapping, since all details were restricted through censorship by the War Office. American newspapers were even more meager with their reportage, many omitting the story entirely, while others buried it in a small caption appearing in the inner pages. However, when the BBC referred to this exploit, it brought delight to its listeners.

The stalwart people of the British Isles had recovered from the savage onslaught of aerial bombardment during the German Blitz of 1940, only to become targets anew of Hitler's formidable secret weapons of destruction, the V-1 and later the V-2 rockets. Yet, in the face of this new terror from the sky, the citizens of England smiled when they heard the news item about the German general's kidnapping. There was something typically British in the daring of that episode.

One particular lady listening to the BBC had a much greater reason to smile than any other person in England. She had not heard from Patrick Leigh Fermor for many months. She knew that he had been involved in the battle for Crete back in May 1941 and that later he was successfully evacuated to Egypt. Then she heard nothing further from him. When his name was announced on BBC radio, she finally learned where "Paddy" was and what he had accomplished. The announcement came like a gift from heaven for her, for the day in which the BBC reported the abduction of the German general was this lady's birthday. This smiling, happy woman was Patrick Leigh Fermor's mother.[2]

Master Sergeant John Alexander, the peripatetic American from Wheeling, West Virginia, reported for duty early on the morning following his arrival at OSS headquarters in Bari. He appeared before the commanding officer of the 2677 Regiment (Provisional) OSS, Colonel Ellery Huntington. The colonel was a well-built, robust individual with the air of an athlete. He had played football as an All-American from Colgate, and as far as he was concerned all men in the OSS should have been football players like himself. When he reviewed Sergeant Alexander's service file, he remarked to his personnel officer that "this kid was a three-letter man in high school, one of which was in football!" It appeared that having been a football player even at the high school level placed Alexander in good stead with this unit commander.

It did not take long for Alexander to discover that the OSS was indeed a very secretive organization, for all United States army and navy personnel in the Bari and Brindisi area were unaware of its existence. In the eyes of the other commands located in the same area, OSS personnel were identified as members of the SBS. Sergeant Alexander later learned that the initials SBS stood for the Strategic Balkan Services, which was a section of the OSS that sent operational missions into the Balkans.

Inasmuch as Alexander had undergone specialized training when he was assigned to Laycock's commando force for the raid on Iraklion airfield, that phase of the OSS training was waived by his new CO. However, he had to undergo routine qualification tests in marksmanship, in radio operation, and in the study of ciphers. Then came the most complex aspect of his new duties with the OSS— political indoctrination.

In the days that followed, he was to undergo several extended and intense briefings in the complex politics of the land in which he was to serve. During those critiques, Alexander realized for the first time that Greece and Crete faced a danger much greater than the presence of the German occupation army. Alexander, who had spent almost a full year on Crete serving with the guerrilla bands and with the SOE, never, in his youthful naivete, realized that there existed such diverse political factions, factions that threatened to create bloody civil strife in that land. These briefings awakened him to the realization that there was much to learn.[3]

In the midst of the German occupation of Greece, after April 1941 and later in Crete after June of the same year, the Central Committee of the Communist party of Greece worked clandestinely to enhance support for its ranks. By 1944, the official Communist party of Greece—the Kommunistikon Komma Ellados, designated simply as the KKE—at the instigation of the Soviet Union, forged an attempt to spread a covert influence over the politically fluid climate of that nation. The KKE shrouded itself under the misleading guise of the Greek National Liberation Front—the Ethnikon Apeleftherotikon Metopon (EAM).

The communist leaders of this organization chose this title in order to give the movement a national and nonpolitical connotation. Its name was a misnomer, for its purpose was neither national nor nonpolitical. It was in reality a partisan group of communists with allegiance to the Soviet Union who sought to take advantage of Greece's weakness during the German occupation and thus convert Greece into a communist satellite state.

To better enforce the political dicta of the EAM, the political leaders of the KKE advised the formation of an army of its own creation. The National People's Liberation Army (translated as the Ethnikos Laikos Apeleftherotikos Stratos, with the acronym ELAS) became the military arm of the EAM from the day of its founding on April 10, 1942.[4]

The EAM-ELAS organization was dominated by a hard core of communist leaders.[5] Their immediate intent was to prevent the return of the monarchy to Greece once the German occupation army had withdrawn. In the political unrest that would follow the German withdrawal, the communists would establish their own national government. The ultimate agenda was the total communization of Greece.

The ELAS recruited into its ranks former officers of the Greek army, disgruntled political hacks, and those who had a grievance with the pre-war government. The remainder of the ranks were filled through the medium of intimidation, threats, fear, and terror. To gain strength through popularity among the very people it intended to enslave, the EAM "supported every patriotic demonstration that took place in spite of the occupation authority's prohibition. It took initiatives useful to the proletariat. It was openly opposed to the first forced transfer of Greek workers to Germany."[6] All these stances had a self-serving purpose.

Beguiled by promises of a future utopia, many duped people of Greece and Crete rushed to join the ranks of the EAM-ELAS. People from all walks of life—priests, teachers, scholars, and even simple, illiterate villagers—soon expanded the rolls of the EAM-ELAS organization. They paid no heed to the Greek king's promise made in a letter to England's prime minister, Winston Churchill, that he had "declared to the people that after liberation they will be invited to determine by means of free elections the form of their government."[7] King George's royal proclamation fell on deaf ears.

Opposing the EAM-ELAS faction was the EDES—the National Army of a Free Democratic Nation—under the command of the portly General Napoleon Zervas, a jovial former army officer, who had been dismissed by the Greek government sixteen years earlier after a failed coup d'etat.

Zervas and his EDES organization was conservative politically, yet did not favor the return of the monarchy. Unlike the leaders of the EAM-ELAS group, Zervas's allegiance was to Greece and not to the Soviet Union.[8]

With the Italian surrender in September 1943, the ELAS acquired most of the Italian war material on the Greek mainland, thus gaining arms superiority over Zervas's EDES. Using these weapons to advantage, the EAM-ELAS forces conveniently forgot that the goal of the guerrilla movement was to stand resolute against the Nazi occupation force as the common foe. Instead, they attacked the EDES. For the whole month of October 1944, a continuous struggle prevailed between the attacking communist ELAS army and the defending republican EDES forces for control of the Greek countryside. The Nazis sat back and watched gleefully, while Greek slew Greek in a mountain warfare that was exemplified by such brutal slaughter that the Nazis pogroms seemed moderate in comparison.

When Churchill realized that the real intent of the EAM-ELAS forces was to communize the Macedonian and Epirus provinces of Greece for the benefit of the Soviet Union's postwar influence over the Balkans, he decided to take an immediate stand to allay the attempt. The British prime minister immediately ordered that no additional military supplies be sent to the ELAS forces, distributing them instead to Zervas's conservative EDES.[9]

With the foresight of the great statesman that he was, Churchill ordered that military missions be sent into Greece with the purpose of restoring peace between the two warring guerrilla factions, and concentrate their efforts against Nazi troop and supply movements. The main purpose in mediating this self-destructive mountain conflict was to prevent it from escalating into a civil war—an event that, in fact, did occur following the German withdrawal from Greece.

The Special Operations Executive agents serving on Crete were warned of the political intentions of EAM-ELAS. SOE agents like Patrick Leigh Fermor and William Stanley Moss were already aware of the traitorous intentions of the EAM-ELAS, having encountered their unscrupulous activity when they threatened to betray them to the Germans during the Kreipe abduction.

When the United States government became involved in the Mediterranean theater of operations, the OSS set up its own headquarters in Bari and Brindisi for its covert operations in the Balkans and in Crete. When the first OSS officers appeared in Greece and in Crete, the British Military Mission was changed to the Allied Military Mission.[10]

At first, the British SOE and the OSS agents were in conflict with the principal objectives of their missions. The British openly favored the conservative EDES, while the leftists of the EAM-ELAS strove to beguile with falsehoods the newly arrived OSS members. Whereas the British labored for the postwar restoration of the Greek monarchy, the Americans were interested only in finishing the war successfully and quickly, with little or no postwar motives.

Many OSS agents were hostile to the men of the SOE, some through Anglophobia, whereas others fell victim to the EAM-ELAS "democratic" propaganda. It was not until the proclamation of the Truman Doctrine on March 12, 1947 that the Americans were finally alerted to the true intentions of those communist forces.[11]

On Crete, 168 air miles south of the Greek mainland, the activities of the communist-directed EAM-ELAS forces influenced only some areas on the western part of the island in the Khania province. These communist forces were under the command of a forceful, mentally unstable leader named John Podias, known and cursed by the Cretans as Yanni Podias.

Podias had originally been a member of Kapetan Manoli Bandouvas's guerrilla band. In his maniacal desire to exert his leadership, and swayed by the misguided propagandistic political proclamation issued by the EAM-ELAS, Podias broke away from Bandouvas and organized a communist guerrilla band based in the White Mountains of Crete.

It was Podias's ELAS group that had threatened in April 1944 to expose Fermor and Moss and the plot to kidnap General Kreipe to the Germans.

Similar in purpose to the EAM-ELAS communist movement on the Greek mainland which instead of fighting Germans fought other Greeks, so it was on Crete, that Yanni Podias and his ELAS band attacked the Bandouvas guerrilla forces. In the bitter, prolonged battle that followed between these two Cretan forces, Podias was killed. Bandouvas ordered that Podias's head be severed from his body, speared, and carried through the villages to educate the local inhabitants about these "traitors of Crete!"[12]

The group that opposed these communist bands of the EAM-ELAS on Crete was the National Organization of Crete—the Ethniki Organosis Kriti (EOK). Its ranks were filled with patriotic, strongly nationalistic men who considered the Nazis, and *not* fellow Cretans with their self-serving political beliefs, to be their only enemy. These patriotic ranks were filled by such leaders as Kapetans Petergeorge, Bandouvas, Grigorakis, and Xilouris, to name only a few, and the hundreds of brave men who fought in their bands.[13]

Others, who served with the British in the SOE, such as George Psychoundakis, Leigh Fermor's runner, and the kidnappers of General Kreipe, Manoli Paterakis, George Tyrakis, and Strati Saviolakis, and the rest, also stood firmly unto death against the EAM-ELAS communist conspiracy in Crete.

Into this cauldron of political strife, turmoil, and unrest, the agents of the OSS were being sent to represent the American armed forces in Greece and in Crete.

When the final briefing on Greek politics concluded, Master

Sergeant John Alexander leaned back, looked at his fellow American agents in the room, and shook his head. Even though he had served on Crete, he knew nothing of all this.

"What the bloody hell are we getting into?" he exclaimed aloud. "I thought the *Nazis* were the enemy!"

The OSS intelligence officer, who had expounded at length on Greek politics, took a sip of water and responded tartly, "Remember, that the *Krauts* are our enemy, and these mountain people must be made to cooperate with us until this God-damned war is over. That will be your job!"[14]

With the briefings concluded, assignment of this contingent of OSS agents to serve behind German lines on the Greek mainland and in Crete was the responsibility of the commanding officer of the OSS unit in Bari, the 2677 Regiment, and his intelligence and operations staff officers.

American agents were already operating in the northern territories of the Greek mainland. One of the first OSS operational groups (OGs) to arrive in Greece was the Chicago Mission led by Major James Kellis, a Greek-American. Other operational groups had been infiltrated into Greece, and by late 1944 seven OGs of twenty to thirty men in each group were working behind German lines.[15] One such OSS agent was George Doundoulakis who had already served in Crete with Patrick Leigh Fermor and was later assigned to an OSS OG in northern Greece, as was his brother Louis.[16]

For the first few months since John Alexander's transfer to the United States army, the rush of events had pushed any thoughts of revenge against Fritz Schubert into the background. When Sergeant Alexander reported for assignment, his CO's first inclination was to attach him to one of the OGs already serving in the mountains and cities of the Greek mainland. Alexander wanted to return to Crete.

The regimental commander's intelligence officer (Alexander never learned his name) emphasized that Alexander's earlier experience on Crete gave him a tremendous advantage with which to operate. His familiarity with the terrain, with its people, and with some of the leaders of the Resistance Movement would prove invaluable in establishing a successful operational environment.

The colonel remained thoughtful and apparently unconvinced. He read through the file once again, while Alexander prayed that the G-2's suggestion would prevail. Finally, the colonel relented.

"O.K., we'll send him to Crete!"

Relieved, John Alexander smiled; but now he was in for an unexpected surprise.

The intelligence officer added that the British SOE agents on Crete were mostly officers, so that to compete equally in rank, the OSS agents on Crete should also have officer rank. Once again, the rivalry that existed between the British SOE and the American OSS was evident. Alexander wondered how this would concern him.

"It would be a temporary rank, of course, only for the duration," the G-2 explained. "There would be no problem with the paperwork, and it is covered by the AR's (Army Regulations Manual) which authorizes the promotion at your discretion for the good of the service."

The colonel stared at Alexander, standing there at ease, for several moments before deciding whether to accept his intelligence officer's suggestion. He squinted thoughtfully and looked down at the file once again, before nodding approval.

"We're going to make you an officer and a gentleman," the colonel remarked sarcastically to Alexander, "all for the good of the service." He made an entry into the file and passed it to his personnel officer.

"As of 0800 hours tomorrow, consider yourself promoted to officer rank as a first lieutenant!"

The G-2 nodded agreement. It was a rank that gave Alexander authority, yet not too high a rank, considering the rapidity with which it was given.

Alexander did not wait for 8:00 A.M. the next day. He stopped off at the PX that same afternoon and purchased two pairs of silver bars. Once in his quarters, he pinned one pair to the collar of his OD shirt and the other to the shoulder epaulets of his jacket.

He studied his reflection in the cracked mirror on his dresser and smiled. It was strange, he reflected, how fate had treated him during his journey through life these past four years. His thoughts flashed back to the Crete of 1940 when he first arrived on a visit as a young teenager just graduated from high school in Wheeling, West Virginia. He had lived through the German paratroop invasion of the island and the occupation that followed; his father's murder by the Gestapo sergeant; his own imprisonment and subsequent escape; his evacuation to Egypt; his loneliness and despair; his enlistment in the British army; his return to Crete with the commando raiding party; his service with the SOE; his transfer to the United States army; his promotion to master sergeant; and now as a first lieutenant, he was going back to Crete where it all began.

"Schubert, you son-of-a-bitch," he muttered to his image in the mirror, "I'm coming back to Crete. I'll get you yet!"[17]

Within a week of his return to Tara, the safe house in Cairo, Patrick Leigh Fermor fell seriously ill with rheumatic fever, though at first it was thought to be a form of paralysis. The many weeks in the cold and dampness of the Cretan mountain caves, hiding from the Germans, had taken their toll. Fermor was hospitalized for almost two months as a result of this illness.

It was while Fermor was sitting up for the first time after entering the hospital that General Sir Bernard Paget, the commanding general in Cairo, arrived to pin the DSO on Fermor's pajama top.[18] William Stanley Moss received his DSO at a more formal ceremony back at headquarters. Both were proud of their decorations, awarded for the successful abduction of the German general. They would have been even more pleased had they known at that time that the Germans had placed a bounty on both their heads. The Germans wanted them dead or alive.

The Oberkommando der Wehrmacht (OKW) had issued an order over Hitler's signature that "All soldiers in uniform . . . whether armed or unarmed, in battle or in flight, are to be slaughtered to the last man."

This order encompassed the possibility of another British commando raid like the one in which Alexander was involved, besides the covert efforts of the SOE agents. The OKW proclamation went on to state that "No pardon is to be granted them on principle . . . if such commandos, such as agents, saboteurs, etc., fall into the hands of the military forces . . . they are to be handed over to the S.D."

The order concluded with the absolute condemnation that "All sabotage troops will be exterminated without exception, to the last man."[19]

In spite of such an edict, and with a German bounty balanced heavily on his head, Captain Moss planned to return to Crete. This time he planned to kidnap Kreipe's successor, General Benthag.

Moss returned to Crete by boat and used the same hideouts as before, while he formulated strategy with the Cretan underground. The new German garrison commander, in the Iraklion district, traveled only with an armed escort in view of what happened to General Kreipe. This made it more critical to put Moss's plan into effect without risking a skirmish during the actual moment of the planned abduction.

Unfortunately for Moss and his team, the plan was betrayed to the Germans by the communist leaders of the ELAS group at Ano Archanes village where the new garrison commander, like Kreipe before him, maintained his headquarters.

When the first letter from the ELAS leaders arrived threatening to expose the plot, Moss, like Leigh Fermor before him during the Kreipe abduction, ignored it. He also ignored the second letter. However, the third one was so strongly worded in its affirmation of betrayal, as to the time, place, and personnel involved, that moss decided to change the date of the kidnapping and the original abduction site.

At dawn the next day, a battalion of 800 German troopers swarmed over the recently vacated abduction site. When Moss realized the apparent danger existing by such betrayals, he decided to abandon the whole project. Once again the communist leadership of the ELAS had proven that they preferred to serve the cause of the Nazis by betraying their own people.[20]

First Lieutenant John Alexander stood on the dock at Brindisi harbor waiting for the arrival of his transportation to Crete. Amidst the hustle and bustle on the quay, there was one other American standing nearby.

"Hello! You're that new fellow who recently joined us!"

Distracted from his thoughts, Alexander turned and recognized one of the officers who had attended the briefings with him two days earlier. He introduced himself as James Simvoulakis from California and said that he was scheduled to sail for Crete with Alexander.

Lieutenant Simvoulakis had earlier served in the Pacific theater of operations. After a brief leave at home, he was transferred to Special Forces and was recruited to serve as an agent of the OSS. After specialized training, he was assigned for duty in the Mediterranean theater with the Strategic Balkan Service, and he was assigned to duty on Crete.

They boarded a small motor launch with sails—a typical Greek caique—that roamed the waters around Greece and Crete like any other fishing boat without attracting special attention from the Germans. Several such caiques were manned by Greek crews and skippered by Greeks, but were commanded by officers of the OSS.

During this voyage across the Mediterranean, both Alexander and Simvoulakis silently studied the caique's commander, who kept to himself throughout the trip. He was a tall, deeply tanned, and heavily bearded, with a familiar ring to his voice. It was a voice that neither Alexander nor Simvoulakis could immediately place. This caique commander bore the name of Captain John Hamilton, United States Marine Corps. They were very close to their destination before they recognized the owner of that famous voice. It belonged to the movie actor Stirling Hayden, who was serving in the OSS. The name of John Hamilton was his nom de guerre![21]

They made shore at a secluded area west of the Cretan capital of Khania, where they were greeted by guerrillas under the command of a Colonel Flotakis. Both Lieutenants Simvoulakis and Alexander were now part of a bigger OSS operation, named the Apple Mission under the command of Lieutenant Colonel Grady McGlasson. The mission's objective was to determine the strength, composition, morale, and dispositions of the German troops on the island, and the numbers and dispositions of the guerrilla forces who opposed them.

The British Intelligence Service had this information available from reports submitted to them by their SOE agents, but the Americans wanted to collect their own. It was odd that the American Apple Mission commander never inquired whether the Allied Military Mission already had such intelligence on file, and the British never voluntarily disclosed their information. Although they were fighting the same enemy in the same war, the rivalry that existed between the two intelligence services was very apparent.

Most of the agents of the Apple Mission were evacuated from Crete in July 1944, after one month of intelligence gathering. Simvoulakis and Alexander, however, remained behind to continue their covert operations. Soon after the two OSS agents parted, each going to his own individual assignment.[22]

John Alexander, disguised as an impoverished villager, traveled over familiar landmarks as he ascended the rocky trails that led deep into the mountain lairs that hid the guerrilla bands. After several days of travel, mostly at night, he arrived at the hideout that housed his old friend Kapetan George Petergeorge.

The tall, aristocratic guerrilla chieftain greeted Alexander warmly with embraces and kisses on both cheeks. That night, amidst the warmth of a cozy fire, good food, and ample wine,

Alexander detailed his story since his departure from Crete. The old chieftain was delighted to learn that Alexander was now an officer in the U.S. army, working for the OSS.

For several months, Kapetan Petergeorge had developed a distrust of the English and the SOE. Although he cooperated fully with their efforts against the Germans, he was wary that the British were laboring for only one political purpose in postwar Crete–the return of the monarchy. Although on many occasions he argued vociferously with Tom Dunbabin, the SOE agent in that area, he would never betray Dunbabin's work or his cause to the enemy. He was too much of a patriot to do so.

On one occasion, Dunbabin insisted that Petergeorge should attack the communist ELAS forces in the area. The guerrilla chieftain refused, for he felt that the Nazis were the common enemy and not his fellow Cretans. He also feared that an attack on the ELAS forces might ignite a civil war.

Thus, when Alexander returned as an American officer in the OSS, Petergeorge felt that now he could work with a person whom he could trust.

One evening, the guerrilla chieftain asked anxiously, "Will the Americans invade this island?" Alexander could not answer that question. Before leaving the Apple Mission, he had learned that General Mark Clark's Fifth U.S. army had captured Rome and that on June 6, the greatest armada in modern history had invaded Hitler's Festung Europa over the beaches of Normandy. Crete had not been mentioned at all in their briefings.

Kapetan Petergeorge nodded understandingly. The Allies were too busy elsewhere to bother with Crete. "We shall carry on alone, until this Nazi devil surrenders," he remarked sadly, accepting the obvious.

The Kapetan gave Alexander permission to use any facility he needed to fulfill his assignment, whereupon the young American set up his radio transmitter in one of the caves above Mount Ida, not far from Petergeorge's headquarters.

The next day, the Kapetan left with his band of guerrillas to attack a German column that had ventured into his area. His guerrillas ambushed the 400 men of the German force in a mountain pass. They fought a bitter battle all day with the Germans, who used machine guns and light mountain artillery against rifles. But guerrilla marksmanship and good deployment had a telling effect on the Germans. With the advent of darkness, the Germans broke off the engagement and withdrew, leaving behind sixty-three dead, which included two officers. Petergeorge's band suffered only one dead and two wounded. The disciplined Germans had been outclassed, outmaneuvered, and outfought by the untrained mountain irregulars![23]

Alexander reported the battle and its outcome to his radio contact in Cairo that same night. In the course of the days that followed, using information obtained for him by Petergeorge's men, he was able to supply the intelligence division of the OSS's Greek Section the information they sought about the German garrison on Crete.

He reported that the Apple Mission's original estimate of 30,000 German troops on Crete was thought to be too high, with 15,000 being a more realistic figure. These troops were assigned to the 22nd and 133rd Infantry Divisions headquartered in Khania, with units of regimental strength deployed in Rethimnon and Iraklion. There were also troops varying in groups of twenty to thirty men in blockhouses stationed at critical points throughout the island.[24]

In action similar to Petergeorge's guerrilla band, other resistance fighters took heart and harassed German dispositions and troop movements on an almost daily basis. Even William Moss took the opportunity to score against the enemy.

Leading a group of fifty Cretans, some of whom were originally part of his kidnap team, they ambushed a German motorized column, destroying ten trucks, killing fifty of the enemy, and taking fifteen prisoners. Moss personally accounted for the destruction of an armored car by jumping on it and dropping a grenade down its turret, killing the crew. He received a cluster (an American military term; a bar, in British) to his Military Cross.

George Psychoundakis had returned to Crete in July 1943 after his evacuation to Egypt to keep him out of the clutches of the Gestapo. No sooner was he back than he resumed where he had left off, running errands for the SOE.

One day he ambled into Vaphe, a village located south of the main northern road that led out of Suda Bay. Surprisingly, he had encountered no Germans on the road, and he found that several roadblocks on the way had been abandoned. In this village, the SOE agents had stored all their supplies, even though Vaphe was in close proximity to German headquarters.

If, by chance, the Germans had raided Vaphe that hour on that day, they would have captured the whole SOE operation on Crete. When Psychoundakis entered the home of his friend, Antoni Vandoulakis, he was surprised to find seated around a long table, Captain Dunbabin, Major Smith-Hughes, Captain Ciclitiras, and Major Fermor. Fermor had returned to Crete after recuperating from his severe illness. They had all gathered at the Vandoulakis house to discuss plans for the next operation against the Germans.

They were eating, drinking, and singing heartily when Psychoundakis walked in. They greeted him warmly with slaps on the back and the usual embraces. Fermor offered him a drink.

"But, Mr. Michali," Psychoundakis objected, "it's midday and I haven't eaten yet."

"George, my boy, have one," Fermor persisted teasingly, his spirits already buoyed by several drinks. "What is a drink meant for? It's no use for anything else. You can't rub it into your scalp or clean your gun with it. You drink it for the sake of *kefi* (well-being), to make you happy and ready to dance and sing and to forget all your worries; in fact, to get drunk . . . that's what it's meant for!"

Then he gave him a glass of a reddish-brown liquid which Psychoundakis assumed to be wine. It was rum, a drink that the young Cretan had never tasted. It went down in one burning gulp not unlike the native drink, raki. Ciclitiras gave him a second glass; Dunbabin, a third; Smith-Hughes, a fourth, and countless more. Then they all sat around eating and smiling knowingly, with all eyes centered on Psychoundakis, waiting for the explosion. It finally came.

Totally drunk but still upright, Psychoundakis bolted out of the house and dashed for the center of the village, much to everyone's amusement. On the road, he ran into a village youth, Manoli Gyparis, an active member of the Resistance Movement. Bobbing and weaving, and crosseyed from too much rum, Psychoundakis drew a revolver from his belt and emptied all six bullets at him, while Gyparis scampered behind some rocks. Psychoundakis viewed Gyparis in multiples of three and luckily fired at every image except the real one. When the pistol was emptied, Gyparis seized Psychoundakis around the waist and carried him back to the house. Everyone watched the scene and was doubled over with laughter at Psychoundakis's antics. When he finally passed out, they carried him in a drunken stupor to the village schoolhouse where all the SOE supplies were kept. There among those stores they let Psychoundakis recuperate from his first introduction to rum.

Humorous moments such as these often helped dispel the tedium of everyday existence and the severity of the dangerous life that these secret agents of the British SOE and the American OSS faced in performing their duties on Crete.[25]

The Gestapo learned from an informant that the SOE's supplies were stored at Vaphe. In December 1944, a detachment of Germans attacked the village at dawn, with an advance element of armored vehicles leading the assault.

Vasili Paterakis (a brother of Manoli, who with Leigh Fermor had bodily seized General Kreipe during the abduction eight months earlier) saw the Germans approaching and opened fire with his Bren machine gun. He held the Germans at bay until the guerrillas in the area rallied and struck back in force. By the end of the day, the Germans withdrew having lost forty men, while the Cretans counted two casualties in the skirmish. Vasili Paterakis had suffered an arm wound in the fracas, but his advance warning and his opening bursts of fire contained the Germans until the guerrillas were able to counterattack.[26]

From his hideout high on Mount Ida, OSS Lieutenant John Alexander looked westward. There beyond the mountain peaks he could see deep black clouds of smoke rising skyward. He knew the meaning of that heavy smoke.

The Germans had set fire to all the villages in the Kedros area, south of the city of Rethimnon. They burned to the ground the villages of Anoghia, Kamares, Yerakari, Vrysses, Kardaki, and Saktouria—to mention only a few of the hundreds that were torched. They proclaimed that this wanton destruction was enacted in order to punish the Cretans for sheltering the kidnappers of General Kreipe, and they distributed leaflets so that *everyone* understood the purpose of their deed. This contention was a falsehood, for this latest act of destruction came months after the actual abduction. The Cretans knew better, and this latest act of bestiality only deepened the hatred that already existed for the enemy.

The Germans had launched this latest campaign in order to terrorize the civilian population of the island and to show them that they still maintained the strength and the will to destroy the very substance of Cretan life. In reality, their proclamation and these latest dreadful deeds of destruction were a subterfuge shielding their real intent.

Constantly harassed by ever-increasing numbers of guerrilla bands, with no new troop reinforcements arriving from Germany to supplement the dwindling garrison, and with little or no replenishment of supplies, the German command on Crete decided to withdraw and concentrate all troops within the Khania city limits and to create the Fortress of Khania.

In withdrawing, the Germans feared that if their weakness due to the shortage of men and material was discovered, all the guerrilla bands on the island would join forces in a combined effort, supplied by the British and the Americans, to launch a massive attack against the remnants of the garrison. Indeed, the whole civilian population might rise in open rebellion to avenge all the suffering exacted on them during the four years of a terror-filled occupation.

In the village of Fres, not far from Vaphe, and several miles inland from the main northern highway that led into Khania, First Lieutenant James Simvoulakis, the OSS officer who had returned to Crete with John Alexander, had set up his radio transmitter in a sheepfold high in the mountain above that village.

He had arrived in Fres dressed in the mangy, dirty garments of a mountain sheepherder. Along the way, he had purchased a small flock of sheep to better disguise the real purpose of his presence in the area.

From his perch high in the mountain, Simvoulakis could see convoy after convoy of troop-laden German vehicles traveling westward along the main northern highway, passing south of Suda Bay and entering the outer limits of the city of Khania. He did not have to use his field glasses to understand that all these movements were going westward into Khania while nothing was being transported eastward away from the capital city.

During his rare descents from his sheepfold into the valley below, he noted (like George Psychoundakis had discovered before him) that many of the sentry posts and blockhouses at vital crossroads had been abandoned. He realized that the Germans were withdrawing their forces completely into Khania. That same night he transmitted that information to his OSS radio contact in Cairo.

In the days that he did descend from his mountain hideout and entered the village, he always took a few sheep with him to further his masquerade. All the villagers soon got to know him and referred to him as "Dimitri the Shepherd."

As the Germans withdrew from the many villages and as their authority waned, political posters appeared everywhere, on walls, doorways, poles, and trees, placed there during the night by communist ELAS representatives denouncing local and civil government as well as Allied officers and their staffs.

On one occasion, Simvoulakis witnessed from his hideout an attack by a faction of ELAS communists against the conservative EOK, which left several killed and wounded. In his report to the OSS, he included the reports of some eyewitnesses to the skirmish, who implied that German uniformed noncoms had led the ELAS forces. He added indignantly that "he was damned tired of Greeks . . . slitting their own throat by shooting each other right under the noses of the Germans."[27]

During his trips into Fres, Simvoulakis often paused at a white, austere, stone house on the outer rim of the village and asked its occupant for food. The white-haired old lady who lived in that house was at first suspicious of this raggedy-looking visitor, for he could have been a Gestapo informant. What softened her attitude toward him was that her mongrel dog never barked or snarled at him, but rather greeted him playfully. That fact impressed her.

Thereafter, each time Dimitri the Shepherd came to her front door, the old lady, whose name was Mrs. Maria, would share with him whatever food she had collected that day, usually legumes or potatoes. Before permitting Dimitri to enter her neat, dirt-floored, single-room home, she would send him to the water trough in the backyard to wash the filth off his face and hands.

On one occasion, while Dimitri sat waiting for the old lady to put the food on the table, a picture hanging on the wall caught his attention. He carefully studied the faces of the people pictured in that family portrait.

"Who is that man in the picture with that little boy next to him?" he asked of the old lady, his grimy finger touching the two faces in the picture.

"That man is my son, and that little boy you are pointing to is my grandson. Only God knows if I shall live long enough to ever see them!"

A trace of a tear glistened in each eye as she looked away.

That night, Dimitri the Shepherd sent his usual evening transmission to Cairo. Appended to Simvoulakis's report was a personal request that a memo be forwarded on his behalf to his father in California. The note was to read: "Your mother is well!"

Chapter 16

The
Confrontation

The war on the European continent was over. After 2,078 days—from the day Adolf Hitler's armies crossed the Polish frontier on September 1, 1939 until Berlin fell to the Russians—all hostilities on the continent had concluded in the complete defeat of the German army.

The war in the Pacific, however, still had 116 days before total peace would reign again in the world, for V-J Day and Japan's surrender did not take place until September 2, 1945 on the deck of the battleship, the USS *Missouri*.

In a cascade of cursory events, Grand Admiral Karl Doenitz announced to the world via Hamburg Radio on May 1, 1945 that Der Fuehrer, Adolf Hitler, was dead and that he, Doenitz, was now the head of the German government. On May 7, the unconditional surrender was signed at 1:41 A.M. at Rheims in the headquarters of the Allied supreme commander, General Dwight Eisenhower. President Harry Truman proclaimed that May 9 be designated officially as V-E Day—victory in Europe.

The people of the former German-occupied lands of Europe were at last free from the yolk of the Nazi oppression. Happiness and hope were evident on their faces as they smiled for the first time in six years. Many hoped to pick up the shattered pieces and resume their lives or what was left after the horror of war and subjugation.

The Nazi swastika, however, continued to flutter from its staff above German headquarters in Khania, Crete, long after the German surrender on the continent. It would not be lowered until May 23, a full fortnight after V-E Day had been proclaimed.

In the interval, Khania had become a fortress with all German troops concentrated in that city and its environs. Only a German could enter, but no German dared exit, for by now the concentration of guerrilla forces had formed a tight ring around the city. The final German troop movement into Khania came on May 7, the day the unconditional surrender had been signed in Rheims.

An incident that occurred that same day on the road leading into Khania typified the brutality of the German four-year occupation.

A Gestapo officer raced his Volkswagen jeep down the main highway toward Khania, hoping to enter the city before darkness. A little boy was crossing the road at the exact moment that the officer's vehicle zoomed around a blind curve. Unable to stop in time, the driver swerved, sending the jeep off the road and into a ditch, bending its fender. The Gestapo officer got out, surveyed the damage, and glared angrily at the boy. Shyly and sheepishly, the frightened boy smiled at the German, shrugging his shoulders apologetically.

The Gestapo officer beckoned to the boy to approach. When the boy came close, the German grabbed him by the arm and snapped it across his knee, breaking it. Then he got back into his vehicle, backed up, and drove off, leaving the little boy screaming in pain. It was yet another barbarous act, even on the eve of surrender.[1]

Although the German occupation forces had departed from Iraklion and Rethimnon for Khania, a new danger confronted the people of those cities—civil war. The political factions of the communist-led EAM issued orders to their military arm, the ELAS, to seize those cities as soon as they were free of Germans. Opposing them, the conservative EOK notified the patriotic guerrilla chieftains of this danger and requested that they assist in keeping the ELAS out of those cities until a formal governing body had been established.

Kapetan George Petergeorge responded immediately to this clarion call to keep Crete free from communist subjugation. "First we had the Germans, now we have these traitorous communists," he confided to one of his lieutenants, George Tzitzikas.[2]

The tall, patriotic Petergeorge led his guerrilla band to Iraklion. In his footsteps, Kapetan Manoli Bandouvas followed with his larger force. Together, the two chieftains situated their men so as to keep the ELAS out of the city. They concentrated their forces on the heights above Iraklion, one group at the western part of the city by the Khania Gate, while the other secured the eastern entrance at the Fortetza Gate. In between the Petergeorge-Bandouvas forces, the ELAS band had deployed its men. The two forces faced each other ready for battle. It was a tinderbox in which the slightest provocation could have caused a bloody conflict between the two factions.

Through diplomatic persuasion, using logic and his powerful personality as a weapon, Kapetan Petergeorge was able to convince the ELAS leaders of the futility of such an armed confrontation, which would lead to bloodshed and cause irreversible strife. The communists, deployed in exposed positions and outnumbered in manpower, relented and departed peacefully. Iraklion was at last free and the celebrations began.

Tom Dunbabin was asked by Petergeorge to remain in the shadows during the conference, lest the ELAS be provoked by the presence of a British representative. Dunbabin now arrived to compliment the aristocratic guerrilla leader on the success of his diplomacy. Petergeorge raised his hand to interrupt Dunbabin in midsentence, shaking his head at the thought of what could have happened if the ELAS group had not withdrawn.

"Now, perhaps you understand, Mr. Tom," Petergeorge remarked to the SOE agent, "why I did not wish to attack the ELAS gang in the mountains, as you had demanded. I outnumbered them and I could have beaten them, but if I had attacked then, we would have no peace today. All you English have in mind is the return of the king. Let's have peace first, then let the people decide who would govern them!"[3]

In the city of Rethimnon, it was a different story.

The mood of the two opposing political factions had become very unyielding. The ELAS forces had taken up positions on the heights above Rethimnon and had established roadblocks at the western and eastern entrances into the city. No one could enter or depart unless he was an EAM-ELAS member. The ELAS forces meant to dominate the city and convert it into a communist stronghold.

Lieutenant Colonel Paul (Pavlo) Gyparis, who commanded the Cretan Brigade of the EOK conservative forces, sent an emissary to the ELAS with the request that they raise the siege of the city and "leave everybody alone."

"It was bad enough we had persecution under the Germans for four years," he wrote in a note to the ELAS leaders, echoing the exact sentiments expressed by Petergeorge at Iraklion. "Must we now do it to ourselves?"

The communists promised that they would withdraw from their positions, but by late afternoon, they had reneged on the promise. Colonel Gyparis sent his youthful nephew, Manoli, and his friend, on a reconnaissance patrol. This was the same Manoli who some days earlier had encountered the inebriated George Psychoundakis in the town of Vaphe, and after ducking from Psychoundakis's aimless shooting spree, had carried him back to Leigh Fermor. Now he and his friend Anastasi Petrakis crept through the tall brush to observe if the ELAS men had kept their promise to withdraw.

The communists noticed his approach and opened fire on him and his friend, killing Manoli. Outraged at this breach of promise, Colonel Gyparis attacked the ELAS group in force and put them to flight, scattering them into the countryside beyond. He had lost his nephew, but in the clash, Gyparis and his men slew the ELAS leaders of Rethimnon, freeing the city.

It was a sad episode for a people who had suffered dreadful persecution during the German occupation, only to face political insurrection just as the bell of freedom was ready to peal.[4]

Major Ciclitiras, who had been serving intermittently on Crete with the SOE, was living temporarily in Kastelli-Kissamou, a sleepy town little bigger than a village, nestled around a deep harbor on the western end of the island, approximately twenty-five miles west of Khania.

Early on the morning of May 8, Ciclitiras received orders via radio from British headquarters set up in liberated Iraklion. Ciclitiras (code named Dionysios) was ordered to contact the German general commanding the force in Khania and to hand him the terms of the unconditional surrender.

Traveling under a white flag of truce, Ciclitiras and his interpreter, Lieutenant Constantine Mitsotakis of the Greek army, approached the western entrance to Khania. Lieutenant Mitsotakis had been sent into Crete from Cairo to help organize the Greek political underground movement for the eventual return of the exiled royal government of King George II. Mitsotakis could not then have foreseen that by the early 1970s the monarchy would be replaced by a parliamentary democracy and that by the late 1980s, he himself would become the prime minister of Greece.[5]

At the guard post, Major Ciclitiras, in full British uniform with his rank evident on his epaulets, stated that he represented the Allied Forces Headquarters and requested a meeting with the commanding general in Khania, General Benthag. A German staff car eventually arrived to take Ciclitiras and Mitsotakis to Benthag's headquarters.[6]

The German commanding general and his chief of staff, Colonel Barge, received the Allied emissary in the general's office, formerly the home of the late great Greek statesman, Eleftherios Venizelos. There was a moment of silence following the formal introductions, and Ciclitiras noted a degree of embarrassment on the general's countenance. It was not easy for a proud German general to discuss such a delicate matter as unconditional surrender.

"I have received orders from Admiral Doenitz at Flensburg to surrender to the local commander of the Allied Forces in Crete," Benthag stated formally, breaking the embarrassing silence that prevailed in the opening moments of the confrontation. "Are you a representative of the Allied Forces commander?" he inquired.[7]

When Mitsotakis completed the interpretation, Ciclitiras nodded affirmatively.

There now arose the problem of protocol. The Geneva Convention on the subject stipulated that a general officer can only surrender to another officer of equal rank. This was the same regulation which dictated that General Angelo Carta could not surrender his Italian command on Crete, back in 1943, to Captain Patrick Leigh Fermor, any more than the abducted General Heinrich Kreipe could do so. Both generals had to wait until they arrived in Egypt before surrendering officially to another general. Ciclitiras could not accept General Benthag's official surrender, for he was only a major, serving in the Special Operations Executive, although he was officially attached to the South Staffordshire Regiment. Other arrangements had to be made.

Both Benthag and British Headquarters Command in Iraklion agreed that the German general would be flown to Iraklion to sign the formal terms of surrender and there accept the official arrangements for the entrance of the liberating army into Khania, and plan the final evacuation of the German garrison as prisoners of war. All this was to be accomplished without anyone knowing that the German garrison commander had left Khania for Iraklion and then returned for the official surrender ceremony.

"I must be assured that in my absence, the Cretan population and the guerrilla bands would not attack my troops," Benthag strongly emphasized. It appeared that the German general feared retribution.

Major Ciclitiras returned the same afternoon to inform the general that he would be flown out in a small aircraft the next morning for Iraklion. All arrangements had been made for the flight to leave Maleme airfield, ten miles west of Khania, site of the airborne struggle in the first days of the German invasion, back on May 20, 1941.

"How did you get your message through so quickly, Major?" General Benthag inquired, rather puzzled.

"Well, Sir, our radio is only three doors away from your headquarters, so I did not have to go far to send my message."

When Mitsotakis translated Ciclitiras's response, Benthag stared incredulously at Ciclitiras, obviously upset by this revelation.

"Only three doors away from here?" he murmured in disbelief. Then the general cast a stern glance at his chief of staff, who looked down in embarrassment.[8]

First Lieutenant Simvoulakis, from Modesto, California, received his orders that same day from his OSS contact in Cairo, to leave his hideout above the village of Fres and go to Iraklion to join the other members of the Allied Military Mission.

He removed the dirty and torn garments that he had worn in his disguise as Dimitri the Shepherd, and he slipped into the uniform of an officer in the United States army. He left the sheepfold that had served as his clandestine wireless headquarters all these weeks, and pushing his flock of a dozen sheep before him, he took the trail down the mountain into Fres.

Before leaving Fres village, he wanted to visit for the last time the white-haired old lady whom everyone called Mrs. Maria. She had been very kind to him, sharing with him, on so many occasions, whatever scant food she had available. Now, he planned to repay that kindness by giving her the twelve sheep of his flock. She could use the wool to make cloth and the mutton for food, until the deprivation wrought by the long German occupation ended and normalcy returned.

He left the trail and took the curving path that led to Mrs. Maria's house. Her dog approached him hesitantly, at first emitting a soft growl. It then sniffed him for a few seconds, and then recognizing him, wagged its tail.

Simvoulakis knocked on Mrs. Maria's door.

"Who are you?" she asked, rather perplexed by the appearance of this young man standing at her doorstep in a strange uniform.

"Don't you recognize me? You have fed me these last four weeks."

A look of recognition appeared on her face.

"Ah! I recognize the *voice*. You are Dimitri the Shepherd! But you are clean!"

Then the ring of surprise in her voice turned to one of anger.

"And where did you steal those clean clothes?" she scolded.

It took many minutes for Simvoulakis to explain to this kind, motherly old lady that he was not really a shepherd; that he was a secret agent, an officer in the American army; that his appearance as a shepherd was only a disguise.

She listened, shaking her head, trying to understand what it all meant.

"Are you hungry?" You usually are, at least Dimitri the Shepherd was," she smiled mockingly. "Eat something before you leave!" And she threw a few scraps of kindling wood into her stove, lit it, and placed a pot of soup on top.

The young American officer watched her with loving eyes and a warm smile, while the old lady puttered around her stove. He rose and took down the family portrait that was still hanging on the wall.

"Tell me, Mrs. Maria, who did you say this man and little boy were in this photograph?"

"I told you the last time you asked," she replied, somewhat annoyed.

"The man is my son, and the little boy is my grandson. They live in America . . . a place called C-a-l-i . . . C-a-l-i-f . . ."

"California," he corrected.

She stirred the soup several times, repeating the wish that she had offered in her nightly prayers, made since the beginning of the German occupation. "God only knows if I shall ever see them. I pray to God at least to see my grandson before I die!"

"Mrs. Maria . . . don't you know me?"

"Know you? Of course! You were Dimitri the hungry, dirty shepherd, and you are now a nice, clean American soldier."

She spooned some soup into a deep plate and placed it on the table. She smiled at him, inviting him to sit and eat before the soup got cold.

"I haven't changed much in my face, except for my moustache, and that I am twenty years older than in the photograph."

The old lady stopped what she was doing, the smile fading from her face, replaced by a look of bewilderment that furrowed her wrinkled brow.

"Who *are* you? You're not . . .?"

"Yes, I am! I am that little boy in the photograph, your grandson!"

The old lady swayed for a moment and sank abruptly into a chair. When she finally understood what she had just heard, a loud exclamation of happiness came forth from her heart and tears of joy ran down her cheeks.

Her prayer had been answered.[9]

Lieutenant Simvoulakis arrived in Iraklion, the tender scene with his grandmother deeply embedded in his heart. He hated to leave her but promised to return before departing from Crete; he also pledged to return some day with his father, her son.

It proved difficult to explain that, while he knew all those weeks that Mrs. Maria was in reality his grandmother, he could not reveal to her his true identity. She could not understand, however, even after he explained that had he been exposed to the Gestapo by an informant that he was actually an American agent and not a mountain shepherd, the revelation could have jeopardized her safety. If it had become known that Mrs. Maria was Simvoulakis's grandmother, the Gestapo would have seized her, tortured her, and probably executed her. In order not to endanger her life, he chose to keep his identity unknown to her all those weeks.

Still, she would not accept his explanation but lovingly scolded him for deceiving her.

In Iraklion, Simvoulakis watched as the people of the city celebrated the joy of liberation. It was a festive, carnival atmosphere. For the first time in four years, the people were smiling, laughing, and dancing in the streets. They were happy to be free at last! It was a heartwarming scene to behold.

On the first night of his arrival, Simvoulakis became unexpectedly involved in the political conflict that existed between the EAM-ELAS forces and those of the EOK. He had been briefed about these political differences back in Bari, as had John Alexander, but this night he came face to face with a paradigm of the strife that threatened to plunge the whole island into a cauldron hotter than that which existed under the German occupation.

A group of guerrillas from the conservative EOK faction had demanded that some ELAS representatives relinquish their weapons upon entering Iraklion, inasmuch as Iraklion was now a liberated city. The ELAS contingent refused, and lines were drawn in an ominous portent of a showdown skirmish.

At that precise moment, Lieutenant Simvoulakis inadvertently strolled into the midst of these two opposing forces.

Together with his commanding officer, Lieutenant Colonel V. J. ("Paz") Pazzetti, the two had left their quarters and were going to the Allied Officers' mess hall, when they encountered the two armed groups. As they approached, one of the ELAS men shouted to another, "Here come two of the bastards!"

Simvoulakis heard the remark and cautioned Colonel Pazzetti of the pending danger. The confrontation appeared serious, and each American casually thrust his hand into the pocket of his field jacket, quietly cocking his pistols, an unofficial Beretta, preparing for any eventuality.

Jim warned "Paz" to stand by while he identified themselves to the leaders of each faction. Once they were acknowledged as "Amerikanoi," both groups lowered their weapons. Then Simvoulakis loosened a seething tirade at them using strong, earthy Greek expletives.

Surprisingly, the leaders of each armed group apologized profusely, after which they all dispersed! At that moment, the two American OSS agents did not realize that their unexpected intervention had snuffed a lit fuse that could have culminated in a bloody battle.[10]

A few days later, Simvoulakis was ordered to travel to the town of St. Nicholas, located on the north coast road, forty-three miles east of Iraklion. He was to set up a temporary OSS station and report his observations. On this assignment, this young American from Modesto, California, for the first time in his life began to appreciate the spiritual sense that peace brings to a land and to its people after the terror of war and subjugation.

From the road that curves southward into St. Nicholas and runs tangent to its harbor, Simvoulakis could see fishing boats peacefully anchored, their masts prismatically reflected in the still waters. And out beyond the jetty of the harbor, fishermen were lazily dangling lines from their bobbing boats. They were at peace, and for the first time in four years they were free from fear and apprehension.

It was a calm, balmy spring day, with a beautiful blue sky the vastness of which was intermittently interrupted by the fleeting passage of fluffy clouds. On shore, young women and children scampered among the rocks of the jetty looking for snails for their evening meal.

Scattered everywhere across the fields were the sprouting flowers of spring, dotting the countryside like a palette of yellow, purple, red, green, and white hues. With each breath came the scent of orange blossoms whose fragrances was lofted across the land by the soft, warm ocean breeze.

Riding over the crest of a hill, Simvoulakis took in the sight of hundreds of windmills in the Lasithi plain beyond, the varicolored sails turning in never-ending circles, pumping water into the cisterns.

It was a sight to behold, and it felt good to be alive and free!

Everywhere, Cretans were digging in their gardens again. They were plowing their fields, spreading manure, mending their fences, and rebuilding their homes.

Peace had brought these people a renewal of life and a new hope for the future. The fear of death and destruction that had cast a black shadow over the whole island was gone. Church bells that had once sounded the alarm back on May 20, 1941, to announce the coming of the invader, now pealed a new tone for the coming of peace to the land of Minos.

Wherever James Simvoulakis traveled, the people smiled and waved. So accustomed were they to the presence of the English, that they greeted Simvoulakis with the joyful shout of "ZITO ENGLEZI!"—"LONG LIVE THE ENGLISH!"

Simvoulakis pointed to the American flag stitched to his sleeve and shouted back, "ZITO AMERIKANI!"—"LONG LIVE AMERICANS!"

Then he would correct them with a smile, adding, "That is what you should say!"

"O.K." was their laughing response.[11]

George Psychoundakis, the lithe, olive-eyed youth from the village of Asi Gonia, south of Rethimnon, was unable to celebrate the liberation of either his home village or the city of Rethimnon. On the day of liberation, he was ordered to remain behind in the mountain hideout and guard the SOE supplies, arms, and wireless sets from the new enemy, now that the Germans had withdrawn the ELAS bands.

For four years, Psychoundakis, like all Cretans, had waited for this day of liberation from Nazi tyranny. Now that the day had come at last, he was not present to participate in the explosive joy of freedom. He did not arrive in Rethimnon until three days after the freedom bell rang, but when he did, he made up for what he had missed the first three days.

Each day, the people of that city held parades, made speeches, and danced in the streets from sunrise to sunset. Sunset did not deter them either, for at night the celebrations continued under torchlight. It was an unending festive atmosphere. For the first time in four years, a free-spirited people who cherished freedom above all else in life were in fact free. They were delirious with happiness.

One day, Psychoundakis was asked to read one of his narrative poems which he had penned while in the mountains, performing his dangerous duties as a runner for the British SOE. Written in a fifteen syllabic meter, he stood on the steps of the local schoolhouse in Rethimnon, before a huge throng of townspeople and related to them the tale of the historic village of Yerakari, painting in words a tableau of a beautiful village before the Nazis destroyed it. The poem, in a sense, also mirrored the tragic tale of Crete and of its people during the four years of the German occupation.

The joy of a liberated people subsided during the oration, replaced momentarily by bitter remembrance. In those minutes, the gleam of happiness changed to the tears of sorrow as Psychoundakis rolled his colorful verses. When Psychoundakis finished, silence prevailed, like Lincoln at Gettysburg. The people were deeply stirred by the words of this village youth from Asi Gonia, whose only schooling had been the school of mountain life under the German occupation.

The final arrangements for the unconditional surrender of the German garrison in Khania were at last completed. The ceremony was to take place officially at noon on May 23—four years and three days after the German parachutists first set foot on Cretan soil.

On May 13, a battalion of the Hampshire Regiment arrived in the capital city of Khania to oversee the surrender. This unit was subsequently joined by elements of the Greek National Guard. The two units were to provide a Guard of Honor during the surrender ceremony and eventually supervise the evacuation of the former German garrison as prisoners of war.

Ten days later, on May 23, the last remaining swastika flag that still fluttered over any land in Europe would be lowered for the final time in the saga of the Second World War.

George Psychoundakis traveled by jeep to Khania in the company of his friend, Pavlo—SOE agent Dick Barnes, now promoted to major.

The road to the capital city was cluttered with milling throngs of villagers who came from all over Crete to witness the surrender ceremony. There were endless columns of vehicles, crawling bumper to bumper, all traveling in the same direction, with the same purpose in mind.

Along the two-laned narrow road that led into Khania from the west, arches of flowers canopied the roadway. Signs were everywhere, wishing a welcome to all liberators. There were also, of course, the ubiquitous political slogans of the EAM-ELAS and the EOK.

Like the residents of Rethimnon and those of Iraklion before them, the people of Khania also demonstrated their happy exuberance. They laughed, they danced, and they sang, for liberation had come at last. Above these joyful shouts and clamor of a free people came the opening chords of a martial band announcing to one and all that the final moment of the official surrender ceremony was approaching.

Psychoundakis leaped from the jeep, with Barnes trailing in his dust, and ran toward the gates of Khania as fast as his wiry legs could move. He did not wish to miss the moment that would conclude forever what had begun four years earlier.[12]

It was this festive air of liberation that reigned when First Lieutenant Alexander entered Khania for his long-awaited rendezvous with Gestapo Sergeant Fritz Schubert.

Two days earlier, Alexander had received instructions from his OSS radio contact in Cairo that he was to proceed to Khania as one of the American representatives of the Allied Military Mission. He was to participate in the formal surrender ceremony.

Escorted by two Cretans from Kapetan Petergeorge's group of guerrillas, the trio drove in a commandeered vehicle toward Khania. Like Psychoundakis and Major Barnes before them, they encountered heavy vehicular traffic on the road and dense masses of happy humanity that slowed their progress to the city's gate.

Alexander's driver swung off the main road, cut across some

fields and goat trails, and after a short, dusty, and bumpy ride reached a less obstructed road that led into the city. They were forced to stop at a wooden barrier manned by a squad of British soldiers from the Hampshire Battalion.

Alexander identified himself as an American officer. The sergeant-of-the-guard studied his identification card carefully and let him pass through. His two escorts were not as fortunate.

"Sorry, Sir," the British sergeant explained, "no armed Resistance Fighters are allowed to go past this point, only official Allied military personnel."

"I don't drive!" Alexander retorted sharply. "How do you expect me to reach my destination? Walk?"

The duty officer overheard the conversation and volunteered his own driver to transport Alexander on the short run to his destination. When the jeep made its turn into the main square, Alexander caught sight of Aleko, Kapetan Petergeorge's senior lieutenant, and wondered—rather marveled—how he of all people had filtered past the guards to this point. He asked the driver to leave him in the plaza in front of the main marketplace, the Agora. Aleko also had spotted Alexander, and the two rushed to greet each other.

It was Aleko who had first greeted Alexander on the sandy beach near Iraklion when he came ashore as a member of the Duncan-Moore commando raiding party. Ironically, Aleko had been a neighbor of the Alexandrakis family on Grigoriou Street in Rethimnon and as such knew Alexander's father well.

It was Aleko who had escorted Alexander to Rethimnon in the failed effort to confront Schubert in his own quarters. And it was Aleko who had guided the young American to Kapetan Petergeorge's home village to visit his mother and sisters. Now, he was here to guide Alexander to his nemesis, Fritz Schubert.

"You are amazing, Aleko," Alexander remarked, greeting him with a warm traditional embrace. "Only military personnel are permitted to enter this area of the city, yet here you are!"

The usually laconic Aleko smiled. "My Kapetan wished it so. So I am here to help you in your quest!"

He took Alexander by the arm and walked with him to the far end of the Agora; they turned down a wide street that angled away from the main plaza.

"Our people inform us that your quarry is still in residence."

"You mean Fritz Schubert?" Alexander asked hopefully.

Aleko nodded.

Alexander's heart pounded faster, honed by this revelation that the man who had killed his father four years ago was now within his grasp. He could feel his pulse beating like a drum in both ears. He gulped hard, then asked, "Where is he?"

Aleko motioned with his nose toward a row of buildings on the left side of the wide street at the far end of the plaza.

"The Gestapo had their offices on that street," he remarked bitterly. "Many of our people suffered in those houses . . . by torture . . . most of them died."

Alexander noticed a tear forming in Aleko's hardened eye. Some of those people were his relatives.

"The man you seek is in that one-storied building, the second house on the left, Number Four."

Alexander studied the front of the building. Aleko read his thoughts. "There is no rear exit, Mr. John," Aleko confirmed, "he is still in there!"

From the day the young American had returned as an officer in the OSS, Aleko no longer addressed him as Alexander, or the more familiar Yanni—John. Now he referred to him respectfully as Mr. Lieutenant or Mr. John.

"Your chance has come again, Mr. John. Your father's spirit calls out to you for revenge. That anathema, that devil from hell, is in there. He has killed thousands of us in four years. Avenge your father; avenge those poor victims!"

Alexander looked deeply into Aleko's pleading eyes, surprised by his emotional outburst. It was so unlike him. Alexander nodded and turned toward the house at "Number Four."

"Good luck, Mr. John!" Aleko muttered softly.

Alexander passed a British sentry post as he entered "death alley"—the name the people of Khania had given this wide street that housed the Gestapo offices. The guards saluted him smartly. Halfway across the street he passed a British officer, a major. Alexander's arm flew up into a snappy salute and continued unhesitatingly toward building Number Four.

The British officer smiled at the American lieutenant, a fellow Allied officer, and continued a few paces, then paused and turned. His eyes followed Alexander as he crossed the street. The major had recognized the American's face; he had met him before, but where?

"Lieutenant?"

Alexander turned, scowled momentarily at the summons, and walked back. When he came close, a smile of recognition crossed the British major's face.

"I know you! You're John Alexander! I knew you as Corporal Alexander, British Signal Corps. It was I, you know, who had recommended you for duty with the Duncan-Moore commando group.

He paused momentarily, eyeing Alexander's uniform. "I see that you are now an American officer. Good show, ol' boy! Good show!"

Alexander had long since recognized the major. It was Denis Ciclitiras, the British SOE officer who had negotiated the German unconditional surrender. They exchanged a few additional pleasantries, some of which were spoken in Greek.

From across the plaza, Aleko watched the meeting, worried that this chance encounter might betray Alexander's intent.

When Alexander finally saluted and departed, Major Ciclitiras walked past Aleko, his mind deep in thought.

"There was something about that young man," Ciclitiras reflected. "There was something about his family . . . his father . . . that's it . . . his father . . . a vow . . . a vow of vengeance!" The name of Fritz Schubert rushed immediately into his mind.

Alexander walked to the front entrance of building Number Four. The British guard at the door made no effort to interdict the American officer, and, in truth, Alexander was in no mood for interdiction. Like a hunter having found the prey he sought, Alexander closed in on Fritz Schubert.

He walked quietly, step by step, the length of the dark corridor, and stopped at the closed door that led to the room beyond. Aleko had mentioned that this door led to "that devil's" office. Alexander unbuttoned the flap to his holster and withdrew his .45 caliber army automatic, pausing a second before entering.

In that second, a panorama of events rushed through his mind from that dreadful day on Grigoriou Street, to his short stay in death-infested Prison Valley, to safety in the Monastery of St. John at Preveli, to this moment! A lifetime in less than a second.

He clenched his teeth, pursed his lips tightly, took a deep breath, and pushed the door open.

There, behind the desk, was SS Sergeant Fritz Schubert!

Alexander stood motionless before him, staring coldly at this man who had murdered his father.

"What do you want?" Schubert snapped angrily, his tone arrogant. He never looked up but continued sorting papers into a briefcase. When at last he did look at Alexander, he recognized the American uniform.

"I plan to surrender to the British, not to you Americans. Now go away!" He uttered his words flippantly, first in German, then in Greek with a heavy Turkish accent.

"I am not here to accept your surrender," Alexander replied in Greek, punctuating his words slowly, annoyed at Schubert's arrogance.

Schubert looked at Alexander, surprised that this American spoke Greek flawlessly. "Then what do you want?"

"I am here to *kill* you!"

Schubert frowned, disbelief apparent in his eyes. "What! You, an American, here to kill *me*! I see you are an American officer, not a Cretan guerrilla seeking revenge!"

"Four years ago," Alexander sneered, hate slowly rising in his voice, "on Grigoriou Street in Rethimnon, you killed in cold blood an American citizen and sent his son to die in Prison Valley."

Schubert put his papers down and leaned on the desk, staring intently at this young American officer. The scene that Alexander described came slowly into focus. After all, so many had died at his command and by his own hand. How could he be expected to remember every one?

"That man," Alexander continued, "was my father, and I was his son. I have sought you for four years. Now, that I have finally found you, I shall execute you like a common criminal!"

Alexander raised his pistol to arms length, cocking it. The sharp click resonated through the quiet room.

For the first time, Schubert's arrogance waned. A tinge of fear flickered in his eyes. That scene of Grigoriou Street now came into better focus. At last he remembered, and he paled, a pallor that showed through his dark complexion. The first drops of cold perspiration appeared on his balding forehead. He blinked once and sat down.

Alexander kept his army automatic at arms length, sighted on the narrow space between Schubert's eyes. One squeeze, one shot, and the vow to his father would be fulfilled.

His finger blanched when it tightened slightly on the trigger. Schubert cringed. He knew it would be useless to beg for his life from a man as determined as this American officer. He sat there staring at the muzzle of the barrel, waiting for the bullet that would blow his head away.

The moment of truth had come and then passed.

"Lieutenant Alexander! Put that pistol down!"

It was the voice of Major Ciclitiras. When he remembered the young American's vow, he noted that Alexander was going to Building Four. There would be only one reason for Alexander to seek out Sergeant Fritz Schubert. Revenge!

"Under the Articles of the Geneva Convention," Ciclitiras reminded Alexander, hoping to stop him from committing a court-martial offense, "this man is considered to be a prisoner of war and must be treated as such."

Alexander remained adamant in his purpose. He stood frozen in place, his pistol still held at full arms length, still aimed at Schubert's head.

"One squeeze; one shot; then the hell with the rest!" he muttered.

Schubert sat breathless, staring at Alexander and at the pistol. Total fear was reflected in his face, and his hand was raised as if to ward off the bullet.

"John," Ciclitiras continued, speaking softly, almost pleadingly, "would you do to him what he has done to us?"

These words finally stirred Alexander out of the darkness of his thoughts and into the presence of reality.

He took a deep breath, gave Schubert a long cold stare, and lowered his arm. He turned and walked out of the room.[13]

The quest was over.

Epilogue

When John Alexander walked out of Fritz Schubert's office, he felt that he had forever forsaken the vow to avenge the wanton murder of his father.

For four long years, Alexander had harbored this emotion of hate for his father's murderer. Yet, in spite of all the animosity that had built up in his heart and nibbled constantly at his very soul, when the actual moment arrived, Alexander could not squeeze the trigger of the pistol. With Ciclitiras's plea echoing in his ears, he realized that two such wrongs do not make one single right. He would not become Schubert's executioner. All that Alexander could do was hope that justice would be served through other avenues, not only for his father's death but also for the many thousands of Cretans who had died by Schubert's hand or by his personal command. In time, it was.

There was, however, one satisfying moment for Alexander during this confrontation with Schubert. He saw the Gestapo sergeant in a light that no other Cretan had ever witnessed. He had seen the German cringe in fear, waiting for the bullet that would end his life, the bullet that never came.

Schubert surrendered to the British that same day and was evacuated with the rest of the German garrison to the mainland for interrogation and subsequent transfer to an Allied prisoner-of-war camp. To avoid detection, Schubert cleverly changed his tunic to one of a Wehrmacht private. The ruse worked well, for he fooled his British interrogators and eventually he was returned to Germany for discharge from the army.

Time, however, was running out on the former Gestapo sergeant, for the scales of justice had begun to tip against him.

While stationed in Crete, Fritz Schubert had fallen in love with a girl whose family had migrated to the island from Salonika. Once settled in Vienna after his discharge, Schubert communicated with her and the two made arrangements to meet in Greece's second largest city. While strolling down the main thoroughfare of Salonika with his fiancée, a young man recognized Schubert and followed the two to the woman's residence. The young man, Anthony Psillakis, was from Rethimnon, and his father and two brothers had been executed on Schubert's orders when caught carrying supplies to Kapetan Petergeorge's guerrillas.[1]

Subsequently, Schubert made certain that Psillakis and three of his cousins would be shipped to Germany to serve as slave laborers. With Germany's capitulation, the four Cretans were repatriated to Greece. They were making plans to sail for Crete from Salonika, when fate willed that they should encounter their nemesis from Rethimnon.

Psillakis and his cousins followed Schubert's movements for several days, confirming the fact that he was, indeed, the man they thought him to be. Once assured, they reported the German to the local constabulary who detained him. When his identification was verified, the authorities remanded him into custody of the War Crimes Commission.[2]

Schubert was placed on trial as a war criminal before the War Crimes Tribunal that convened in Salonika a few months later. During the trial, hundreds of witnesses arrived to give testimony relative to the bestial atrocities perpetrated by this former Gestapo sergeant. *One of the witnesses was John Alexander.*

Born Peter Constantine (Petros Constantinidis) of Hellenic parentage in Izmir, Turkey, with an inexplicable hatred for anything Greek, Fritz Schubert was found guilty as charged for the "high crime of murder against humanity." He was executed by firing squad on a dreary day in October 1947.

One of the persons invited to witness the execution, as a member of the Allied Military Commission, was John Alexander.

Alexander stood to one side of the prison yard with the other Allied witnesses and watched as Schubert was escorted to the stake. The prisoner's hands were tied behind him, and a blindfold was placed over his eyes. On the command, bullets from the firing squad tore into his body. Schubert lurched momentarily from the impact, and then fell to the ground, dead.

Alexander noted that a bullet had torn off the blindfold. Another bullet had pierced Schubert's forehead between the eyes. Ironically, it was the same target on which Alexander had sighted his pistol, many months before, but was loath to pull the trigger.

When the rifles barked, Alexander winced and lowered his head, his heart filled with emotion. Tears welled up in his eyes and ran down his cheek. A moment later he looked up in time to see an officer giving Schubert the coup de grace. Quietly he muttered to himself, "Father, it is done."[3]

Justice at last had been served.

Alexander left the army in early 1948 and returned to the United States with his mother and two sisters. They settled in their old neighborhood in Wheeling, West Virginia, and resumed their lives after an absence of eight years. However, life without the patriarch of the family was not the same; there were too many happy prewar memories everywhere. To get away from these memories, they moved to New York. His mother never fully recovered from the shock she endured in Crete in witnessing her husband's murder and eventually died from the persistent lament of a broken heart. The oldest sister followed the mother a few years later.

Presently, Alexander lives in retirement in Florida with his widowed second sister.

The elderly abbot of the Monastery of St. John at Preveli, the Reverend Father Lagouvardos, who back in 1941 had given the young 18-year-old refugee from Prison Valley sanctuary in his monastery and later insisted that Alexander be evacuated to Egypt for his own safety, was himself eventually evacuated when the Germans discovered his underground activities.

Father Lagouvardos had a chance meeting with Alexander—then a corporal in the British Signal Corps—while in Cairo in 1942. The Reverend Father died a short time after a second reunion with Alexander, during the hot summer of 1944.[4]

Commander Francis Pool of the Royal Navy, in whom Father Lagouvardos entrusted John Alexander's safe evacuation to Cairo and out of Fritz Schubert's clutches, was the recipient of the Distinguished Service Cross and the Distinguished Service Order for his exemplary work with the SOE. After Germany's surrender, he was serving as a member of the Allied Commission in Athens, when he died suddenly in 1947.[5]

The guerrilla chieftain who developed a paternal affection for Alexander—from the moment he first met him as an interpreter for the Duncan-Moore commando team in the raid on Iraklion airfield, up to their final farewell in Iraklion—Kapetan George Petergeorge continued a life of service in postwar Crete.

Although suffering from severe rheumatism caused by his many months in the damp and cold mountains during the Resistance, he resumed his life as a businessman in peacetime. He moved to Iraklion and built factories in order to provide employment and thus help develop the economy of the impoverished district.

He successfully ran for Parliament and later—still an ardent foe of communism and the communist movement in Crete and on the mainland—he accepted the presidency of the pro-western National Organization of Crete, the EOK. Throughout his active years as a Resistance leader, as a businessman, and as a member of Parliament, he gained the respect of everyone, even his enemies. He received many decorations from his own as well as the British and American governments for his wartime and postwar services. He died in Iraklion at age 82 and was honored even in death with a state funeral.

An episode involving the Petergeorge family in the postwar years nearly brought the island of Crete to the brink of civil war. The event had nothing to do with the prevailing insurgency of the communist movement at the time.

George Petergeorge's daughter, Tassoula, was kidnapped by her fiancé—it was actually an elopement—and taken to the seclusion of a mountain hideout. There she married him without the presence of her family, which was an inexcusable and unacceptable circumstance in the social structure of Cretan family life in that period of time. Inasmuch as the bride's family were ardent Venizelists (followers of Cretan-born republican statesman Eleftherios Venizelos of the prewar years), while the groom's family were strong royalists who favored the monarchy, the whole island took sides. So strong and dominating were the long-existing political differences between the two that this division brought the two factions to the verge of a blood-feud. Fortunately, cooler minds prevailed, and bloodshed was prevented.

This romantic love story of the abduction, however, made good copy for the news media of the world at that time. It also made the Petergeorge name a household word among romanticists.[6]

Kapetan Petergeorge's senior lieutenant, Aleko Vandoukakis, who had been a guide for John Alexander on several occasions, had developed a brotherly affection for the young American throughout their association on the island. He cried openly when Aleko and Alexander parted after the war, never destined to see each other again.

Aleko returned to his village, married, and raised seven children. He still lives there amidst a host of grandchildren.[7]

The other American OSS officer who arrived on Crete with Alexander, First Lieutenant James Simvoulakis from Modesto, California, never had the occasion to return to Crete and revisit his grandmother, Mrs. Maria, as he had promised.

He did keep one part of his promise to her, however: in later years he sent his father to the village of Fres.

James's father arrived in the village to visit his mother after an absence of many years. He took the familiar curving dirt path to her house, supported by a cane. When the hardy Mrs. Maria spied her son using a cane, she admonished him and ordered him to discard it. After all, she reasoned, she was much older than he and *she* did not use a cane, so why should her son. He had to discard it, at least in her presence. Even in her old age, the hearty and high-spirited Mrs. Maria gave everyone around her a youthful outlook on life.

When she saw her son, after all those years, she cried tears of joy as she had when she first met her grandson, James. Now she felt that her life was complete; her prayers had been fulfilled; she had met her grandson for the first time, and she was seeing her son once again.

After his discharge from the army, James Simvoulakis returned to Modesto and married his fiancée, Penelope Pallios, to whom he had written endless letters during his many months in service. A successful businessman, he raised a fine family and lived in that city until his death in 1985.[8]

Following his last mission on Crete, Patrick Leigh Fermor returned to the safe house in Cairo. His friends and fellow residents of Tara were there, and he spoke laughingly with William Stanley Moss about the episode when he got George Psychoundakis drunk on the young Cretan's first taste of rum.

It was Christmas 1944, and although the American army was fighting a bloody winter battle in the bitter cold and snow of the Ardennes in Belgium, the war was actually rushing to a victorious conclusion for the Allies.

After the war, Fermor resumed his great love for travel, starting with a tour of postwar Germany. In the years that followed, he wrote several books based on his journeys, including *The Traveller's Tree* about travel in the West Indies; *A Time to Keep Silence* and *The Violin of St. Jacques*, a novel: *Mani*, a book about his travels through the southern Peloponnesus of Greece, and its companion book, *Roumeli*; *A Time of Gifts*, an enthralling account of his prewar travels on foot from Rotterdam to Hungary; and on to Constantinople with *Between the Woods and the Water*. Most of his books have earned literary awards.

Fermor never wrote an extensive account of the kidnapping of General Heinrich Kreipe, except for a short article entitled, "How to Steal a General" which appeared in a seven-volume history of the Second World War.

His name is well known among the wartime generation. As a philhellene, he has been honored by Hellenic academia, which appointed him a visiting member of the prestigious National Academy of Athens.

Presently, he lives with his wife in a house of his own design in the Peloponnesus, near the city of Kalamata, where they spend most of their year. This blissful buccaneer lives his life fully and in good style. He sails, swims, fishes, and walks over the mountain trails of southern Greece, which must give him a nostalgia for Crete. The rest of the time he continues to write.

It is ironic, that having served four years within the beautiful landscape of Crete, he chose to reside in the less volatile countryside of the Peloponnesus.[9]

His friend and comrade-in-arms on Crete, William Stanley Moss, returned to Cairo after his aborted plan to kidnap General Kreipe's successor. No sooner had he settled into the comforts of Tara when he was summoned to army headquarters, briefed for a new assignment, and within thirty-six hours sent to join the British Military Mission in Macedonia. There, he was to serve under Colonel C. M. Woodhouse in the attempt to persuade the EAM-ELAS forces to cooperate with the conservative EDES for a common front against the German foe.

When the war ended, Moss married a resident of Tara, the Polish countess Sophie Tarnowska, and left to sail in the Mediterranean on their newly acquired yacht.

During his stay in Crete, Moss penned a diary of the kidnapping of General Kreipe. He tried to publish it in 1945 but was prohibited through censorship by the War Office. It was finally published in 1950 as an exciting tale of adventure entitled *Ill Met by Moonlight*. It is the only authentic day-by-day account of that adventure in the mountains of Crete.

The head of the Cretan Section of the Special Operations Executive, Major Jack Smith-Hughes—known as Yanni to the Cretans, and in effect both Leigh's and Moss's commanding officer during their service in Crete—became a consul in Crete after the war. He married a Cretan girl, and returned to the military as a lawyer and an author until retirement.

Xan Fielding—the SOE agent nicknamed Aleko by the Cretans— wrote about his escapades on Crete in his book *The Stronghold* (1963). Sandy Rendel—Alexis—worked for the *London Times* after the war and produced an excellent account of his adventures in the eastern part of the island in *Appointment in Crete*.

For the other agents of the SOE, service on Crete left them with vivid memories of adventure, danger, and good times which lingered long after the war concluded.

The Falstaffian character of Athanasios Bourdzalis, the guerrilla chieftain who had arrived to assist Fermor and Moss in the abduction of General Kreipe, left a deep impression on both leaders of the kidnapping team. Bourdzalis was a true patriot in the war against the Nazis and was always available to render assistance to the SOE agents who served on Crete.

He was executed by the ELAS communists in October of 1944, in an act of great injustice.

In Cretan lore, the honor of a woman in a family household is the honor of that family. The Bourdzalis family was dishonored when their daughter was taken forcibly to the mountains by a fellow Cretan, John Podias. He had promised her marriage but, instead, turned her into a camp-follower. This was the same Yanni Podias who later broke away from the Bandouvas guerrilla group and formed his own band with allegiance not to Crete's liberation but to the communist insurgency.

The father of the girl, Athanasios Bourdzalis, swore vengeance to the death against Podias for violating his family's honor.

After the liberation of Iraklion, Bourdzalis had a chance encounter with Podias on a street of that city and shot him. Because the weapon was deflected by a bystander, Podias was only wounded. When rumor spread that Podias had been killed by Bourdzalis, Bourdzalis was arrested. Using this accusation as a ploy to gain political advantage for the communist ELAS over the conservative EOK, the communist leaders demanded at the court trial that Bourdzalis be found guilty.

Strange as it may seem, Kapetan Manoli Bandouvas, the guerrilla chieftain with whom Bourdzalis had served, concurred with the communist leaders. Believing Bourdzalis expendable, he urged that he be found guilty and executed, thereby salving the communists' fury and preventing a civil war. In a "kangaroo" trial, the court found the defendant guilty, and Athanasios Bourdzalis was executed the next day.[10]

It was an appalling conclusion to a tragic story. When you consider that for generations such private feuds were affairs that tolerated no interference from outsiders, this trial and verdict represented a mockery of justice. It concluded in the death of a patriarch who was merely defending his family's honor. Indeed, this was an example of politics making strange bedfellows.

General Heinrich Kreipe, the object of the famous abduction by Patrick Leigh Fermor and William Stanley Moss, remained a British prisoner of war until after the end of hostilities. In the years that followed the war, Kreipe seldom referred to that embarrassing episode in an otherwise unblemished military career.

Twenty-eight years later, on May 7, 1972, the abduction team of Fermor, Paterakis, Tyrakis, Saviolakis, Athanassakis, and Akoumianakis, among others, gathered to celebrate what had become one of the most legendary tales to come out of the Second World War—the kidnapping of a German general.

Heinrich Kreipe was also in attendance at the reunion. A glaring absence was that of Fermor's fellow officer, Stanley Moss, who had died.

During the banquet, Fermor, speaking in fluent Greek and German, stated that "after twenty-eight years, General, we apologize to you for what happened then . . . but war is war."

The white-haired general, sitting with his wife, smiled benignly and nodded in agreement. He replied in French, which had not improved since the days of his abduction, saying "C'est la guerre!"[11] During the reunion, Kreipe did admit that if fate had not deigned that he be kidnapped, then perhaps he, too, might have faced the same postwar criminal charges that led to the executions of many of his predecessors.[12]

Kreipe's predecessors—General Alexander Andre, who had replaced Kurt Student after the battle; General Walter Mueller, who had commanded in the Iraklion area and continued Andre's pogroms; and General Bruno Brauer, who was the commanding general of Fortress Kreta and who had commanded the First Parachute Regiment at Iraklion during the battle for Crete—were tried before the War Crimes Tribunal in Athens in December 1945 as war criminals for the brutal mass executions of hapless Cretan civilians during the four-year occupation. They were executed on the anniversary of the invasion of Crete on May 20, 1947—six years to the day after this saga began.[13]

When the liberation celebration finally subsided, George Psychoundakis, the lithe and energetic Cretan runner, decided to return to his village of Asi Gonia, ready to resume the life he had left off when the Germans invaded the island. He felt satisfied that he had served well in the struggle against the Germans as a member of the Resistance Movement and as a messenger for the British SOE.

Unfortunately for him, however, the documents relating to his war service had been lost during the upheaval caused by the occupation, and Psychoundakis was arrested as a deserter. He had been decorated by the British in 1945 with the Medal of the British Empire—the BEM—but the newly formed Greek government would not accept this award as evidence of his service. As a result, Psychoundakis was unjustly imprisoned and spent many months locked in cells with the thieves, murderers, and communists of the mainland.

After only three days of bewilderment, confusion, and misery brought on by this miscarriage of justice, Psychoundakis completely lost his abundant mop of black hair.

When Fermor learned of this injustice, he came to his defense, writing a strongly worded letter to the appropriate authorities in which he described the young Cretan's invaluable service with the SOE and with the Resistance Movement. The letter brought immediate results. Although the bureaucratic government authorities saw fit to correct their error, Psychoundakis still was made to serve two years in the National Military Service. Those two years were spent fighting the EAM-ELAS communist insurgents in the bitter civil war that took place in the mountains of northern Greece.

It was a sad story for this young, heroic Cretan, who, having served in the Resistance Movement against the Germans on Crete, now had to fight another war on the mainland, while his family lived in poverty on Crete. Yet, in spite of all his misfortune, Psychoundakis rose above all these obstacles.

During his imprisonment, he began to write a diary of his activities with the guerrillas and with the SOE. He put it aside during his military service on the mainland and continued it upon his official discharge. At a reunion with his old comrade-in-arms, Patrick Leigh Fermor, many years later, he gave the diary to him to read. Fermor was impressed, for it described with poignant clarity the troglodytic life of the men who fought in the mountains, chronicling their personal conflicts, the dangers they faced, their happy moments and their sad ones. Fermor translated the diary into English and had it published abroad for his young Cretan friend. It was an immediate literary success. The book was appropriately titled, *The Cretan Runner*.[14]

George Psychoundakis returned to Crete after completing his military service, married, and settled in the village of Tavronitis on the northern main road west of Khania, where he raised his family. At this writing, he still resides there, going to his home village of Asi Gonia only on special occasions.

He continues to write poetry, and in 1989, he was presented an award by the National Academy of Athens for his literary works. This was a great achievement considering that this simple mountain villager never had any formal schooling.[15]

Among the Cretan members of the abduction team that kidnapped the German general, the name of Manoli Paterakis has become legendary. His name is respected among those historians of World War II who have written about the Partisans of Europe and of their resistance to the German occupation.

Even in the United States, where the tale of the general's abduction received little reportage, and the deeds of the Cretan Resistance Movement—the first officially documented resistance against Nazism—were never related, the name of Manoli Paterakis is highly regarded by those who served there.

After the war, Great Britain awarded Paterakis the Military Medal of the British Empire. King George II and King Paul of the Hellenes (when Greece was a monarchy) further honored him with decorations from the Greek government. The walls of his home are adorned with letters of commendation from such famous historical personages of that war as Sir Winston Churchill and Field Marshal Sir Harold Alexander. Even the Germans recognized Paterakis's heroic feats by honoring him with a commemorative plaque.[16]

This gallant man died in a hunting accident in 1986. He was given a state funeral, as all of Crete mourned his untimely death. This modest hero of the Resistance would have blushed had he been able to witness all those who came to Crete to attend his funeral, including former English, Australian, New Zealand, and American comrades-in-arms.

He died in the mountains where he was born, where he spent all his life, and where he fought the war for liberation from oppression.

In 1974, the West German government purchased the ground of Kazvakia Hill at the village of Maleme, better known as Hill 107, the site of the famous battle that took place for Maleme airfield on May 20, 1941. On this field, the Germans constructed a military cemetery in which under a huge wooden cross, they buried more than 5,000 of their kinsmen who were killed during the battle and died during the occupation that followed. Their bodies, which had been buried haphazardly all over the island, were reinterred in this new military cemetery—the Deutscher Soldatenfriedhof.

In 1974, the president of the West German Veterans Association was none other than Heinrich Kreipe! It was he who had suggested that the caretakers of this newly opened German military cemetery be two Cretans of his acquaintance: George Psychoundakis and Manoli Paterakis.

It was an ironic twist of fate that these two Cretans, who had fought the enemy invader from the first day of battle and later played such a major role in the Resistance Movement against this oppressor of their land, were selected to tend the graves of those who came to Crete to stay forever. As General Kreipe remarked at the reunion in 1972. "C'est la guerre."

Notes

INTRODUCTION

1. Archer, *The Balkan Journal*, 117 - 120.
2. Papagos, *The Battle of Greece*, 275.
3. Trevor-Roper, *Hitler's War Directives, 1939 - 1945*, 90.

CHAPTER 1

1. Farrar-Hockley, *Student*, 88
2. Frischauer, *Rise and Fall of Hermann Goering*, 187.
3. Halder, Franz, *Kriegstagebuch*, entry April 24, 1941.
4. Trevor-Roper, *Hitler's War Directives*, 117.
5. Churchill, *The Second World War*, Vol. 3, 226.
6. Ibid., Vol. 2, 548.
7. Ibid., Vol. 3, 272.
8. Clark, *The Fall of Crete*, 33.
9. Kurowski, *Der Kampf Um Kreta*, 18.
10. Clark, 71.
11. Ibid., 99.
12. Kippenberger, *Infantry Brigadier*, 50.
13. Aristides Kritakis. Interview, Athens, July 15, 1978.
14. Kippenberger, 65.
15. Manolikakis, *The Golgotha of Crete*, 72.
16. Churchill, Vol. 3, 299.

CHAPTER 2

1. Stewart, *The Struggle for Crete*, 316.

2. Kostas Mavridakis. Interview, Kontomari, Crete, July 1984.
3. Mathiopoulos, *Death of a Village*, 31 - 46.
4. Rev. S. Frantzeskakis, Personal archives to author, Paleochora, Crete, July 14, 1980.
5. Manolis Manolakakis. Interview of brother, Khania, Crete, July 10, 1978.
6. Theodore Patsourakis. Interview, Khania, Crete, July 11, 1982.
7. Kostas Tsanakis. Interview, Khania, Crete, July 9, 1982.
8. Manolikakis, *The Golgotha of Crete*, 96 - 98.
9. Mrs. A. Progoulis. Interview, Platanias, Crete, July 15, 1980.

CHAPTER 3

1. Manolikakis, *The Golgotha of Crete*, 103.
2. Xirouhakis, *National Archives of Crete*, Vol. 2, 33.
3. Manolikakis, 104 - 106.
4. Kiriakopoulos, *Ten Days to Destiny*, 346.
5. Olga Kastrinakis. Interview, New York, September 9, 1988.
6. Alexander Karvoulakis. Interview, New York, September 10, 1988.
7. Manolikakis, 111.
8. John Alexander. Interview, New York, October 3, 1988.
9. Ibid., October 6, 1988.
10. George Psychoundakis. Interview, Tavronitis, Crete, July 1980.
11. Tsirimonakis, *The National Resistance in Rethimnon*, 101.
12. Paterakis, *Kapetan Petergeorge*, 66.

CHAPTER 4

1. Miller, *The Resistance*, 40.
2. Foot, *The SOE*, 19.
3. Ibid., 21.
4. Miller, 41.
5. Foot, 13.
6. Pychoundakis, *The Cretan Runner*, 9.
7. Ibid., 11.
8. Ibid., 10.
9. Ibid., 38 - 47.

CHAPTER 5

1. Moss, *Ill Met by Moonlight*, 13.
2. George Psychoundakis. Interview, Tavronitis, Crete, July 1980.
3. Psychoundakis, *The Cretan Runner*, 2 - 3.

4. Kiriakopoulos, *Ten Days to Destiny*, 365.
5. Ibid., 366.
6. Clark, *The Fall of Crete*, 189.
7. Ibid., 190.
8. Maria Babcock. Interview, Los Angeles, Calif., October 1982.
9. Eugenia Torakis. Interview, New York, October 1987.
10. Papadakis, *The Monastery of Preveli in Crete*, 25.
11. Psychoundakis, 77.
12. John Alexander. Interview, New York, October 1988.

CHAPTER 6

1. John Alexander. Interview, New York, October 1988.
2. Ladd, *Commandos and Rangers of World War II*, 114.
3. Ibid., 118.
4. Davin, *Crete*, 446.
5. John Alexander. Interview, New York, October 1988.
6. John Alexander. Interview, New York, May 1989.

CHAPTER 7

1. Harold Feldman. Interview, London, July 1989.
2. John Alexander. Interview, New York, May 1989.

CHAPTER 8

1. James Tsangarakis. Interview, Rethimnon, Crete, July 1988.
2. Brigadier General Charles Duncan-Moore (retired). Interview, London, July 1989.
3. Harold Feldman. Interview, London, July 1989.
4. Charles Duncan-Moore. Interview, London, July 1989.
5. James Tsangarakis. Interview, Rethimnon, Crete, July 1988.
6. Charles Duncan-Moore. Interview, London, July 1989.
7. John Alexander. Interview, New York, May 1989.

CHAPTER 9

1. John Alexander. Interview, New York, May 1989.
2. Manolikakis, *The Golgotha of Crete*, 99.
3. P. L. Fermor. Interview, New York, May 1983.
4. Ibid.
5. Psychoundakis, *The Cretan Runner*, 112.
6. Ibid., 45.

7. Ibid., 55.
8. Churchill, *The Second World War*, Vol. 5, 532.
9. Psychoundakis, 58.
10. Ibid., 58.
11. Ibid., 89.
12. John Alexander. Interview, New York, May 1989.
13. Psychoundakis, 70 - 73.
14. Ibid., 98 - 100.
15. Ibid., 115.

CHAPTER 10

1. Parton, *American Heritage Chronology of World War II*, August 1942.
2. Paterakis, *Kapetan Petergeorge*, 24.
3. John Alexander. Interview, New York, May 1989.
4. Ibid.
5. Psychoundakis, *The Cretan Runner*, 37.
6. Mrs. M. Adamakis. Interview, Modesto, Calif., November 1988.
7. John Alexander. Interview, New York, May 1989.

CHAPTER 11

1. Charakopos, *The Abduction of General Kreipe*, 35.
2. Hadjipateras-Fafalios, *Crete, 1941: Eyewitnessed*, 306.
3. Charakopos, 41.
4. Psychoundakis, *The Cretan Runner*, 167.
5. Ibid., 86.
6. Ibid., 168.

CHAPTER 12

1. John Alexander. Interview, New York, May 1989.
2. Psychoundakis, *The Cretan Runner*, 115.
3. Moss, *Ill Met by Moonlight*, 183.
4. Ibid., 184.
5. John Alexander. Interview, New York, May 1989.
6. Hymoff, *The OSS in World War II*, 366.
7. Ibid., 20 - 26.
8. Ibid., 41.
9. Ibid., 76.
10. Ibid., 365.
11. Smith, *The OSS: The Secret History of America's First Central Intelligence Agency*, 6.

12. John Alexander. Interview, New York, May 1989.
13. P. L. Fermor. Interview, New York, May 1983.

CHAPTER 13

1. P. L. Fermor, "How to Steal a General": *History of the Second World War*, Vol. 4, p. 1900.
2. Moss, *Ill Met by Moonlight*, 67.
3. Fermor, 1900.
4. Moss, 38.
5. Hadjipateras and Fafalios, *Crete 1941*, 307.
6. Moss, 31.
7. Ibid., 43.
8. Fermor, 1900.
9. Ibid.
10. Moss, 95.
11. Ibid., 97.

CHAPTER 14

1. Moss, *Ill Met by Moonlight*, 99.
2. Ibid., 101.
3. Ibid., 76.
4. Ibid., 77.
5. Ibid., 112.
6. Ibid., 111.
7. Manoli Paterakis. Interview, Khania, Crete, July 1984.
8. Moss, 124.
9. Ibid., 133.
10. Manoli Paterakis. Interview, Khania, Crete, July 1984.
11. Moss, 155.
12. Ibid., 157.
13. Ibid., 174.
14. Ibid., 177.

CHAPTER 15

1. Moss, *Ill Met by Moonlight*, 183.
2. P. L. Fermor. Interview, New York, May 1983.
3. John Alexander. Interview, New York, May 1989.
4. Averoff-Tossizza, *By Fire and Axe*, 76.
5. Churchill, Vol. 5, 534.

6. Averoff-Tossizza, 75.
7. Churchill, *The Second World War*, Vol. 5, 536.
8. Ronald Bailey, *World War II: Partisans and Guerrillas*, 153.
9. Churchill, Vol. 5, 538.
10. Hymoff, *The OSS in World War II*, 261.
11. Smith, R. Harris, 127.
12. Psychoundakis, *The Cretan Runner*, 183.
13. George Tzitzikas. Interview, Modesto, Calif., November 1988.
14. John Alexander. Interview, New York, May 1989.
15. Hymoff, 261.
16. Louis Doundoulakis. Interview, New York, September 1990.
17. John Alexander. Interview, New York, May 1989.
18. Moss, 187.
19. Ibid., 186.
20. Ibid., 187.
21. John Alexander. Interview, New York, May 1989 (also cited in Hymoff, 262).
22. Office of Strategic Services, File 226, National Archives, Washington, D.C.
23. Paterakis, *Kapetan Petergeorge*, 59.
24. John Alexander. Interview, New York, May 1989.
25. Psychoundakis, 225.
26. Ibid., 226.
27. James Simvoulakis, Letter to Penelope Pallios, April 1945.

CHAPTER 16

1. John Tsifakis. Interview, Platanias, Crete, July 1987.
2. George Tzitzikas. Interview, Modesto, Calif., November 1988.
3. Paterakis, *Kapetan Petergeorge*, 77.
4. Gyparis, *Heroes and Heroism in the Battle of Crete*, 105.
5. Constantine Mitsotakis. Interview, New York, March 1990.
6. Hadjipateras and Fafalios, *Crete 1941*, 314.
7. Ibid., 315.
8. Ibid., 314.
9. Mrs. Penelope Simvoulakis. Interview, Modesto, Calif., November 1988.
10. James Simvoulakis, Letter to Penelope (Pallios) Simvoulakis, May 1945.
11. Ibid.
12. Psychoundakis, *The Cretan Runner*, 233.
13. John Alexander. Interview, New York, May 1989.

EPILOGUE

1. Manolikakis, *The Golgotha of Crete*, 111.
2. Psillakis, Anthony. Interview, Montreal, Canada, May 1991.
3. John Alexander. Interview, New York, May 1989.
4. Manolikakis, 126.
5. Psychoundakis, *The Cretan Runner*, 36 (Fermor's notation).
6. Hercules Petergeorge. Interview, Iraklion, Crete, August 1989.
7. Ibid.
8. Penelope Simvoulakis. Interview, Modesto, Calif., November 1988.
9. Fermor. Interview, New York, May 1983.
10. George Tzitzikas. Interview, Modesto, Calif., November 1988.
11. Charakopos, *The Abduction of General Kreipe*, 316.
12. Manolis Paterakis. Interview, Khania, Crete, May 1983.
13. Manolikakis, 120.
14. Psychoundakis, 6 (Fermor's notation).
15. George Psychoundakis. Interview, Tavronitis, Crete, July 1989.
16. Manolis Paterakis. Interview, Khania, Crete, July 1984.

Bibliography

Archer, Laird. *The Balkan Journal*. New York: W. W. Norton, 1944.

Argyropoulos, Katy. *From Peace to Chaos*. New York: Vantage Press, 1975.

Averoff-Tossizza, Evangelos. *By Fire and Axe*. New York: Caratzas, 1978.

Bailey, George. *Germans*. New York: Avon, 1972.

Bailey, Ronald, ed. *World War II: Partisans and Guerrillas*. Alexandria, Va.: Time-Life Books, 1978.

Baldwin, Hanson. *Battles Lost and Won: Crete—The Winged Invasion*. New York: Avon, 1968.

Barry, Gerald. *The Parachute Invasion*. London: Blackwoods, 1944.

Bohmler, Rudolf. *Fallschirmjäger*. Munich: Verlag Hans-Henning Podzun, 1961. (in German)

Buckley, Christopher. *Greece and Crete 1941*. London: Her Majesty's Stationery Office, 1977.

Charakopos, George. *The Abduction of General Kreipe*. Athens: IDH, 1970.

Churchill, Winston S. *The Second World War, Vol. 2: Their Finest Hour*. Boston: Houghton Mifflin, 1950.

Churchill, Winston S. *The Second World War, Vol. 3: The Grand Alliance*. Boston: Houghton Mifflin, 1950.

Churchill, Winston S. *The Second World War, Vol. 4: The Hinge of Fate*. Boston: Houghton Mifflin, 1950.

Churchill, Winston S. *The Second World War, Vol. 5: Closing the Ring*. Boston: Houghton Mifflin, 1950.

Clark, Alan. *The Fall of Crete*. London: Anthony Blond Ltd., 1962.

Comeau, M. G. *Operation Mercury*. London: Kimber, 1961.

Cunningham, Admiral of the Fleet Viscount of Hyndhope. *A Sailor's*

Odyssey. New York: E. P. Dutton, 1951.

Davin, Daniel M. *Crete. (Official history of New Zealand in the Second World War, 1939-1945)*. Wellington, New Zealand: Department of Internal Affairs, War History Branch, 1953.

Davis, Brian L. *German Parachute Forces, 1935-1945*. New York: Arco Publishing Co., 1974.

Delarue, Jacque. *The Gestapo*. New York: William Morrow, 1964.

Dobiasch, Sepp. *Gebirgsjäger Auf Kreta*. Berlin: Stocker, 1942. (in German)

Farrar-Hockley, Anthony. *Student*. New York: Ballantine Books, 1973.

Feist, Uwe, et al. *Fallschirmjäger in Action*. Michigan: Squadron-Signal Publications, 1973.

Fergusson, Bernard. *Wavell: Portrait of a Soldier*. London: Collins, 1961.

Fermor, Patrick Leigh. "How to Steal a General." *History of the Second World War*, Vol. 4, p. 1900. Cavendish, U.S.A.: 1973.

Fielding, Xan. *The Stronghold*. London: Secker and Warburg, 1963.

Fitzgibbon, Constantine. *Secret Intelligence in the Twentieth Century*. New York: Stein and Day, 1977.

Foot, M. R. D. *The S.O.E.* New York: University Publications of America, 1986.

Frischauer, Willi, *The Rise and Fall of Hermann Goering*. New York: Ballantine Books, 1951.

Gericke, Walter. *Da Gibt Es Kein Zurück*. Munster: Fallschirmjäger Verlag, 1955. (in German)

Gyparis, Paul. *Heroes and Heroism in the Battle of Crete*. Athens: 1954. (in Greek)

Hadjipateras, C. and Fafalios, M. *Crete 1941: Eyewitnessed*. Athens: Efstathiadis, 1988.

Halder, Col. Gen. Franz. *Kriegstagebuch*. Stuttgart: Kohlhammer, 1963. (in German)

Howell, Edward. *Escape to Live*. London: Longmans, 1947.

Hymoff, Edward. *The OSS in World War II*. New York: Ballantine Books, 1972.

Keegan, John. *The Second World War*. New York: Viking, 1989.

Kippenberger, Major General Sir Howard. *Infantry Brigadier*. London: Oxford University Press, 1949.

Kiriakopoulos, G. C. *Ten Days to Destiny—The Battle for Crete, 1941*. New York: Franklin Watts, 1985.

Koutsoulas, Dimitrios. *The Price of Freedom*. New York: Syracuse University Press, 1953.

Kunhardt, Philip, ed. *World War II*. New York: Little, Brown, 1990.

Kurowski, Franz. *Der Kampf Um Kreta*. Bonn: Maximilian-Verlag, 1965. (in German)

Ladd, James. *Commandos and Rangers of World War II*. New York: St Martin's Press, 1978.

Lavra, Stephen. *The Greek Miracle*. London: Hastings House, 1943.

Lewin, Ronald. *The Chief: Field Marshal Lord Wavell 1939-1947*. New York: Farrar, Straus and Giroux, 1980.

Liddell Hart, Basil. *History of the Second World War, Vol. 4*. London: Marshall Cavendish Ltd., 1973.

Macksey, Kenneth. *The Partisans of Europe in Second World War*. New York: Stein and Day, 1975.

Manolikakis, I. G. *The Golgotha of Crete*. Athens: Efstathiadis, 1951. (in Greek)

Manvell, Roger. *Goering*. New York: Ballantine Books, 1972.

Mathiopoulos, V. *Death of a Village*. Athens: Postman Magazine, 1980. (in Greek)

Mathioulakis, C. Z. *Crete: Mythology and History*. Athens: 1974. (in Greek)

Meyer, Kurt. *Battle for the Stronghold of Crete*. Berlin: 1941. (in German)

Miller, Russell, ed., *The Resistance*. Alexandria, Va.: Time-Life, 1979.

Moss, William Stanley. *Ill Met by Moonlight*. New York: Macmillan Co., 1950.

Mourellos, J. D. *Battle of Crete*. Iraklion: Erotocritos, 1950. (in Greek)

Muller, Gunther. *Sprung Über Kreta*. Oldenberg: Stalling, 1944. (in German)

Office of Strategic Services. *Crete*. Washington, D.C.: National Archives, 1945.

Papadakis, Michel. *The Monastery of Preveli in Crete*. Athens, 1978. (in Greek)

Papagos, General Alexander. *The Battle of Greece*. New York: New World Publishers, 1946. (in Greek)

Parton, James. *American Heritage Chronology of World War II*. New York: American Heritage Publishing Co., 1966.

Paterakis, George. *Kapetan Petergeorge*. Iraklion, 1983.

Psychoundakis, George. *The Cretan Runner*. London: John Murray, 1955.

Rokakis, Manousos. *The Story of Crete, 1941-1945*. Khania, Crete, 1953.

Singleton-Gates, Peter. *General Lord Freyberg, V. C.* London: Joseph, 1963.

Smith, Michael Llewellyn. *The Great Island: A Study of Crete*. London: Longman, Green and Co., 1965.

Smith, R. Harris. *The OSS: The Secret History of America's First Central Intelligence Agency*. Los Angeles: University of California Press, 1972.

Stephanides, Theodore. *Climax in Crete*. London: Faber and Faber, 1946.

Stewart, I. McD. G. *The Struggle for Crete, 20 May-1 June*. London:

Oxford University Press, 1966.

Student, General Kurt. *Crete*. South Africa: Ministry of Defense, 1952.

Theodorakis, A. *The National Resistance in Crete, 1941-1945*. Iraklion, 1970.

Trevor-Roper, H. R., ed. *Hitler's War Directives, 1939-1945*. New York: Holt, Rinehart and Winston, 1965.

Tsirimonakis, E. *The National Resistance in Rethimnon, 1941-1944*. Athens, 1985. (in Greek)

Von der Heydte, Baron F. *Daedalus Returned*. London: Hutchinson and Co., 1958.

Warlimont, General Walter. *Inside Hitler's Headquarters, 1939-1945*. New York: Praeger, 1964.

Wason, Betty. *Miracle in Hellas*. New York: Macmillan Co., 1943.

Whipple, A. B. C., ed. *World War II: The Mediterranean*. Alexandria, Va.: Time-Life Books, 1978.

Whiting, Charles. *The War of the Shadows*. New York: Ballantine Books, 1973.

Whiting, Charles. *Hunters from the Sky*. New York: Ballantine Books, 1974.

Winterstein, Ernst, and Jacobs, Hans. *General Meindl und Seine Fallschirmjäger*. Munich: Gesammelt und Neidergeschrieben, 1949. (in German)

Woodhouse, C. M. *The Struggle for Greece: 1941-1949*. London: Hart-Davis, MacGibbon, 1976.

Wunderlich, Hans Georg. *The Secret of Crete*. New York: Macmillan Co., 1974.

Xirouhakis, A. *National Archives of Crete*. Khania, Crete, Vol. 2, 33.

Young, Brigadier Peter. *Atlas of the Second World War*. New York: Berkley Publishing Corp. 1977.

Young, Brigadier Peter. *Commando*. New York: Ballantine Books, 1969.

Zotos, Stephanos. *Greece: The Struggle for Freedom*. New York: Thomas Crowell Co., 1967.

Index

About the Author

G. C. KIRIAKOPOULOS is a Professor of Dentistry at Columbia University. He is a highly decorated combat veteran of World War II, and is a Fellow of the Royal Society of Health of Great Britain. His first book, *Ten Days to Destiny: The Battle for Crete, 1941* has been acclaimed internationally as the most authentic documentation of that battle by those who fought it.